Book

Sixth Edition

The Humanistic Tradition

Romanticism, Realism, and the Nineteenth-Century World

Sixth Edition

Book 5

The Humanistic Tradition

Romanticism, Realism, and the
Nineteenth-Century World

Gloria K. Fiero

Connect
Learn
Succeed™

Boston   Burr Ridge, IL   Dubuque, IA   New York   San Francisco   St. Louis
Bangkok   Bogotá   Caracas   Kuala Lumpur   Lisbon   London   Madrid   Mexico City
Milan   Montreal   New Delhi   Santiago   Seoul   Singapore   Sydney   Taipei   Toronto

THE HUMANISTIC TRADITION, BOOK 5
ROMANTICISM, REALISM, AND THE NINETEENTH-CENTURY WORLD

Published by McGraw-Hill, an imprint of The McGraw-Hill Companies, Inc.,
1221 Avenue of the Americas, New York, NY, 10020.

This book is printed on acid-free paper.

1 2 3 4 5 6 7 8 9 0 / 0

Library of Congress Cataloging-in-Publication Data

Fiero, Gloria K.
    The humanistic tradition / Gloria K. Fiero.– 6th ed.
        p. cm.
    Includes bibliographical references and index.
    ISBN-13: 978-0-07-352397-2 (bk. 1 : alk. paper)
    ISBN-10: 0-07-352397-6 (bk. 1 : alk. paper)
      1. Civilization, Western–History–Textbooks.
      2. Humanism–History–Textbooks.
      I. Title.

CB245.F47 2009
909'.09821–dc22

2009027018

Permissions Acknowledgments appear on page 142,
and on this page by reference.

Publisher: *Chris Freitag*
Director of Development: *Rhona Robbin*
Associate Sponsoring Editor: *Betty Chen*
Editorial Coordinator: *Sarah Remington*
Marketing Manager: *Pamela Cooper*
Managing Editor: *David Staloch*
Senior Production Supervisor: *Tandra Jorgensen*
Typeface: *10/12 Goudy*
Printer: *Phoenix Offset, Hong Kong*

http://www.mhhe.com

 This book was designed and produced by
Laurence King Publishing Ltd., London
www.laurenceking.com

Commissioning Editor: *Kara Hattersley-Smith*
Senior Editor: *Melissa Danny*
Production Controller: *Simon Walsh*
Picture Researcher: *Emma Brown*
Designer: *Robin Farrow*

Front cover
Casper David Friedrich, *Two Men Looking at
the Moon* (detail), 1819–1820. Oil on panel,
13¾ x 17¼ in. Gemäldegalerie Neue Meister,
Dresden.

Back cover
Kunisada, triptych showing the different
processes of printmaking (detail), early
nineteenth century. Japanese woodblock
color print. Courtesy of the Trustees of the
Victoria and Albert Museum, London.

Frontispiece
Edouard Manet, *Zola*, exhibited 1868. Oil
on canvas, 57 x 45 in. Louvre, Paris. ©
Photo Josse, Paris.

Series Contents

Book 5 Contents

Preface

Each generation leaves a creative legacy, the sum of its ideas and achievements. This legacy represents the response to our effort to ensure our individual and collective survival, our need to establish ways of living in harmony with others, and our desire to understand our place in the universe. Meeting the challenges of *survival, communality,* and *self-knowledge*, we have created and transmitted the tools of science and technology, social and political institutions, religious and philosophic systems, and various forms of personal expression—the totality of which we call *culture*. Handed down from generation to generation, this legacy constitutes the humanistic tradition, the study of which is called *humanities*.

The Humanistic Tradition originated more than two decades ago out of a desire to bring a global perspective to my humanities courses. My fellow humanities teachers and I recognized that a western-only perspective was no longer adequate to understanding the cultural foundations of our global world, yet none of the existing texts addressed our needs. At the time, the challenge was daunting—covering the history of western poetry and prose, art, music, and dance was already an ambitious undertaking for a survey course; how could we broaden the scope to include Asia, Africa, and the Americas without over-packing the course? What evolved was a thematic approach to humanities, not as a collection of disciplines, but as a discipline in itself. This thematic approach considers the interrelatedness of various forms of expression as they work to create, define, and reflect the unique culture of a given time and place. It offers a conceptual framework for students to begin a study of the humanistic tradition that will serve them throughout their lives. I am gratified that others have found this approach to be highly workable for their courses, so much so that *The Humanistic Tradition* has become a widely adopted book for the humanities course.

The Humanistic Tradition pioneered a flexible six-book format in recognition of the varying chronological range of humanities courses. Each slim volume was also convenient for students to bring to classes, the library, and other study areas. The sixth edition continues to be available in this six-book format, as well as in a two-volume set for the most common two-term course configuration.

The Sixth Edition of *The Humanistic Tradition*

While the sixth edition of *The Humanistic Tradition* contains a number of new topics, images, and selections, it remains true to my original goal of offering a manageable and memorable introduction to global cultures. At the same time, I have worked to develop new features that are specifically designed to help students master the material and critically engage with the text's primary source readings, art

reproductions, and music recordings. The integration of literary, visual, and aural primary sources is a hallmark of the text, and every effort has been made to provide the most engaging translations, the clearest color images, and the liveliest recorded performances, as well as the most representative selections for every period. The book and companion supplements are designed to offer all of the resources a student and teacher will need for the course.

New Features that Promote Critical Thinking

New to the sixth edition are special features that emphasize connections between time periods, styles, and cultures, and specific issues of universal significance. These have been added to encourage critical thinking and classroom discussion.

- **Exploring Issues** focuses on controversial ideas and current debates, such as the battle over the ownership of antiquities, the role of the non-canonical Christian gospels, the use of optical devices in Renaissance art, the dating of African wood sculptures, and creationism versus evolution.
- **Making Connections** brings attention to contrasts and continuities ibetween past and present ideas, values, and styles. Examples include feudalism East and West, Classical antiquities as models for Renaissance artists, and African culture as inspiration for African-American artists.

New Features that Facilitate Learning and Understanding

The sixth edition provides chapter introductions and summaries that enhance the student's grasp of the materials, and a number of features designed to make the materials more accessible to students:

- **Looking Ahead** offers a brief, preliminary overview that introduces students to the main theme of the chapter.
- **Looking Back** closes each chapter with summary study points that encourage students to review key ideas.
- **Iconographic "keys"** to the meaning of images have been inset alongside selected artworks.
- **Extended captions** to illustrations throughout the text provide additional information about artworks and artists.
- **Chronology boxes** in individual chapters place the arts and ideas in historical background.
- **Before We Begin** precedes the Introduction with a useful guide to understanding and studying humanities.

Organizational Improvements and Updated Content

The sixth edition responds to teachers' requests that the coverage of Mesopotamia precede Egypt and other ancient African cultures in the opening chapters. The global coverage has been refined with revised coverage of the early Americas, new content on archeological discoveries in ancient Peru, a segment on the role of the West in the Islamic Middle East, and a discussion of China's global ascendance. Chapters 36 through 38 have been updated and reorganized: Ethnicity and ethnic identity have been moved to chapter 38 (Globalism and the Contemporary World), which brings emphasis to recent developments in digital technology, environmentalism, and global terrorism. Other revisions throughout the text also respond to teacher feedback; for example, a description of the *bel canto* style in music has been added; Jan van Eyck's paintings appear in both chapters 17 and 19 (in different contexts); and T. S. Eliot's works are discussed in both chapters 32 and 35.

Among the notable writers added to the sixth edition are William Blake, Jorge Luis Borges, Seamus Heaney, and John Ashbury. New additions to the art program include works by Benozzo Gozzoli, Buckminster Fuller, Kara Walker, Jeff Wall, Damien Hirst, El Anatsui, and Norman Foster.

Beyond *The Humanistic Tradition*

Connect Humanities

Connect Humanities is a learning and assessment tool designed and developed to improve students' performance by making the learning process more efficient and more focused through the use of engaging, assignable content, which is text-specific and mapped to learning objectives, and integrated tools. Using this platform, instructors can deliver assignments easily online, and save time through an intuitive and easy to use interface and through modifiable pre-built assignments.

Connect provides instructors with the Image Bank, a way to easily browse and search for images and to download them for use in class presentations.

Visit mcgrawhillconnect.com

Traditions: Humanities Readings through the Ages

Traditions is a new database conceived as both a standalone product as well as a companion source to McGraw-Hill's humanities titles. The collection is broad in nature, containing both western and non-western readings from ancient and contemporary eras, hand-picked from such disciplines as literature, philosophy, and science. The flexibility of Primis Online's database allows the readings to be arranged both chronologically and by author.

Visit www.primisonline.com/traditions

Music Listening Compact Discs

Two audio compact discs have been designed exclusively for use with *The Humanistic Tradition*. CD One corresponds to the music listening selections discussed in Books 1–3 (Volume I), and CD Two contains the music in Books 4–6 (Volume II). Music logos (right) that appear in the margins of the text refer to the Music Listening Selections found on the audio compact discs. The compact discs can be packaged with any or all of the six books or two-volume versions of the text.

Online Learning Center

A complete set of web-based resources for *The Humanistic Tradition* can be found at

www.mhhe.com/fieroht6e

Materials for students include an audio pronunciation guide, a timeline, research and writing tools, links to select readings, and suggested readings and Web sites. The instructor side of the Online Learning Center includes discussion and lecture suggestions, music listening guides, key themes and topics, and study questions for student discussion and review and written assignments.

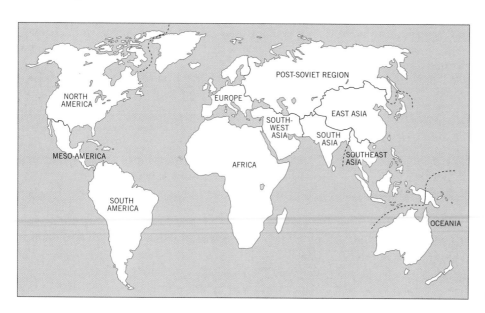

Key map indicating areas shown as white highlights on the locator maps

Acknowledgments

Personal thanks go to my discerning editor, Betty Chen (McGraw-Hill), and to the editorial and production staff of Laurence King Publishing. As with former editions, my colleague and husband, James H. Dormon, read all parts of the manuscript and made substantive editorial suggestions. This edition is dedicated to him. I am also grateful to Eric C. Shiner (curator and art historian) for his assistance in contemporary Asian art.

In the preparation of the sixth edition, I have benefited from the suggestions and comments generously offered by Donald F. Andrews (Chattanooga State Technical Community College), Samuel Barnett (University of Maryland), Bobbie Bell (Seminole Community College), Marjorie Berman (Red Rocks Community College), Terri Birch (Harper College), Pat Bivin (International Academy of Design and Technology), Casey Blanton (Daytona Beach Community College), Diane Boze (Northeastern State University), Nellie Brannan (Brevard Community College), Diane S. Brown (Valencia Community College, Osceola), Joyce Caldwell Smith (University of Tennessee at Chattanooga), Cynthia Clegg (Pepperdine University), Harry S. Coverston (University of Central Florida), Julie deGraffenried (Baylor University), Ann Dunn (University of North Carolina, Asheville), Renae Edge (Norwalk Community College), Monika Fleming (Edgecombe Community College), A. Flowers (College of Alameda), Rod Freeman (Estrella Mountain College), Arby L. Frost (Roanoke College), Samuel Garren (North Carolina A&T University), Caryl Gibbs (Rose State College), Robin Hardee (Santa Fe College), Melissa T. Hause (Belhaven College), Barbara A. Hergianto (South Florida Community College), Dale Hoover (Edison College), Ron Israel (San Diego Mesa College), Marian Jacobson (Albany College of Pharmacy), Theresa James (South Florida Community College), Judith Jamieson (Providence College), Keith W. Jensen (William Rainey Harper College), Jerry Jerman (University of Oklahoma), Patrick Kiley (Marian College), Donald Koke (Butler County College), Jayson Larremore (Oral Roberts University), Bonnie Loss (Glendale Community College), Diana Lurz (Rogers State University), Eldonna Loraine May (Wayne State University), Barbara J. Mayo (Northeast Lakeview College), Susan McClung (Hillsborough Community College), Trudy McNair (Valencia Community College), Richard Middleton-Kaplan (Harper College), Yvonne J. Milspaw (Harrisburg Area Community College), Maureen Moore (Cosumnes River College), Sean P. Murphy (College of Lake County), Judy Navas (Sonoma State University), Jack L. Nawrocik (St. Philip's College), James Norwood (University of Minnesota), Craig Payne (Indian Hills College), Randall M. Payne (South Florida Community College), Laurel S. Peterson (Norwalk Community College), Richard W. Peyton (Florida Agricultural and Mechanical University), Anne L. Pierce (Hampton University), William H. Porterfield (West Virginia State Community & Technical College), Judith Poxon (Sacramento City College), Robin Poynor (University of Florida), Verbie Lovorn Prevost (University of Tennessee at Chattanooga), Andreas W. Reif (Southern New Hampshire University), Denise M. Rogers (University of Louisiana at Lafayette), Karen Rumbley (Valencia Community College), Maria Rybakova (San Diego State University), John Scolaro (Valencia Community College), Vanessa Sheldon (College of the Desert), Mary Slater (Missouri Valley College), Linda Spain (Linn-Benton Community College), Hartley S. Spatt (SUNY Maritime College), Lisa Stokes (Seminole Community College), Alice Taylor (West Los Angeles College), Andreia Thaxton (Florida Community College at Jacksonville), Randall K. Van Schepen (Roger Williams University), Andrew Vassar (Northeastern State University), John Michael Vohlidka (Gannon University), Laura Wadenpfuhl (New Jersey City College), John R. Webb (Highland Community College), Jason Whitmarsh (Florida State College at Jacksonville), and Linda Woodward (Lone Star Montgomery College).

—Gloria K. Fiero

BEFORE WE BEGIN

Studying humanities engages us in a dialogue with *primary sources*: works original to the age in which they were produced. Whether literary, visual, or aural, a primary source is a text; the time, place, and circumstances in which it was created constitute the context; and its various underlying meanings provide the subtext. Studying humanities from the perspective of text, context, and subtext helps us understand our cultural legacy and our place in the larger world.

Text

The *text* of a primary source refers to its medium (that is, what it is made of), its form (its outward shape), and its content (the subject it describes).

Literature: Literary form varies according to the manner in which words are arranged. So, *poetry*, which shares rhythmic organization with music and dance, is distinguished from *prose*, which normally lacks regular rhythmic patterns. Poetry, by its freedom from conventional grammar, provides unique opportunities for the expression of intense emotions. Prose usually functions to convey information, to narrate, and to describe.

Philosophy, (the search for truth through reasoned analysis), and *history* (the record of the past) make use of prose to analyze and communicate ideas and information.

In literature, as in most forms of expression, content and form are usually interrelated. The subject matter or form of a literary work determines its *genre*. For instance, a long narrative poem recounting the adventures of a hero constitutes an *epic*, while a formal, dignified speech in praise of a person or thing constitutes a *eulogy*.

The Visual Arts: The visual arts employ a wide variety of media, ranging from the traditional colored pigments used in painting, to wood, clay, marble, and (more recently) plastic and neon used in sculpture, to a wide variety of digital media, including photography and film. The form or outward shape of a work of art depends on the manner in which the artist manipulates the elements of color, line, texture, and space. Unlike words, these formal elements lack denotative meaning.

The visual arts are dominantly spatial, that is, they operate and are apprehended in space. Artists manipulate form to describe or interpret the visible world (as in the genres of portraiture and landscape), or to create worlds of fantasy and imagination. They may also fabricate texts that are non-representational, that is, without identifiable subject matter.

Music and Dance: The medium of music is sound. Like literature, music is durational: it unfolds over the period of time in which it occurs. The major elements of music are melody, rhythm, harmony, and tone color—formal elements that also characterize the oral life of literature.

However, while literary and visual texts are usually descriptive, music is almost always nonrepresentational: it rarely has meaning beyond sound itself. For that reason, music is the most difficult of the arts to describe in words.

Dance, the artform that makes the human body itself the medium of expression, resembles music in that it is temporal and performance-oriented. Like music, dance exploits rhythm as a formal tool, and like painting and sculpture, it unfolds in space as well as in time.

Studying the text, we discover the ways in which the artist manipulates medium and form to achieve a characteristic manner of execution or expression that we call *style*. Comparing the styles of various texts from a single era, we discover that they usually share certain defining features and characteristics. Similarities between, for instance, ancient Greek temples and Greek tragedies, or between Chinese lyric poems and landscape paintings, reveal the unifying moral and aesthetic values of their respective cultures.

Context

The *context* describes the historical and cultural environment of a text. Understanding the relationship between text and context is one of the principal concerns of any inquiry into the humanistic tradition. To determine the context, we ask: In what time and place did our primary source originate? How did it function within the society in which it was created? Was it primarily decorative, didactic, magical, or propagandistic? Did it serve the religious or political needs of the community? Sometimes our answers to these questions are mere guesses. For instance, the paintings on the walls of Paleolithic caves were probably not "artworks" in the modern sense of the term, but, rather, magical signs associated with religious rituals performed in the interest of communal survival.

Determining the function of the text often serves to clarify the nature of its form, and vice-versa. For instance, in that the Hebrew Bible, the *Song of Roland*, and many other early literary works were spoken or sung, rather than read, such literature tends to feature repetition and rhyme, devices that facilitate memorization and oral delivery.

Subtext

The *subtext* of a primary source refers to its secondary or implied meanings. The subtext discloses conceptual messages embedded in or implied by the text. The epic poems of the ancient Greeks, for instance, which glorify prowess and physical courage, suggest an exclusively male perception of virtue. The state portraits of the seventeenth-century French king Louis XIV bear the subtext of unassailable and absolute power. In our own time, Andy Warhol's serial adaptations of Coca-Cola bottles offer wry commentary on the commercial mentality of American society. Examining the implicit message of the text helps us determine the values of the age in which it was produced, and offers insights into our own.

Chapter
27

The Romantic View of Nature
ca. 1780–1880

"Beauty in art is truth bathed in an impression received from nature."
Corot

Figure 27.1 JOHN CONSTABLE, *The Haywain*, 1821. Oil on canvas, 4 ft. 3½ in. × 6 ft. 1 in. The artist originally titled this painting *Landscape: Noon.* On the specificity of time and place, he remarked, "No two days are alike, not even two hours; neither were there ever any two leaves alike since the creation of the world."

LOOKING AHEAD

The nineteenth century is often called "the Romantic era." The term "Romanticism" describes a movement in the history of culture, an aesthetic style, and an attitude of mind. As a cultural *movement*, Romanticism reacted against the rationalism of the Enlightenment and the depersonalizing effects of Western industrialization. Spanning the late eighteenth century and continuing well into the twentieth, the Romantic movement revolted against academic convention, and authority, and opposed the limitations to freedom in personal, political, and artistic life.

As a *style*, Romanticism provided an alternative to the Enlightenment values of order, clarity, and rational restraint. In place of Neoclassical formality and the objective exercise of the intellect, Romanticism celebrated spontaneity and the subjective exercise of the imagination. In all of the arts, the Romantics abandoned traditional formal constraints to explore new, imaginative avenues of expression.

As an *attitude of mind*, Romanticism may be seen as an assertion of intuitive individualism and the primacy of feeling. Romantics did not reject the value of reason as such, but they regarded emotions (and the role of the senses) as equally important to human experience—and as essential to creativity. They looked to nature as a source of divine inspiration and seized on the tumultuous events of their time: the exotic, the catastrophic, and the fantastic. They often indulged in acts of nonconformity that alienated them from conventional society.

The lives and works of the Romantics were marked by deep subjectivity—even self-indulgence. If their perceptions and passions were intense, their desire to devise a language adequate to that intensity of feeling often drove them to frustration, melancholy, despair, and early death: the poets Shelley, Keats, and Byron; the composers Chopin and Schubert; and the painters Gros and Géricault, all died before the age of forty.

The Progress of Industrialization

During the nineteenth century, the population of Europe doubled in size. At the same time, material culture changed more radically than it had in the previous 1000 years. The application of science to practical invention, begun in the eighteenth century, had already sparked the beginnings of the Industrial Revolution—the mass production of material goods by machine (see chapter 25). The first phase of industrialization occurred in mid-eighteenth-century England, with the development of the steam engine and the machinery for spinning and weaving textiles (see chapter 25). Monopolized by the English for a half-century, the Industrial Revolution spread to the rest of Europe and to the United States by the 1830s. As increasing production of coal, iron, and steel encouraged the further expansion of industry and commerce, the West was transformed from an agrarian to an industrially based society. Goods that had been hand-produced in homes and workshops were increasingly manufactured in newly constructed factories, mills, and mines. Industrialization demanded enormous investments of capital and the efforts of a large labor force; it stimulated growth in Europe's urban centers. And ultimately, it provided the basis for the West's controlling influence over the rest of the world (see chapter 30).

Early Nineteenth-Century Thought

Romanticism found its formal philosophers largely among nineteenth-century German intellectuals. Gottlieb Fichte (1762–1814), Friedrich Schisler (1775–1854), and Arthur Schopenhauer (1788–1860) followed the philosophic idealism of Immanuel Kant, who exalted the role of the human mind in constructing an idea of the world (see chapter 25). According to the German idealists, the truths of empirical experience were not self-evident, as Locke had argued, and the truths of the mind were not clear and distinct, as Descartes had held. Much like Rousseau (see chapter 25) and the Romantic poets (discussed later in this chapter), the idealists prized the powers of human instinct and viewed nature in deeply subjective terms.

Schopenhauer defended the existence of a "life-will," a blind and striving impersonal force whose operations are without purpose or design, and whose activities give rise to disorder and delusion. In Schopenhauer's view, the only escape from malignant reality was selfless contemplation of the kind described in Hindu literature and the mystical treatises of Johannes Eckhart (see chapter 15). Welcoming the influence of Indian religious philosophy, Schopenhauer wrote, "Sanskrit literature will be no less influential for our time than Greek literature was in the fifteenth century for the Renaissance."

While Schopenhauer perceived existence as devoid of reason and burdened by constant suffering, others moved in the direction of mysticism. Some allied with notable visionaries, such as Friedrich von Hardenberg, better known as Novalis (1772–1801). Novalis shaped the German Romantic movement through poems and essays that expressed longing for the lost mythic past and a spiritually inspired future. "If God could become man," wrote Novalis, "then He can also become stone, plant, animal, and element and perhaps in this way there is redemption in Nature." The Romantic reawakening of religion embraced the doctrines of mysticism, confessional emotionalism, and pantheism, the last of which stressed the unity of God, man, and nature. According to the foremost German

Protestant theologian and preacher, Friedrich E. D. Schleiermacher (1768–1834), the object of religion is "to love the spirit of the world" and "to become one with the infinite."

Hegel and the Hegelian Dialectic

The most influential philosopher of the nineteenth century was Georg Wilhelm Friedrich Hegel (1770–1831). A professor of philosophy at the university of Berlin, Hegel taught that the world consists of a single divine nature, which he termed "absolute mind" or "spirit." Spirit and matter obey an evolutionary process impelled by spirit seeking to know its own nature. He explained the operation of that process, or **dialectic**, as follows: every condition (or "thesis") confronts its opposite condition (or "antithesis"), which then generates a synthesis. The synthesis in turn produces its opposite, and so on, in a continuing evolution that moves toward the ultimate goal of spiritual freedom. For Hegel, all reality is a process that operates on the principle of the dialectic—thesis, antithesis, and synthesis—a principle that governs the realm of ideas, artistic creation, philosophic understanding . . . indeed, history itself. "Change in nature, no matter how infinitely varied it is," wrote Hegel, "shows only a cycle of constant repetition. In nature, nothing new happens under the sun."

Hegel's dense prose work *The Philosophy of History* (1807), a compilation of his own and his students' lecture notes, advances the idea that the essence of spirit is freedom, which finds its ultimate expression in the nation-state. According to Hegel, human beings possess free will (thesis), which, though freely exercised over property, is limited by duty to the universal will (antithesis). The ultimate synthesis is a stage that is reached as individual will comes into harmony with universal duty. This last stage, which represents real freedom, manifests itself in the concrete institutions of the state and its laws. Hegel's view of the state (and the European nation-state in particular) as the last stage in the development of spirit and the Hegelian dialectic in general had considerable influence on late nineteenth-century nationalism, as well as on the economic theories of Karl Marx (see chapter 30).

Darwin and the Theory of Evolution

Like Hegel, the British scientist Charles Darwin (1809–1882) perceived nature as constantly changing. A naturalist in the tradition of Aristotle, Darwin spent his early career amassing enormous amounts of biological and geological data, partly as the result of a five-year voyage to South America aboard the research vessel HMS *Beagle*. Darwin's study of fossils on the Galápagos Islands of the Pacific Ocean confirmed the view of his predecessors that complex forms of life evolved from a few extremely simple organic forms. The theory of evolution did not originate with Darwin—Goethe, for example, had already suggested that all forms of plant life had evolved from a single primeval plant, and the French biologist Jean-Baptiste de Lamarck (1744–1829) had shown that fossils give evidence of perpetual change in all species. Darwin, however, substantiated the theory of evolution by explaining the process by which evolution occurs. Observing the tendency of certain organisms to increase rapidly over time while retaining traits favorable to their survival, he concluded that evolution operates by means of *natural selection*.

By natural selection, Darwin meant a process whereby nature "prunes away" unfavorable traits in a given species, permitting the survival of those creatures most suited to the struggle for life and to reproduction of that species. The elephant's trunk, the giraffe's neck, and the human brain were evidence, he argued, of adaptations made by each of these species to its environment and proof that any trait that remained advantageous to continuity would prevail. Failure to develop such traits meant the ultimate extinction of less developed species; only the "fittest" survived.

In 1859 Darwin published his classic work, *The Origin of Species by Means of Natural Selection, or the Preservation of the Favored Races in the Struggle for Life*. Less than a year later, a commentator observed, "No scientific work that has been published within this century has excited so much general curiosity." But curiosity was among the milder responses to this publication, for Darwin's theory of evolution, like Newton's law of gravity, challenged traditional ideas about nature and the world order. For centuries, most Westerners had held to the account of the Creation described in Scripture. Some, in fact, accepted the chronology advanced by the Irish Catholic Bishop James Ussher (1581–1656), which placed earthly creation at 4004 B.C.E. Most scholars, however, perceived the likelihood of a far greater age for the earth and its species.

Darwin's thesis did not deny the idea of a divine creator—indeed, Darwin initially speculated "it is just as noble a conception of the Deity to believe that He created a few original forms capable of self-development into other and needful forms, as to believe that He required a fresh act of creation to supply the voids caused by the action of His laws." But Darwin's theory implied that natural selection, not divine will, governed the evolutionary process. By suggesting that nature and its operations were impersonal, continuous, and self-governing, the theory of natural selection challenged the creationist view (supported by the Bible) that God had brought into being a fixed and unchanging number of species. Equally troubling was Darwin's argument (clarified in his later publication, *The Descent of Man*, 1871) that the differences between humans and less complex orders of life were differences of degree, not

Science and Technology

1799	paleontologist William Smith (British) theorizes that rock strata may be identified by fossils characteristic to each
1830	Charles Lyell (British) provides foundations for the modern study of geology in his *Principles of Geology*
1859	Darwin publishes *The Origin of Species*

kind, and that all creatures were related to one another by their kinship to lower forms of life. The most likely ancestor for *Homo sapiens*, explained Darwin, was "a hairy, tailed quadruped, probably arboreal in its habits . . ." (Figure **27.2**).

Clearly, Darwin's conclusions (which nurtured his own reluctant agnosticism) toppled human beings from their elevated place in the hierarchy of living creatures. If the cosmology of Copernicus and Galileo had displaced earth from the center of the solar system, Darwin's theory robbed human beings of their pre-eminence on the planet. At a single blow, Darwin shattered the harmonious worldviews of both Renaissance humanists and Enlightenment *philosophes*.

Figure 27.2 Spoofing evolution, a cartoon of the day portrays an apelike Charles Darwin explaining his controversial theory of evolution to an ape with the help of a mirror. The work appeared in the *London Sketch Book* in May 1874, captioned by two suitable quotations from the plays of Shakespeare: "This is the ape of form" and "Four or five descents since."

Yet, the theory of evolution by natural selection complemented a view of nature in keeping with Romanticism. As Thoreau (see Reading 27.7) mused, "Am I not partly leaves and vegetable mould myself?" And numerous passages from the writings of Wordsworth, Shelley, Emerson, and Whitman (the Romantics treated in this chapter) exhibit a similar pantheistic sentiment. At the same time, Darwin's ideas encouraged the late nineteenth-century movement of "scientism" (the proposition that the methods of the natural sciences should be applied in all areas of rational investigation). Darwin's writing also stimulated the rise of natural history museums, which, unlike the random collections of previous centuries, gave evidence of the common order of living things.

The consequences of Darwin's monumental theory were far-reaching, but his ideas were often oversimplified or misinterpreted. Among some thinkers, the theory of evolution provided the rationale for analyzing civilizations as living organisms with identifiable stages of growth, maturity, and decline. Then too, Darwin's use of the phrase "Favored Races" in the subtitle of his major work contributed to the theory of *social Darwinism*, which freely applied some of his ideas to political, economic, and cultural life.

The term "social Darwinism" did not come into use until 1879, but the idea that natural selection operated to determine the superiority of some individuals, groups, races, and nations over others was effective in justifying European policies of imperialism (see chapter 30). By their intelligence and wealth, argued the social Darwinists, Westerners (and white people in general) were clearly the "fittest," and therefore destined to dominate the less fit. Since Darwin meant by "fitness" the reproductive success of a species, not simply its survival, most applications of his work to contemporary social conditions represented a distortion of his ideas. Nevertheless, social Darwinism, expanded on by political theorists, would provide "scientific" justification for European colonialism. It also anticipated more threatening and extreme theories, such as **eugenics** (which focused on the elimination of society's "less fit" members) and the racist ideology of Adolf Hitler.

In the course of the twentieth century, modern biology, and particularly the science of molecular genetics (the study of the digital information preserved in DNA), has provided evidence to support Darwin's theory of natural selection. Nevertheless, today's scientists continue to probe the origins of life—where and how it first came into being. In the context of the nineteenth century, however, Darwin remains a leading figure. Like all Romantics, he was a keen and curious observer of nature, which he described as vast, energetic, and unceasingly dynamic. In *The Origin of Species*, he exults:

> When we no longer look at an organic being as a
> savage looks at a ship, as something wholly beyond
> his comprehension; when we regard every production
> of nature as one which has had a long history; when
> we contemplate every complex structure and instinct

as the summing up of many contrivances, each useful to the possessor, in the same way as any great mechanical invention is the summing up of the labor, the experience, the reason, and even the blunders of numerous workmen; when we thus view each organic being, how far more interesting . . . does the study of natural history become!

And in the final paragraph of his opus, Darwin brings romantic fervor to his description of nature's laws:

It is interesting to contemplate a tangled bank, clothed with many plants of many kinds, with birds singing on the bushes, with various insects flitting about, and with worms crawling through the damp earth, and to reflect that these elaborately constructed forms, so different from each other, and dependent upon each other in so complex a manner, have all been produced by laws acting around us. These laws, taken in the largest sense, being Growth and Reproduction; Inheritance which is almost implied by reproduction; Variability from the indirect and direct action of the conditions of life, and from use and disuse; a Ratio of Increase so high as to lead to a Struggle for Life, and as a consequence to Natural Selection, entailing Divergence of Character and the Extinction of less-improved forms. Thus, from the war of nature, from famine and death, the most exalted object which we are capable of conceiving, namely, the production of the higher animals, directly follows. There is grandeur in this view of life, with its several powers, having been originally breathed by the Creator into a few forms or into one; and that, whilst this planet has gone cycling on according to the fixed law of gravity, from so simple a beginning endless forms most beautiful and most wonderful have been, and are being evolved.

Nature and the Natural in European Literature

Nature and the Natural in European Literature

One of the central features of nineteenth-century Romanticism was its love affair with nature. In nature, with its shifting moods and rhythms, the Romantics found solace, inspiration, and self-discovery. To Enlightenment thinkers, "nature" meant universal order, but to the Romantics, nature was the wellspring of divinity, the phenomenon that bound humankind to God. "Natural man" was one who was close to nature, unspoiled (as Rousseau had argued) by social institutions and imperatives.

The Romantics lamented the dismal effects of growing industrialization. In rural settings, they found a practical refuge from urban blight, smoke-belching factories, and poverty-ridden slums. The natural landscape, unspoiled and unpolluted, revealed the oneness of God and the universe. This **pantheistic** outlook, more typical of Eastern than Western religious philosophy, came to pervade the literature of European and American Romantics.

Wordsworth and the Poetry of Nature

In 1798, William Wordsworth (1780–1850) and his British contemporary Samuel Taylor Coleridge (1772–1834) produced the *Lyrical Ballads*, the literary work that marked the birth of the Romantic movement in England. When the book appeared in a second edition in 1800, Wordsworth added a preface that formally explained the aims of Romantic poetry. In this manifesto, Wordsworth described poetry as "the spontaneous overflow of powerful feelings," which takes its origin "from emotion recollected in tranquillity." The object of the poet is,

to choose incidents and situations from common life [and] to throw over them a certain colouring of the

EXPLORING ISSUES

Creationism versus Evolution

Darwin's *Origin of Species* generated much controversy in its own time and long thereafter. In the last 150 years, fossil research and molecular biology have provided overwhelming evidence to support the theory of evolution. Nevertheless, controversy continues. The debate centers on the question of origins, that is, whether human beings were divinely created or are the product of a series of biological "accidents" governed by natural selection. Creationists hold that biological design argues for the existence of a Designer whose intelligent contrivance produced the world as we know it. While the defenders of Intelligent Design view Darwin's theory as evidence for a random and undirected universe, Darwin himself, observing the "grandeur in this view of life, with its several powers, having been originally breathed by the Creator . . ."

speculated that natural selection and biological evolution might be part of a divine design.

Many religious faiths have no difficulty in accepting the idea that biological evolution governs the diversity of living things over billions of years, and thus find evolution and religious belief compatible. However, those who hold to the literal truth of Scripture find Darwin's theories in direct contradiction of their religious beliefs. The ongoing controversy, which flourishes mainly in the United States, centers on public education: whether creationism should be taught along with evolution in the classroom. The debate has provoked a number of related issues, including the definition and validity of "good science," and contemporary interpretations of the Book of Genesis.

imagination . . . and above all, to make these incidents and situations interesting by tracing in them, truly though not ostentatiously, the primary laws of our nature.

The leading nature poet of the nineteenth century, Wordsworth was born in the English Lake District. He dated the beginning of his creative life from the time—at age fourteen—when he was struck by the image of tree boughs silhouetted against a bright evening sky. Thereafter, what he called "the infinite variety of natural appearances" became his principal source of inspiration and the primary subject of his poetry. Nature, he claimed, could restore to human beings their untainted, childhood sense of wonder. Moreover, through nature (as revealed to us by way of the senses), one might commune with the elemental and divine forces of the universe.

Wordsworth championed a poetic language that resembled "the real language of men in a state of vivid sensation." Although he did not always abide by his own precepts, his rejection of the artificial diction of Neoclassical verse in favor of this "real language" anticipated a new, more natural voice in poetry—one informed by childhood memories and deeply felt experiences. Wordsworth's verse reflects his preference for **lyric poetry**, which—like art song—describes deep personal feeling.

One of the most inspired poems in the *Lyrical Ballads* is "Lines Composed a Few Miles Above Tintern Abbey," the product of Wordsworth's visit to the ruins of a medieval monastery situated on the banks of the Wye River in southwest England (Figure **27.3**). The 159-line poem constitutes a paean to nature. Wordsworth begins by describing the sensations evoked by the English countryside; he

Figure 27.3 J. M. W. TURNER, *Interior of Tintern Abbey*, 1794. Watercolor, 12⅜ × 9⅞ in. At age nineteen, Turner explored the Wye Valley in search of picturesque subjects. This thirteenth-century abbey had fallen into ruin after the dissolution of the monasteries by Henry VIII in the 1530s.

then muses on the pleasures these memories provide as they are called up in recollection. The heart of the poem, however, is a joyous celebration of nature's moral value: nature allows the poet to "see into the life of things" (line 49), infusing him with "the still, sad music of humanity" (line 91), and ultimately bringing him into the sublime presence of the divine spirit. Nature, he exults, is the "anchor" of his purest thoughts, the "nurse" and "guardian" of his heart and soul (lines 109–110). In the final portion of the extract (lines 111–134), Wordsworth shares with his "dearest Friend," his sister Dorothy, the joys of his mystical communion with nature and humankind. "Tintern Abbey" set forth three of the key motifs of nineteenth-century Romanticism: the redemptive power of nature, the idea of nature's sympathy with humankind, and the view that one who is close to nature is close to God.

READING 27.1 From Wordsworth's "Lines Composed a Few Miles Above Tintern Abbey" (1798)

Five years have passed; five summers, with the length   1
Of five long winters! and again I hear
These waters, rolling from their mountain-springs
With a soft inland murmur. Once again
Do I behold these steep and lofty cliffs,   5
That on a wild secluded scene impress
Thoughts of more deep seclusion; and connect
The landscape with the quiet of the sky.
The day is come when I again repose
Here, under this dark sycamore, and view   10
These plots of cottage-ground, these orchard tufts,
Which at this season, with their unripe fruits,
Are clad in one green hue, and lose themselves
'Mid groves and copses. Once again I see
These hedge-rows, hardly hedge-rows, little lines   15
Of sportive wood run wild: these pastoral farms,
Green to the very door; and wreaths of smoke
Sent up, in silence, from among the trees!
With some uncertain notice, as might seem
Of vagrant dwellers in the houseless woods,   20
Or of some Hermit's cave, where by his fire
The hermit sits alone.
               These beauteous forms,
Through a long absence, have not been to me
As is a landscape to a blind man's eye;
But oft, in lonely rooms, and 'mid the din   25
Of towns and cities, I have owed to them
In hours of weariness, sensations sweet,
Felt in the blood, and felt along the heart;
And passing even into my purer mind,
With tranquil restoration:—feelings too   30
Of unremembered pleasure: such, perhaps,
As have no slight or trivial influence
On that best portion of a good man's life,
His little, nameless, unremembered acts
Of kindness and of love. Nor less, I trust,   35

To them I may have owed another gift,
Of aspect more sublime; that blessed mood,
In which the burthen[1] of the mystery,
In which the heavy and the weary weight
Of all this unintelligible world,   40
Is lightened—that serene and blessed mood,
In which the affections gently lead us on—
Until, the breath of this corporeal frame
And even the motion of our human blood
Almost suspended, we are laid asleep   45
In body, and become a living soul;
While with an eye made quiet by the power
Of harmony, and the deep power of joy,
We see into the life of things.
                If this
Be but a vain belief, yet, oh! how oft—   50
In darkness and amid the many shapes
Of joyless daylight; when the fretful stir
Unprofitable, and the fever of the world,
Have hung upon the beatings of my heart—
How oft, in spirit, have I turned to thee,   55
O sylvan[2] Wye! thou wanderer through the woods,
How often has my spirit turned to thee!

   And now, with gleams of half-extinguished thought,
With many recognitions dim and faint,
And somewhat of a sad perplexity,   60
The picture of the mind revives again;
While here I stand, not only with the sense
Of present pleasure, but with pleasing thoughts
That in this moment there is life and food
For future years. And so I dare to hope,   65
Though changed, no doubt, from what I was when first
I came among these hills; when like a roe
I bounded o'er the mountains, by the sides
Of the deep rivers, and the lonely streams,
Wherever nature led: more like a man   70
Flying from something that he dreads than one
Who sought the thing he loved. For nature then
(The coarser pleasures of my boyish days,
And their glad animal movements all gone by)
To me was all in all—I cannot paint   75
What then I was. The sounding cataract[3]
Haunted me like a passion; the tall rock,
The mountain, and the deep and gloomy wood,
Their colours and their forms, were then to me
An appetite; a feeling and a love,   80
That had no need of a remoter charm,
By thought supplied, nor any interest
Unborrowed from the eye. That time is past,
And all its aching joys are now no more,
And all its dizzy raptures. Not for this   85
Faint I, nor mourn nor murmur; other gifts
Have followed; for such loss, I would believe,

---

[1] Burden.
[2] Wooded.
[3] A descent of water over a steep surface.

Abundant recompense. For I have learned
To look on nature, not as in the hour
Of thoughtless youth; but hearing oftentimes   90
The still, sad music of humanity,
Nor harsh nor grating, though of ample power
To chasten and subdue. And I have felt
A presence that disturbs me with the joy
Of elevated thoughts; a sense sublime   95
Of something far more deeply interfused,
Whose dwelling is the light of setting suns,
And the round ocean and the living air,
And the blue sky, and in the mind of man:
A motion and a spirit, that impels   100
All thinking things, all objects of all thought,
And rolls through all things. Therefore am I still
A lover of the meadows and the woods,
And mountains; and of all that we behold
From this green earth; of all the mighty world   105
Of eye, and ear—both what they half create,
And what perceive; well pleased to recognize
In nature and the language of the sense,
The anchor of my purest thoughts, the nurse,
The guide, the guardian of my heart, and soul   110
Of all my moral being.
                    Nor perchance,
If I were not thus taught, should I the more
Suffer my genial spirits to decay:
For thou art with me here upon the banks
Of this fair river; thou my dearest Friend,[4]   115
My dear, dear Friend; and in thy voice I catch
The language of my former heart, and read
My former pleasures in the shooting lights
Of thy wild eyes. Oh! yet a little while
May I behold in thee what I was once,   120
My dear, dear Sister! and this prayer I make,
Knowing that Nature never did betray
The heart that loved her; 'tis her privilege,
Through all the years of this our life, to lead
From joy to joy: for she can so inform   125
The mind that is within us, so impress
With quietness and beauty, and so feed
With lofty thoughts, that neither evil tongues,
Rash judgments, nor the sneers of selfish men,
Nor greetings where no kindness is, nor all   130
The dreary intercourse of daily life,
Shall e'er prevail against us, or disturb
Our cheerful faith, that all which we behold
Is full of blessings. . . .

Q What does Wordsworth mean when he calls
nature "the anchor of my purest thoughts?"

Q Which lines in this selection best capture the
sublime aspects of nature?

[4] Wordsworth's sister, Dorothy.

The Poetry of Shelley

Like Wordsworth, the English poet Percy Bysshe Shelley (1792–1822) embraced nature as the source of sublime truth, but his volcanic personality led him to engage the natural world with greater intensity and deeper melancholy than his older contemporary. A prolific writer and a passionate champion of human liberty, he provoked the reading public with a treatise entitled *The Necessity of Atheism* (1811), the circulation of which led to his expulsion from Oxford University. His pamphlet on the subject of the French Revolution, *A Declaration of Rights* (1812), endorsed a radical creed for political equality: "A Christian, a Deist, a Turk, and a Jew, have equal rights [in the benefits and burdens of government]."

Shelley was outspoken in his opposition to marriage, a union that he viewed as hostile to human happiness. He was as unconventional in his deeds as in his discourse: while married to one woman (Harriet Westbrook), with whom he had two children, he ran off with another (Mary Godwin). A harsh critic of Britain's rulers, he chose permanent exile in Italy in 1818 and died there four years later in a boating accident.

Shelley's *Defence of Poetry* (1821), a manifesto of the writer's function in society, hails poets as "the unacknowledged legislators of the world." Such creatures take their authority from nature, the fountainhead of inspiration. Shelley himself found in nature metaphors for the inconstant state of human desire. In "Ode to the West Wind" he appeals to the wind, a symbol of creativity, to drive his visions throughout the universe, as the wind drives leaves over the earth (stanza 1), clouds through the air (stanza 2), and waves on the seas (stanza 3). In the last stanza, he compares the poet to a lyre, whose "mighty harmonies," stirred by the wind of creativity, will awaken the world. Then, finally, he seeks his identity with the wind and nature itself: "Be thou, spirit fierce/My spirit! Be thou me, impetuous one!" By means of language that is itself musical, Shelley defends the notion of poetry as the music of the soul. Consider, for instance, his frequent use of the exclamatory "O" and the effective use of **assonance** and tonal color in lines 38 to 40: "while far below/The sea-blooms and the oozy woods which wear/The sapless foliage of the ocean, know."

READING 27.2 Shelley's "Ode to the
West Wind" (1819)

1

O wild West Wind, thou breath of Autumn"s being   1
Thou, from whose unseen presence the leaves dead
Are driven, like ghosts from an enchanter fleeing,

Yellow, and black, and pale, and hectic red,
Pestilence-stricken multitudes: O thou,   5
Who chariotest to their dark wintry bed

The wingèd seeds, where they lie cold and low,
Each like a corpse within its grave, until
Thine azure sister of the spring shall blow

Her clarion o'er the dreaming earth, and fill   10

(Driving sweet buds like flocks to feed in air)
With living hues and odours plain and hill:

Wild Spirit, which art moving everywhere;
Destroyer and preserver; hear, oh, hear!

2

Thou on whose stream, 'mid the steep sky's commotion,   15
Loose clouds like earth's decaying leaves are shed,
Shook from the tangled boughs of Heaven and Ocean,

Angels of rain and lightning: there are spread
On the blue surface of thine aëry surge,
Like the bright hair uplifted from the head   20

Of some fierce Maenad,[1] even from the dim verge
Of the horizon to the zenith's height,
The locks of the approaching storm. Thou dirge

Of the dying year, to which this closing night
Will be the dome of a vast sepulchre,[2]   25
Vaulted with all thy congregated might

Of vapours, from whose solid atmosphere
Black rain, and fire, and hail will burst: O, hear!

3

Thou who didst waken from his summer dreams
The blue Mediterranean, where he lay,   30
Lulled by the coil of his crystalline streams,

Beside a pumice isle in Baiae's bay,[3]
And saw in sleep old palaces and towers
Quivering within the wave's intenser day,

All overgrown with azure moss and flowers   35
So sweet, the sense faints picturing them! Thou
For whose path the Atlantic's level powers

Cleave themselves into chasms, while far below
The sea-blooms and the oozy woods which wear
The sapless foliage of the ocean, know   40

Thy voice, and suddenly grow grey with fear,
And tremble and despoil themselves: O, hear!

4

If I were a dead leaf thou mightest bear;
If I were a swift cloud to fly with thee;
A wave to pant beneath thy power, and share   45

The impulse of thy strength, only less free
Than thou, O uncontrollable! If even
I were as in my boyhood, and could be

The comrade of thy wanderings over heaven,
As then, when to outstrip thy skiey speed   50
Scarce seemed a vision; I would ne'er have striven

As thus with thee in prayer in my sore need.
Oh! lift me as a wave, a leaf, a cloud!
I fall upon the thorns of life! I bleed!

A heavy weight of hours has chained and bowed   55

One too like thee: tameless, and swift, and proud.

5

Make me thy lyre, even as the forest is:
What if my leaves are falling like its own!
The tumult of thy mighty harmonies

Will take from both a deep, autumnal tone,   60
Sweet though in sadness. Be thou, spirit fierce,
My spirit! Be thou me, impetuous one!

Drive my dead thoughts over the universe
Like withered leaves to quicken a new birth!
And, by the incantation of this verse,   65

Scatter, as from an unextinguished hearth
Ashes and sparks, my words among mankind!
Be through my lips to unawakened earth

The trumpet of a prophecy! O, Wind,
If Winter comes, can Spring be far behind?   70

Q How would you describe the function of color in this poem?

Q What does this poem reveal about the personality of the poet?

The Poetry of Keats

The poetry of John Keats (1795–1821), the third of the great English nature poets, shares Shelley's elegiac sensibility. Keats lamented the fleeting nature of life's pleasures, even as he contemplated the brevity of life. He lost both his mother and his brother to tuberculosis, and he himself succumbed to that disease at the age of twenty-five. The threat of imminent death seems to have produced in Keats a heightened awareness of the virtues of beauty, human love, and friendship. He perceived these phenomena as fleeting forms of a higher reality made permanent only in art. For Keats, art is the great balm of the poet. Art is more than a response to the human experience of love and nature; it is the transmuted product of the imagination, a higher form of nature that triumphantly outreaches the mortal lifespan. These ideas are central to Keats' "Ode on a Grecian Urn." The poem was inspired by ancient Greek artifacts Keats had seen among those brought to London by Lord Elgin in 1816 and placed on display in the British Museum (see chapter 5).

In the "Ode," Keats contemplates a Greek vase (much like the one pictured in Figure **27.4**), whose delicately drawn figures are shown enjoying transitory pleasures. Frozen in time on the surface of such a vase, the fair youths will never grow old, the music of the pipes and lyres will never cease to sound, and the lovers will never cease to love. The "little town by river" and the other pastoral vignettes in the poem probably did not belong to any one existing Greek vase; yet Keats describes the imaginary urn (his metaphoric "Cold Pastoral") as a symbol of all great works of art, which, because of their unchanging beauty, remain eternally "true." The poem concludes with the joyous pronouncement: beauty and truth are one.

---

[1] A female attendant of Dionysus; a bacchante (see chapter 26).
[2] Tomb.
[3] An ancient resort in southwest Italy.

Figure 27.4 SISYPHUS PAINTER, south Italian volute krater with women making music and centaur fight, late fifth century B.C.E. Red-figure pottery.

READING 27.3 Keats' "Ode on a Grecian Urn"
(1818)

1

Thou still unravished bride of quietness,   1
   Thou foster-child of Silence and slow Time,
Sylvan historian, who canst thus express
   A flowery tale more sweetly than our rhyme:
What leaf-fringed[1] legend haunts about thy shape   5
   Of deities or mortals, or of both,
    In Tempe[2] or the dales of Arcady?[3]
   What men or gods are these? What maidens loth?
What mad pursuit? What struggle to escape?
   What pipes and timbrels? What wild ecstasy?   10

2

Heard melodies are sweet, but those unheard
   Are sweeter; therefore, ye soft pipes, play on;
Not to the sensual ear, but, more endeared,
   Pipe to the spirit ditties of no tone:
Fair youth, beneath the trees, thou canst not leave   15
   Thy song, nor ever can those trees be bare;
    Bold Lover, never, never canst thou kiss,

Though winning near the goal—yet, do not grieve;
   She cannot fade, though thou hast not thy bliss,
    For ever wilt thou love, and she be fair!   20

3

Ah, happy, happy boughs! that cannot shed
   Your leaves, nor ever bid the Spring adieu;
And, happy melodist, unweariéd,
   For ever piping songs for ever new;
More happy love! more happy, happy love!   25
   For ever warm and still to be enjoyed,
    For ever panting, and for ever young;
All breathing human passion far above,
   That leaves a heart high-sorrowful and cloyed,
    A burning forehead, and a parching tongue.   30

4

Who are these coming to the sacrifice?
   To what green altar, O mysterious priest,
Lead'st thou that heifer lowing at the skies,
   And all her silken flanks with garlands drest?
What little town by river or sea shore,   35
   Or mountain-built with peaceful citadel,
    Is emptied of this folk, this pious morn?
And, little town, thy streets for evermore
   Will silent be; and not a soul to tell
    Why thou art desolate, can e'er return.   40

5

O Attic[4] shape! Fair attitude! with brede[5]
   Of marble men and maidens overwrought,
With forest branches and the trodden weed;
   Thou, silent form, dost tease us out of thought
As doth eternity: Cold Pastoral!   45
   When old age shall this generation waste,
    Thou shalt remain, in midst of other woe
Than ours, a friend to man, to whom thou say'st,
   "Beauty is truth, truth beauty,"—that is all
Ye know on earth, and all ye need to know.   50

Q How does this work of art—the painted urn—lead Keats to a perception of truth?

Blake: Romantic Mystic

The British poet, painter, and engraver William Blake (1757–1827) shared the Romantic disdain for convention and authority. Blake, however, introduced a more mystical view of nature, God, and humankind. Deeply spiritual, he claimed "To see nature in a Grain of Sand,/ And Heaven in a Wild flower." This divine vision he brought to his

---

[1] A reference to the common Greek practice of bordering vases with stylized leaf forms (see Figure 27.4).
[2] A valley sacred to Apollo between Mounts Olympus and Ossa in Thessaly, Greece.
[3] Arcadia, the pastoral regions of ancient Greece (see Poussin's *Arcadian Shepherds*, Figure 21.13).
[4] Attica, a region in southeastern Greece dominated by Athens.
[5] Embroidered border.

poetry and his paintings. Indeed, his poetry was conceived along with visual images that he himself drew. Trained in the graphic arts, he prepared all aspects of his individual works, designing, illustrating, engraving, and hand-coloring each page (Figure 27.5).

Blake's early poems featured singular images with clear and vivid (and often) moral messages. "The Lamb," a short poem from his *Songs of Innocence* (1789), envisions that animal as a symbol of God's gentle goodness. In his *Songs of Experience* (1794), childlike lyricism gives way to the disillusionment of maturity. The most famous poem in this collection, "The Tiger," asks whether goodness must be accompanied by evil, and whether God is responsible for both.

READING 27.4 Blake's "The Tiger"

Tiger! Tiger! Burning bright
In the forest of the night,
What immortal hand or eye
Could frame thy fearful symmetry?

In what distant deeps or skies
Burnt the first of thine eyes?
On what wings dare he aspire?
What the hand dare seize the fire?

And what shoulder, and what art,
Could twist the sinews of thy heart?
And when thy heart began to beat,
What dread hand? And what dread feet?

What the hammer? What the chain?
In what furnace was thy brain?
What the anvil? What dread grasp
Dare its deadly terrors clasp?

When the stars threw down their spears,
And watered heaven with their tears,
Did he smile his work to see?
Did he who made the Lamb make thee?

Tiger! Tiger! Burning bright
In the forests of the night,
What immortal hand or eye,
Dare frame thy fearful symmetry.

Q **What kind of Creator does Blake envision? What preconceptions color Blake's view of nature?**

Blake's poetic imagination took much from the Bible and Milton's *Paradise Lost* (see chapter 22)—some scholars see in the fifth stanza of "The Tiger" an allusion to Milton's powerful Satan. Regardless of whether one perceives the Maker as satanic or divine or both, the poem seems to assert the typically Romantic view of the artist as sharing God's burden of creation and the creative process.

Figure 27.5 WILLIAM BLAKE, *The Tyger*, ca. 1815–1826. Etching, ink and watercolor, 11 × 4 in.

Nature and the Natural in Asian Literature

Although no literary movement in Chinese history has been designated "Romantic," there are clear examples of the Romantic sensibility in Chinese literature of the nineteenth century, especially in those works that exalt the emotional identification of the individual with nature. The Chinese writer Shen Fu (1763–1809) shares with Wordsworth, Shelley, and Keats the reflective view of nature and a heightened sensitivity to its transient moods. A bohemian spirit, Shen Fu failed the district civil examinations that guaranteed financial success for Chinese intellectuals. Often in debt and expelled from his family by an overbearing father, he found brief but profound joy in his marriage to a neighbor's daughter, Zhen Yuen. Shen Fu's autobiography, *Six Chapters from a Floating Life* (1809), is a confessional record of their life together, a life in which poverty is balanced by the pleasures of married love and an abiding affection for nature.

In the following excerpt from Shen's autobiography—a favorite with Chinese readers to this day—the writer describes the simple pleasures he and Zhen Yuen derived from growing flowers and designing "rockeries": natural arrangements of rocks and soil that resemble miniature gardens. The tender story of the destruction of the "Place of Falling Flowers," the couple's tiny version of the natural landscape, anticipates the central event of Shen's intimate life history: the death of his beloved wife. The story also functions as a reminder that all of nature is fragile and impermanent.

As a young man I was excessively fond of flowers and loved to prune and shape potted plants and trees. When I met Chang Lan-p'o he began to teach me the art of training branches and supporting joints, and after I had mastered these skills, he showed me how to graft flowers. Later on, I also learned the placing of stones and designing of rockeries. [1]

The orchid we considered the peerless flower, selecting it as much for its subtle and delicate fragrance as for its beauty and grace. Fine varieties of orchids were very difficult to find, especially those worthy of being recorded in the Botanical [10] Register. When Lan-p'o was dying he gave me a pot of spring orchids of the lotus type, with broad white centres, perfectly even "shoulders," and very slender stems. As the plant was a classic specimen of its type, I treasured its perfection like a piece of ancient jade. Yuen took care of it whenever my work as yamen secretary[1] called me away from home. She always watered it herself and the plant flourished, producing a luxuriant growth of leaves and flowers.

One morning, about two years later, it suddenly withered and died. When I dug up the roots to inspect them, I saw that [20] they were as white as jade, with many new shoots beginning to sprout. At first, I could not understand it. Was I just too unlucky, I wondered, to possess and enjoy such beauty? Sighing despondently, I dismissed the matter from my mind. But some time later I found out what had really happened. It seemed that a person who had asked for a cutting from the plant and had been refused, had then poured boiling water on it and killed it. After that, I vowed never to grow orchids again.

Azaleas were my second choice. Although the flowers had no fragrance they were very beautiful and lasted a long time. [30] The plants were easy to trim and to train, but Yuen loved the green of the branches and leaves so much that she would not let me cut them back, and this made it difficult for me to train them to correct shapes. Unfortunately, Yuen felt this way about all the potted plants that she enjoyed.

Every year, in the autumn, I became completely devoted to the chrysanthemum. I loved to arrange the cut flowers in vases but did not like the potted plants. Not that I did not think the potted flowers beautiful, but our house having no garden, it was impossible for me to grow the plants myself, and those for [40] sale at the market were overgrown and untrained; not at all what I would have chosen.

One day, as I was sweeping my ancestral graves in the hills, I found some very unusual stones with interesting streaks and lines running through them. I talked to Yuen about them when I went home.

"When Hsüan-chou stones are mixed with putty and arranged in white-stone dishes, the putty and stones blend well and the effect is very harmonious," I remarked. "These yellow stones from the hills are rugged and old-looking, but if [50] we mix them with putty the yellow and white won't blend. All the seams and gaps will show up and the arrangement will look spotty. I wonder what else we could use instead of putty?"

"Why not pick out some of the poor, uninteresting stones and pound them to powder," Yuen said. "If we mix the powdered stones with the putty while it is still damp, the colour will probably match when it dries."

After doing as she suggested, we took a rectangular I-hsing pottery dish and piled the stones and putty into a miniature [60] mountain peak on the left side of it, with a rocky crag jutting out towards the right. On the surface of the mountain, we made criss-cross marks in the style of the rocks painted by Ni Tsan[2] of the Yuan dynasty. This gave an effect of perspective and the finished arrangement looked very realistic—a precipitous cliff rising sharply from the rocks at the river's edge. Making a hollow in one corner of the dish, we filled it with river mud and planted it with duckweed. Among the rocks we planted "clouds of the pine trees," bindweed. It was several days before the whole thing was finished. [70]

Before the end of autumn the bindweed had spread all over the mountain and hung like wistaria from the rocky cliff. The flowers, when they bloomed, were a beautiful clear red. The duckweed, too, had sprouted luxuriantly from the mud and was now a mass of snowy white. Seeing the beauty of the contrasting red and white, we could easily imagine ourselves in Fairyland.

Setting the dish under the eaves, we started discussing what should be done next, developing many themes: "Here there should be a lake with a pavilion—" "This spot calls for a [80] thatched summerhouse—" "This is the perfect place for the six-character inscription 'Place of Falling Flowers and Flowing Water'"—"Here we could build our house—here go fishing—here enjoy the view"; becoming, by this time, so much a part of the tiny landscape, with its hills and ravines, that it seemed to us as if we were really going to move there to live.

One night, a couple of mis-begotten cats, fighting over food, fell off the eaves and hit the dish, knocking it off its stand and smashing it to fragments in an instant. Neither of us could help crying. [90]

"Isn't it possible," I sighed, "to have even a little thing like this without incurring the envy of the gods?"

Q What aspects of this selection reflect East Asian attitudes toward nature and the natural?

Q How does Shen Fu suggest the fragility of life?

Romantic Landscape Painting

Landscape painting originated as an independent genre not in the West, but in the East. While the ancient Romans had devised naturalistic settings for mythological subjects (see Figure 6.28), it was in tenth-century China that landscape painting first became a subject *in and of itself*

---

[1] A government clerk.

[2] A famous landscape painter (1301–1374) of the Yuan dynasty (1279–1368).

(see Figures 14.15 and 14.16). By the thirteenth century, the Chinese landscape had overtaken figure painting in popularity. The genre soon spread to Japan and other parts of East Asia. Typically vast and sweeping, Chinese landscapes achieve a cosmic unity of air, earth, and water that dwarfs the human figure (see Figure 27.6). Such landscapes are not literal imitations of reality, but expressions of a benign natural harmony. Executed in monochrome ink on silk, bamboo, or paper scrolls, they were intended as sources of personal pleasure and private retreat. Whether vertical or horizontal in format, they are "read" from a number of viewpoints, rather than from a single vantage point. In all of these features, Chinese landscapes differ from those of European artists.

In Europe, it was not until the Renaissance—among such painters as Leonardo da Vinci, Dürer, and Brueghel—that the natural landscape became a subject in its own right. Most Renaissance landscapes were visual records of a specific time and place (see Figure 19.12). During the seventeenth century, French academic painters cultivated the ideal landscape, a genre in which nature became the stage for mythological and biblical subjects (see Figure 21.14). The composition was conceived in the studio; key motifs, such as a foreground tree or a meandering road (often drawn from nature), were then incorporated into the design. Seventeenth-century Dutch masters, on the other hand, rejected the ideal landscape: Vermeer and Rembrandt rendered empirically precise views of the physical world as perceived by the human eye (see Figure 23.10).

MAKING CONNECTIONS

Chinese landscape paintings generally achieve a sweeping unity of air, earth, and water that dwarfs the human figure. In one typically Chinese ink-on-paper album leaf, the artist Shen Zhou (1427–1509) pictures a solitary figure (possibly himself) atop a rugged cliff, overlooking a vast natural expanse (Figure **27.6**). To the painting, he has added these lines:

> White clouds encircle the waist of the hills like a belt;
> A stony ledge soars into the world, a narrow path into space.
> Alone, I lean on my thornwood staff and gaze calmly into the distance,
> About to play my flute in reply to the song of this mountain stream.*

The paintings of the nineteenth-century German artist Caspar David Friedrich (1774–1840), while not directly influenced by Chinese art, share some of its basic features. Friedrich's views of wintry graveyards and Gothic ruins usually show distant figures contemplating (with what the artist called "our spiritual eye") the mysteries of time and nature. In one of Friedrich's most notable paintings, two men stand at the brink of a steep cliff, overlooking an unseen valley (Figure **27.7**). A craggy, half-uprooted tree is silhouetted against the glowing, moonlit sky. Somber colors enhance a mood of poetic loneliness. While Shen Zhou's cosmic vista makes nature itself the subject matter, Friedrich's landscape—more closely focused and detailed—draws our attention to the figures. Nevertheless, both artists capture nature's power to free the individual from the confines of the material world. In spaces smaller than 2 feet square, they record the universal dialogue between humankind and nature.

*Translated by Daniel Bryant

Figure 27.6 SHEN ZHOU, *Poet on a Mountain Top*, from the "Landscape Album" series, ca. 1495–1500. Album leaf mounted as a handscroll: ink on paper or ink and light color on paper, 15¼ × 23¾ in.

Figure 27.7 CASPAR DAVID FRIEDRICH, *Two Men Looking at the Moon*, 1819–1820. Oil on panel, 13¾ × 17¼ in.

During the following century, topographic landscapes—detailed descriptions of popular or remote locales—served the public as the picture postcards of their time. It was not until the nineteenth century, however, that the landscape became a primary vehicle for the expression of an artist's shifting moods and private emotions. Romantic painters translated their native affection for the countryside into scenes that ranged from the picturesque to the sublime. Like Wordsworth and Shelley, these artists discovered in nature a source of inspiration and a mirror of their own sensibilities.

Constable and Turner

 English artists took the lead in the genesis of the Romantic landscape. John Constable (1776–1837) owed much to the Dutch masters; yet his approach to nature was uncluttered by tradition. "When I sit down to make a sketch from nature," he wrote, "the first thing I try to do is to forget that I have ever seen a picture." Constable's freshly perceived landscapes celebrate the physical beauty of the rivers, trees, and cottages of his native Suffolk countryside even as they describe the mundane labors of its inhabitants (see Figure 27.1). Like Wordsworth, who favored "incidents and situations from common life," Constable chose to paint ordinary subjects—"water escaping from mill-dams, willows, old rotten planks, slimy posts, and brickwork"—as he described them. And like Wordsworth, he drew on his childhood experiences as sources of inspiration. "Painting," Constable explained, "is with me but another word for feeling and I

associate 'my careless boyhood' with all that lies on the banks of the Stour [River]; those scenes made me a painter, and I am grateful."

Constable brought to his landscapes a sensitive blend of empirical detail and painterly freedom. Fascinated by nineteenth-century treatises on the scientific classifications of clouds, he made numerous oil studies of cloud formations, noting on the reverse of each sketch the time of the year, hour of the day, and direction of the wind. "The sky," he wrote, "is the source of light in nature, and governs everything." He confessed to an "over-anxiety" about his skies and feared that he might destroy "that easy appearance which nature always has in all her movements." In order to capture the "easy appearance" of nature and the fugitive effects of light and atmosphere, he often stippled parts of the landscape with white dots (compare Vermeer; see chapter 23)—a device critics called "Constable's snow." His finished landscapes thus record not so much the "look" of nature as its fleeting moods.

In *Wivenhoe Park, Essex*, Constable depicts cattle grazing on English lawns that typically resemble well-manicured gardens (Figure **27.8**). From the distant horizon, the residence of the owners overlooks a verdant estate. Brilliant sunshine floods through the trees and across the fields onto a lake that is shared by swans and fishermen. But the real subject of the painting is the sky, which, with its windblown clouds, preserves the spontaneity of Constable's oil sketches.

If Constable's landscapes describe the gentle spirit of the English countryside, those of his English contemporary Joseph Mallord Turner (1775–1851) invest nature with theatrical fervor. Trained in architectural draftsmanship,

Figure 27.8 JOHN CONSTABLE, *Wivenhoe Park, Essex*, 1816. Oil on canvas, 22⅛ in. × 3 ft. 3⅛ in.
While Constable often made his sketches outdoors where he was able to capture the effects of light in the landscape setting, he finished his paintings in his studio.

Figure 27.9 J. M. W. TURNER, *The Slave Ship (Slavers Throwing Overboard the Dead and Dying: Typhoon Coming On)*, 1840. Oil on canvas, 35¾ in. × 4 ft. ¼ in. Turner infused many of his paintings with a golden glow, achieved by working from a white (rather than a dark) ground and by the use of new yellow pigments commercially available after 1817. His detractors accused Turner of "yellow fever."

Turner began his career by making elegant drawings of Gothic ruins and popular tourist sites in England and Wales. These he sold to engravers, who mass-produced and marketed them. One of his early drawings, an intricate pencil sketch of the ruined monastery of Tintern Abbey, captures with some nostalgia the transient beauty of the medieval past (see Figure 27.3). Between 1814 and 1830, Turner traveled extensively throughout England and the Continent, making landscape studies of the mountains and lakes of Switzerland, the breathtaking reaches of the Alps, and the picturesque cities of Italy. His European tours inspired hundreds of rapid pencil sketches and luminous, eloquent studies executed in the spontaneous (and portable) medium of watercolor. His large-scale paintings of Venice, glorious explorations of the play of light on water, were among the most sought after of his travel canvases.

In his mature style, the lyricism of Turner's early works gave way to impassioned studies of nature's more turbulent moods. Natural disasters—great storms and Alpine avalanches—and human catastrophes, such as shipwrecks and fires, became metaphors for human vulnerability before the forces of nature. Such expressions of the "sublime"—the terror human beings experience in the face of nature's overpowering forces—occupied the Romantic imagination. The sea, a symbol of nature's indomitable power,

prevails as a Romantic theme in Samuel Taylor Coleridge's *Rime of the Ancient Mariner* (1798), Herman Melville's monumental novel *Moby Dick* (1851), and Théodore Géricault's *The Raft of the "Medusa"* (see Figure 29.4), which Turner had seen in London.

In *The Slave Ship* of 1840 (Figure **27.9**), the glowing sunset, turbulent seas, impending storm, and fantastic fish (that appear to devour the remains of the shackled body in the right foreground) do not immediately reveal the horror of the subject described in the original title: *Slavers Throwing Overboard the Dead and Dying: Typhoon Coming On*. While Britain had finally abolished slavery throughout its colonies in 1838, popular literature on the history of the slave trade published in 1839 recounted in some detail the notorious activity that inspired Turner's painting: the transatlantic traders' practice of throwing overboard the malnourished and disease-ridden bodies of African slaves, and then collecting insurance money on "goods lost" at sea. On the threshold of rising British commercialism (see chapter 30), Turner seems to suggest that the human capacity for evil rivals nature's cruelest powers.

Two years later, in *Snowstorm* (Figure **27.10**), Turner mounted his own Romantic engagement with nature: the 67-year-old artist claimed that, at his request, sailors lashed him to the mast of a ship caught for hours in a storm at sea so that he might "show what such a scene was like." He subtitled the painting "Steamboat off a Harbour's Mouth making Signals in Shallow Water . . . the Author was in this Storm on the Night the Ariel left Harwich." Since no ship by that name is listed in the records of the port of Harwich, Turner's imagination may have exceeded his experience. Nevertheless, as with many of Turner's late works, *Snowstorm* is an exercise in sensation and intuition. A swirling vortex of wind and waves, it is the imaginative transformation of an intense physical experience, which, recollected thereafter, evokes—as Wordsworth declared—"a sense sublime/Of something far more deeply interfused,/ Whose dwelling place is the light of setting suns,/And the round ocean and the living air,/And the blue sky, and in the mind of man." Turner's "landscapes of the sublime" come closer to capturing the spirit of Wordsworth's nature mysticism than do Constable's gentler views of the physical landscape. Their expanding and contracting forms and startling bursts of color, comparable to the impassioned rhythms and brilliant dynamics of much Romantic music, were daringly innovative. Critics disparagingly called Turner's transparent veils of color—resembling his beloved watercolors—"tinted steam" and "soapsuds." In hundreds of canvases that he never dared to exhibit, Turner all but abandoned recognizable subject matter; these experiments in light and color anticipated those of the French impressionists by more than three decades.

Landscape Painting in France

On the Continent, the artists of the Barbizon School— named after the picturesque village on the edge of the forest of Fontainebleau near Paris—were among the first to take their easels out of doors. Working directly from nature (though usually finishing the canvas in the studio), they painted modest landscapes and scenes of rural life. These unsentimental views of the local countryside were highly successful in capturing nature's moods.

The greatest French landscape painter of the mid nineteenth century, Jean-Baptiste-Camille Corot (1796–1875), shared the Barbizon preference for working outdoors, but he brought to his compositions a breathtaking sense of harmony and order. Corot's early landscapes, executed for the most part in Italy, are as formally composed as the paintings of Poussin and David; they are, however, more personal and more serene. Corot's luminescent late paintings are intimate and contemplative (Figure **27.11**). He called them *souvenirs*, that is, "remembrances," to indicate that they were recollections of previous visual experiences, rather than on-the-spot accounts. Like many artists, Corot kept notebooks in which he jotted his everyday thoughts. One passage perfectly captures the Romantic point of view:

> Be guided by feeling alone. We are only simple mortals, subject to error, so listen to the advice of others, but follow only what you understand and can unite

Figure 27.10 J. M. W. TURNER, *Snowstorm: Steamboat off a Harbour's Mouth*, 1842. Oil on canvas, 3 × 4 ft. Turner's claim that he was lashed to the mast may have been inspired by a similar event in the Greek epic the *Odyssey*. The English writer John Ruskin described *Snowstorm* as "one of the very grandest statements of sea motion, mist, and light that has ever been put on canvas."

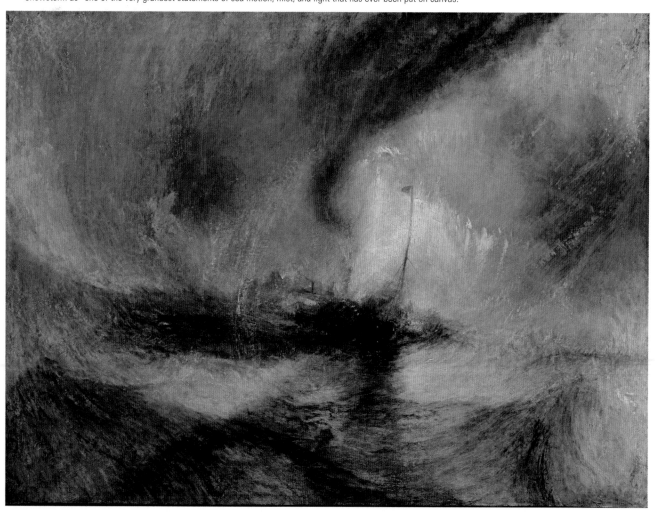

Figure 27.11 JEAN-BAPTISTE-CAMILLE COROT, *Ville d'Avray*, 1870. Oil on canvas, 21⅝ × 31½ in. Even in his own time, forgeries of Corot's late paintings were produced in great numbers. Some of these were the result of Corot's practice of allowing his students to copy his works. One French collection is said to contain almost 2500 Corot forgeries.

in your own feeling . . . Beauty in art is truth bathed in an impression received from nature.

Corot's poetic landscapes, filled with feathery trees and misty rivers, and bathed in nuances of silver light, became so popular in France and elsewhere that he was able to sell as many canvases as he could paint.

American Romanticism

Transcendentalism

Across the Atlantic, along the eastern shores of the rapidly industrializing American continent, Romanticism took hold both as an attitude of mind and as a style. Romanticism infused all aspects of nineteenth-century American culture: it distinguished the frontier tales of James Fenimore Cooper (1789–1851), the mysteries of Edgar Allan Poe (1809–1849), and the novels of Nathaniel Hawthorne (1804–1864) and Herman Melville (1819–1891). But it found its purest expression in the cultural movement known as *transcendentalism*. The group of New England Unitarian ministers who formed the first Transcendental Club took its name from a treatise by the German philosopher Friedrich Schiller (1775–1854). Schiller's *System of Transcendental Idealism* (1800) defended the oneness of Spirit and Nature and encouraged the realization of the higher spiritual self through sympathy with

nature. The American transcendentalists—descendants of the English Puritans—held that knowledge gained by way of intuition transcended knowledge based on reason and logic. Reacting against the material excesses of advancing industrialization, they found sympathetic ideals in such mystical philosophies as Neoplatonism, and in the religions of East Asia, introduced into the Boston area in the early nineteenth century. From Hinduism and Buddhism, they adopted a holistic philosophy based in pantheism and in the ideal of a "universal brotherhood" shared by humanity, nature, and God.

The prime exemplar of the transcendentalists was Ralph Waldo Emerson (1803–1882), whose essays powerfully influenced nineteenth-century American thought. The son and grandson of clergymen, Emerson was ordained as a Unitarian minister when he was in his twenties. Like Wordsworth, he courted nature to "see into the life of things" and to taste its cleansing power. In the essay entitled "Nature" (1836), Emerson sets forth a pantheistic credo:

In the woods is perpetual youth. Within these plantations of God, a decorum and sanctity reign, a perennial festival is dressed, and the guest sees not how he should tire of them in a thousand years. In the woods, we return to reason and faith. There I feel that nothing can befall me in life—no disgrace, no calamity (leaving my eyes), which nature cannot repair. Standing on the bare ground—my head bathed by the blithe air and uplifted into infinite space—all mean egotism vanishes. I become a transparent eyeball; I am nothing; I see all; the currents of the Universal Being circulate through me; I am part or parcel of God.

Although best known for his essays, especially those on the virtues of self-reliance and nonconformity, Emerson was a poet of considerable talent. He shared with Coleridge and Wordsworth (both of whom he had met in England) a mystic reverence for nature; but he also brought to his poetry a unique appreciation of Asian philosophy, which he had acquired by reading some of the central works of Hindu literature, including the *Bhagavad-Gita* (see chapter 3). In Emerson's short poem "Brahma," the voice of the Absolute Spirit and World Creator reminds the reader that a single identity—Brahma him/her/itself—underlies all apparent differences in nature. All universal forces, explains Brahma—even death and birth ("shadow and sunlight")—are one, the knowledge of which supersedes Heaven.

READING 27.6 Emerson's "Brahma" (1856)

If the red slayer[1] think he slays,	1
Or if the slain think he is slain,	
They know not well the subtle ways	
I keep, and pass, and turn again.	
Far or forgot to me is near;	5
Shadow and sunlight are the same;	
The vanished gods to me appear;	
And one to me are shame and fame.	
They reckon ill who leave me out;	
When me they fly, I am the wings;	10
I am the doubter and the doubt,	
And I the hymn the Brahmin[2] sings.	
The strong gods[3] pine for my abode,	
And pine in vain the sacred Seven;[4]	
But thou, meek lover of the good!	15
Find me, and turn thy back on heaven.	

Q **What aspects of Hindu religion does Emerson's poem suggest? How do they compare with typical Western religious beliefs?**

Emerson's friend Henry David Thoreau (1817–1862) set into practice many of the antimaterialist ideals of the transcendentalists. In his youth, Thoreau earned a bachelor's degree at Harvard University and made his way in the world by tutoring, surveying, and making pencils. An avid opponent of slavery, he was jailed briefly for refusing to pay a poll tax to a pro-slavery government. In an influential

---

[1] Shiva, the Hindu god who represents the destructive (and also the recreative) force in nature; with Brahma and Vishnu, one of the three central deities in the Hindu pantheon.
[2] Hindu priest.
[3] Devas or angelic beings.
[4] The seven highest Hindu saints.

essay on civil disobedience, Thoreau defended the philosophy of passive resistance and moral idealism that he himself practiced—a philosophy embraced by the twentieth-century leaders Mohandas Karamchand Gandhi and Martin Luther King.

In 1845 Thoreau abandoned urban society to live in the Massachusetts woods near Walden Pond—an experiment that lasted twenty-six months. He described his love of the natural world, his nonconformist attitude toward society, and his deep commitment to monkish simplicity in his "handbook for living," called *Walden, or Life in the Woods*. In this intimate yet forthright diary, Thoreau glorifies nature as innocent and beneficent—a source of joy and practical instruction.

READING 27.7 From Thoreau's *Walden* (1854)

Near the end of March, 1845, I borrowed an axe and went   1
down to the woods by Walden Pond, nearest to where I
intended to build my house, and began to cut down some tall,
arrowy white pines, still in their youth, for timber. . . . It was a
pleasant hillside where I worked, covered with pine woods,
through which I looked out on the pond, and a small open field
in the woods where pines and hickories were springing up. The
ice in the pond was not yet dissolved, though there were some
open spaces, and it was all dark-colored and saturated with
water. There were some slight flurries of snow during the days   10
that I worked there; but for the most part when I came out on
to the railroad, on my way home, its yellow sand-heap
stretched away gleaming in the hazy atmosphere, and the rails
shone in the spring sun, and I heard the lark and pewee and
other birds already come to commence another year with us.
They were pleasant spring days, in which the winter of man's
discontent was thawing as well as the earth, and the life that
had lain torpid began to stretch itself. One day, when my axe
had come off and I had cut a green hickory for a wedge, driving
it with a stone, and had placed the whole to soak in a pond-   20
hole in order to swell the wood, I saw a striped snake run into
the water, and he lay on the bottom, apparently without
inconvenience, as long as I stayed there, or more than a
quarter of an hour; perhaps because he had not yet fairly come
out of the torpid state. It appeared to me that for a like reason
men remain in their present low and primitive condition; but if
they should feel the influence of the spring of springs arousing
them, they would of necessity rise to a higher and more
ethereal life. I had previously seen the snakes on frosty
mornings in my path with portions of their bodies still numb   30
and inflexible, waiting for the sun to thaw them. On the 1st
of April it rained and melted the ice, and in the early part of
the day, which was very foggy, I heard a stray goose groping
about over the pond and cackling as if lost, or like the spirit of
the fog. . . .

I went to the woods because I wished to live deliberately, to
front only the essential facts of life, and see if I could not learn
what it had to teach, and not, when I came to die, discover that
I had not lived. I did not wish to live what was not life, living is
so dear; nor did I wish to practice resignation, unless it was   40
quite necessary. I wanted to live deep and suck out all the
marrow of life, to live so sturdily and Spartan-like as to put to

rout all that was not life, to cut a broad swath and shave close, to drive life into a corner, and reduce it to its lowest terms, and, if it proved to be mean, why then to get the whole and genuine meanness of it, and publish its meanness to the world; or if it were sublime, to know it by experience, and be able to give a true account of it in my next excursion. For most men, it appears to me, are in a strange uncertainty about it, whether it is of the devil or of God, and have *somewhat hastily* concluded   **50** that it is the chief end of man here to "glorify God and enjoy him forever." . . .

Simplicity, simplicity, simplicity! I say, let your affairs be as two or three, and not a hundred or a thousand; instead of a million count half a dozen, and keep your accounts on your thumb-nail. . . . Instead of three meals a day, if it be necessary eat but one; instead of a hundred dishes, five; and reduce other things in proportion. . . .

The indescribable innocence and beneficence of Nature,— of sun and wind and rain, of summer and winter,—such health,   **60** such cheer, they afford forever! and such sympathy have they ever with our race, that all Nature would be affected, and the sun's brightness fade, and the winds would sigh humanely, and the clouds rain tears, and the woods shed their leaves and put on mourning in midsummer, if any man should ever for a just cause grieve. Shall I not have intelligence with the earth? Am I not partly leaves and vegetable mould myself? . . .

Q **Was Thoreau's retreat to Walden Pond an adventure in practical survival or an extended mystical experience?**

Q **What might Thoreau mean by "the indescribable innocence and beneficence of nature"?**

Walt Whitman's Romantic Individualism

Though technically not a transcendentalist, Walt Whitman (1818–1892; Figure **27.12**) gave voice to the transcendental world-view and to the Emersonian credo of self-reliance. He worked as a Brooklyn printer and newspaper editor, a teacher, and a nurse in the American Civil War. His essays and poems, which have become an influential part of the American canon, assert his affection for the American landscape and its human inhabitants.

Like Wordsworth, Whitman took everyday life as his subject; he too had little use for the artificiality of traditional poetic diction. What he referred to as his "barbaric yawp" found ideal expression in **free verse** (poetry based on irregular rhythmic patterns rather than on the conventional use of meter). His unmetrical rhythms and sonorous cadences are rich in **alliteration**, assonance, and repetition. He loved Italian opera, and his style often simulates the musical grandeur of that genre.

The prevailing themes in Whitman's poetry are nationalism and democracy. He embraced the ordinary individual and sympathized with marginal people, felons, and prostitutes. Claiming to be a poet of the body as well as the soul, he defended an honest recognition of the physical self. The American scene was the source of endless inspiration for the sprawling, cosmic images that dominate his

Figure 27.12 THOMAS EAKINS, *Walt Whitman*, 1888. Oil on canvas, 30⅛ × 24¼ in.

autobiographical masterpiece, *Leaves of Grass* (1855). The first edition of this collection of poems was met with strident criticism for its freewheeling verse forms and its candid celebration of all forms of sexuality—one reviewer attacked the book as "a mixture of Yankee transcendentalism and New York rowdyism." "Song of Myself," the longest of the lyric poems included in *Leaves of Grass*, proclaims the expansive individualism of America's Romantic movement. At the same time, it voices Whitman's impassioned plea for unity with nature and with all humankind.

READING 27.8 From Whitman's
            "Song of Myself" (1855)

1

I celebrate myself, and sing myself,   **1**
And what I assume you shall assume,
For every atom belonging to me as good belongs to you.

I loaf and invite my soul,
I learn and loaf at my ease observing a spear of summer grass.   **5**

My tongue, every atom of my blood, form'd from this soil, this
    air,
Born of parents born here from parents the same, and their
    parents the same,
I, now thirty-seven years old in perfect health begin,
Hoping to cease not till death.

Creeds and schools in abeyance,   **10**
Retiring back a while sufficed at what they are, but never
   forgotten,
I harbor for good or bad, I permit to speak at every hazard,
Nature without check with original energy.

24

Walt Whitman, a kosmos, of Manhattan the son,   **1**
Turbulent, fleshy, sensual, eating, drinking and breeding,
No sentimentalist, no stander above men and women or apart
   from them,
No more modest than immodest.

Unscrew the locks from the doors!   **5**
Unscrew the doors themselves from their jambs!
Whoever degrades another degrades me,
And whatever is done or said returns at last to me.
Through me the afflatus surging and surging, through me the
   current and index.

I speak the pass-word primeval, I give the sign of democracy,   **10**
By God! I will accept nothing which all cannot have their
   counterpart of on the same terms.

Through me many long dumb voices,
Voices of the interminable generations of prisoners and slaves,
Voices of the diseas'd and despairing and of thieves and
   dwarfs,

Voices of cycles of preparation and accretion,   **15**
And of the threads that connect the stars, and of wombs and
   of the father-stuff,
And of the rights of them the others are down upon,
Of the deform'd, trivial, flat, foolish, despised,
Fog in the air, beetles rolling balls of dung.

Through me forbidden voices,   **20**
Voices of sexes and lusts, voices veil'd and I remove the veil,
Voices indecent by me clarified and transfigur'd.

I do not press my fingers across my mouth,
I keep as delicate around the bowels as around the head and
   heart,
Copulation is no more rank to me than death is.   **25**
I believe in the flesh and the appetites,
Seeing, hearing, feeling, are miracles, and each part and tag of
   me is a miracle.

Divine am I inside and out, and I make holy whatever I touch
   or am touch'd from,
The scent of these arm-pits aroma finer than prayer,
This head more than churches, bibles, and all the creeds.   **30**

52

The spotted hawk swoops by and accuses me, he complains of
   my gab and my loitering.   **1**

Figure 27.13 THOMAS COLE, *The Oxbow (View from Mount Holyoke, Northampton, Massachusetts, After a Thunderstorm)*, 1836. Oil on canvas, 4 ft. 3½ in. × 6 ft. 4 in. The loop made by the Connecticut River at Northampton was a well-known early nineteenth-century tourist spot. At the lower center of the canvas, Cole is pictured at his easel; his signature is found on his portfolio at the lower edge of the painting.

Figure 27.14 ALBERT BIERSTADT, *The Rocky Mountains, Lander's Peak*, 1863. Oil on canvas, 6 ft. 1 in. × 10 ft. ¾ in.

I too am not a bit tamed, I too am untranslatable,
I sound my barbaric yawp over the roofs of the world.

The last scud of day holds back for me,
It flings my likeness after the rest and true as any on the
    shadow'd wilds,   5
It coaxes me to the vapor and the dusk.

I depart as air, I shake my white locks at the runaway sun,
I effuse my flesh in eddies, and drift it in lacy jags.
I bequeath myself to the dirt to grow from the grass I love,
If you want me again look for me under your boot-soles.   10

You will hardly know who I am or what I mean,
But I shall be good health to you nevertheless,
And filter and fibre your blood.

Failing to fetch me at first keep encouraged,
Missing me one place search another,   15
I stop somewhere waiting for you.

Q How does Whitman's poetry (and personality)
compare with that of the European romantics
(Readings 27.1 to 27.4)?

American Landscape Painting

Landscape painters in America mirrored the sentiments of
the transcendentalists by capturing what Thoreau
described as "the indescribable innocence and beneficence
of nature." No less than the European Romantics,
American artists took clear delight in the beauty of nature
and its fleeting moods. But they also brought to their art a
nationalistic infatuation with one of their young nation's
unique features—its unspoiled and resplendent terrain.
Mountain ranges, broad lakes and rivers, and verdant
forests are precisely and lovingly documented. It is as if
these painters felt compelled to record with photographic
precision the majesty and moral power of the American
continent and, at the same time, capture the magnitude of
its untamed wilderness. Panorama and painstaking detail
are features found in the topographic landscapes of the
Hudson River School—a group of artists who worked
chiefly in the region of upstate New York during the 1830s
and 1840s.

One of the leading figures of the Hudson River School
was the British-born Thomas Cole (1801–1848), whose
Oxbow (Figure **27.13**) offers a view of the Connecticut
River near Northampton, Massachusetts. In this landscape, Cole achieved a dramatic mood by framing the
brightly lit hills and curving river of the distant vista with
the darker motifs of a departing thunderstorm and a blight-
ed tree.

Intrigued by America's drive to settle the West,
the German-born Albert Bierstadt (1830–1902) made
panoramic depictions of that virginal territory. Bierstadt's
landscape of the Rocky Mountains, which includes a
Native American encampment in the foreground, reflects
his fascination with the templelike purity of America's vast,
rugged spaces along the Western frontier (Figure **27.14**).

Figure 27.15 FREDERIC EDWIN CHURCH, *Niagara*, 1857. Oil on canvas, 42½ × 90½ in. Grand scale and fine detail characterize this typically nineteenth-century American painting. A contemporary newspaper critic exulted, "We know of no American landscape which unites as this does the merits of composition and treatment."

The isolated settlement, dwarfed and enshrined by snow-capped mountains, a magnificent waterfall, and a looking-glass lake—all bathed in golden light—is an American Garden of Eden, inhabited by tribes of unspoiled "noble savages." Bierstadt gave cosmic breadth to the ancient Roman genre of the idyllic landscape, in which humankind and nature flourish in perfect harmony. The huge dimensions of the painting (some 6 x 10 feet) heralded the official establishment of landscape as a respectable genre, comparable to historical and religious subjects that, in academic tradition, commanded a large-size canvases. Such "frontier landscapes" also gave public evidence of American expansionism and ascending nationalism.

Most nineteenth-century American artists visited Europe and spent years studying abroad; however, for the ordinary public, panoramic landscapes depicting remote locales were substitutes for actual travel, and viewers were known to carry binoculars to their showings, admission to which usually required entrance fees. Such was in fact the case with the paintings of Frederic Edwin Church (1826–1900), a pupil of Thomas Cole. Church's celebrated vista of Niagara Falls, displayed in a ticketed exhibition in New York City, was visited by more than 100,000 spectators (Figure **27.15**). His rendering of the Falls as seen from the Canadian side includes almost no foreground, thus putting viewers at the brink of the rushing water. The sky-borne rainbow, one of Church's favorite devices, would have been recognized as a symbol of divine benevolence and harmony. One critic called *Niagara* "the finest picture ever painted on this side of the Atlantic." Other Church landscapes, illustrating tropical storms, erupting volcanoes,

and gigantic icebergs, transported American gallery patrons to the exotic places—Brazil, Ecuador, Newfoundland—the artist himself had visited. Such scenes, produced in the age of polar exploration and ocean shipwrecks, conjured awe and a sense of the Romantic sublime. Called by his contemporaries "the Michelangelo of landscape art," Church became the most famous American painter of his time.

America and Native Americans

The Romantic fascination with unspoiled nature and "natural man" also inspired documentary studies of Native Americans (Figure **27.16**), such as those executed by the artist–ethnologist George Catlin (1796–1872). During the 1830s, Catlin went to live among the Native Americans of the Great Plains. Moved by what he called the "silent and stoic dignity" of America's tribal peoples, he recorded their lives and customs in literature, as well as in hundreds of drawings and paintings. Catlin's "Gallery of Indians," exhibited widely in mid nineteenth-century Europe, drew more acclaim abroad than it did in his own country. Catlin popularized the image of Native Americans as people who deeply respected nature and the natural world (see chapter 18). He described exotic rituals designed to honor the Great Spirit (or Great Sun) and promote health and fertility. Observing that most tribes killed only as much game as was actually needed to feed themselves, Catlin brought attention to Native Americans as the first ecologists.

Harmony with nature and its living creatures was central to Native American culture, whose pantheistic idealism is eloquently conveyed in the proverbial teachings of the northwestern tribes: "The Earth does not belong to us; we belong to the earth . . . We did not weave the web of life; we are merely a strand in it. Whatever we do to the web, we do to ourselves." Following ancestral tradition, Native Americans looked upon living things—plants, animals, and human beings—as sacred parts of an all-embracing, spiritually charged environment. Their arts, which for the most part served religious and communal purposes, reflect their need, at the same time, to protect the balance between these natural forces, and to take spiritual advantage of their transformative and healing powers. Woodcarving, pottery, basket-weaving, beadwork embroidery, sand painting, and other Native American crafts make significant use of natural imagery, but do so in ways that are profoundly different from the artistic enterprises of European and American Romantics: whereas Western artists perceived nature from "without," as a source of moral and aesthetic inspiration, Native American artists perceived nature from "within," as a power to be harnessed and respected. A polychrome water jar from the Zuni Pueblos of the American Southwest is treated as a living being whose spirit or breath may escape from the bowl by means of an

opening in the path (the double line) painted around the vessel's shoulder (Figure **27.17**). In the body of the deer represented on the bowl, a "spirit" line links heart and mouth—a convention that derives from prehistoric pottery decoration.

Not the panoramic landscape, but the natural forces and living creatures immediate to that landscape, preoccupied native artists. As Catlin observed while living with the Plains Indians, natural forms embellished all ceremonial objects, one of the most important of which was the carved stone pipe. Pipes were often presented as gifts to seal tribal alliances. They were believed to be charged with supernatural power, and pipe-smoking—both public and private—was a sacred act. Among the Plains Indians, pipes were considered "activated" when the stem (symbolic of male power) was joined to the bowl (symbolic of the maternal earth). Often produced jointly by men and women, Plains pipes were carved out of catlinite, a red-colored stone quarried in southwestern Minnesota (so named because Catlin was the first to bring east samples of this distinctive mineral). Legend identified the stone variously as the flesh of a mythical tribal people or the congealed blood of all dead

Figure 27.16 GEORGE CATLIN, *The White Cloud, Head Chief of the Iowas*, 1844–1845. Oil on canvas, 28 × 22⅞ in. Catlin considered the Native Americans of the northern plains, the frontier between the United States and Canada, the least corrupted by contact with other Americans. In paintings introduced to Europeans, he presented them as "nature's sovereign nobility."

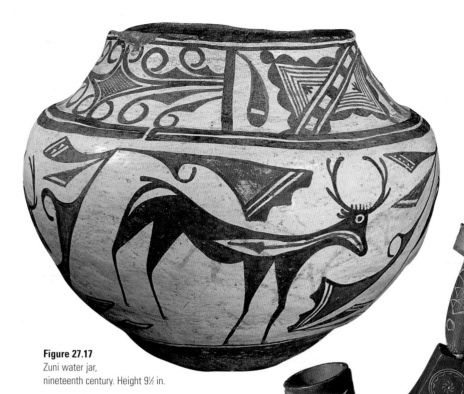

Figure 27.17
Zuni water jar,
nineteenth century. Height 9½ in.

Figure 27.18 Catlinite pipe (possibly a specialized medicine pipe or one for women's use) representing a fanged and crested water spirit, with fish effigy stem, 1850–1860. Sioux tribe, carved in Minnesota. Length 8⅝ in. After the Europeans introduced the horse to Native American culture, this animal joined the more traditional motifs used to ornament ritual pipes.

Indians and dead buffalo. Catlinite pipes served in rituals for healing. They usually bear effigies of legendary birds, bears, or water creatures (Figure **27.18**).

Popularizing the culture of the Native American in literature, the American poet Henry Wadsworth Longfellow (1807–1882) offered a sentimental picture of American Indian life in his narrative poem *The Song of Hiawatha* (1885). This fictional tale is based on the life of a sixteenth-century Mohawk statesman. Unfortunately, neither Longfellow nor Catlin, nor the achievements of the Native Americans themselves, impeded the wholesale destruction of Native American cultures. Beginning in the 1830s, under pressure from the United States government, tribes were forced to cede their homelands and their hunting grounds to white settlers and to move into unoccupied lands in the American West. The perception of the Native American as the "devil savage" prevailed over the Romantic notion of the "noble savage" and came to justify America's effort to "civilize" its "savage" populations through policies (strongly criticized by Catlin and others) that forced most tribes to take up residence on "reservations" and, more often than not, to abandon their native languages, religions, and traditions. Persecution, humiliation, outright physical attack, and the continuing effects of disease further accelerated the decline and near extinction of America's indigenous peoples.

American Folk Art

American folk artists produced some of the most interesting artworks of the nineteenth century. Unlike professionally trained artists like Cole and Church, folk artists lacked technical schooling in the visual arts. Nevertheless, they were inspired to adorn their everyday surroundings with objects that often manifested extraordinary sensitivity to design and affection for natural detail.

One of the most distinctive of nineteenth-century folk art genres was the hand-stitched quilt, a utilitarian object produced almost exclusively by women. Unlike academic art objects, quilts were often communal projects. Several women embroidered or appliquéd designs onto individual fabric patches salvaged from leftover sewing materials. Then, at popular quilting "bees," they assembled the patches into bedcovers some 9 by 8 feet in size. Quilt motifs, frequently drawn from nature, were stylized and brightly colored (Figure **27.19**). Many became standardized patterns that were passed from mother to daughter and from household to household. Patchwork quilts might commemorate religious or family occasions (such as weddings) or public events, but they rarely narrated a story. Rather, quilts conveyed meaning through abstract signs and symbols. A folk record of nature and the natural, quilt-making and related textile arts constitute a decorative yet intimate nineteenth-century American artform.

The Romantic sanctification of nature is even more vividly configured in *The Peaceable Kingdom* (Figure **27.20**), a painting by the American folk artist Edward Hicks (1780–1849). A Quaker minister in Bucks County, Pennsylvania, Hicks was also a popular sign-painter. His inspiration for more than 100 versions of this utopian subject came from the Book of Isaiah (11: 6–9): "The wolf also shall dwell with the lamb, and the leopard shall lie down with the kid . . . and a little child shall lead them." Hicks set his charming, wide-eyed beasts and weightless, diminutive children in a verdant landscape. In the background, at the

Figure 27.19 SARAH ANNE WHITTINGTON LANKFORD, probably Mary Evans, and possibly others, Baltimore Albion Quilt, ca. 1850. Appliqué, 7 ft. × 8 ft. 3 in. At the top of the quilt is pictured an American war memorial and a schematic rendering of the newly completed United States Capitol.

far left, Hicks' fellow Quaker William Penn displays the peace treaty signed with the Lenape tribe (an event that had received treatment in academic American art). The decorative handling of the composition and its disregard for traditional perspective contributes to its visual immediacy; but it is in the gestures of the children, reaching out lovingly to the wild creatures in their midst, that Hicks establishes the link between natural innocence and peace.

Figure 27.20 EDWARD HICKS, *The Peaceable Kingdom*, ca. 1834. Oil on canvas, 30 × 35½ in.

Glossary

alliteration a literary device involving the repetition of initial sounds in successive or closely associated words or syllables

assonance a literary device involving similarity in sound between vowels followed by different consonants

dialectic in Hegelian philosophy, the process by which every condition (or "thesis") confronts an opposite condition (or "antithesis") to resolve in synthesis

eugenics the science of improving human beings by

means of genetic manipulation

free verse poetry that is based on irregular rhythmic patterns rather than on the conventional and regular use of meter

lyric poetry "lyric" means accompanied by the lyre, hence, verse that is meant to be sung

rather than spoken; poetry marked by individual and personal emotion (see also chapter 6)

pantheism the belief that a divine spirit pervades all things in the universe

LOOKING BACK

The Progress of Industrialization

- Nineteenth-century Europe experienced a population boom; increased production of coal, iron, and steel encouraged expansion of industry and commerce in the West. In this industrially based society, goods were increasingly made at factories rather than in homes.
- Advancing industrialization encouraged urbanization and spurred Western efforts to find markets and resources in other parts of the world.

Early Nineteenth-Century Thought

- German philosophers, influenced by Asian philosophy and Kantian idealism, viewed nature subjectively and in the direction of mysticism.
- Hegel proposed a dialectical model according to which all reality, all history, and all ideas progressed toward perfect freedom.
- Darwin argued that by means of natural selection, all living things, including human beings, evolved from a few simple forms: species either develop into higher forms of life or fail to survive.
- While the theory of natural selection displaced human beings from their elevated place in the hierarchy of living creatures, it advanced the idea of the unity of nature and humankind.

Nature and the Natural in European Literature

- Nature provided both a metaphor for the Romantic sensibility and a refuge from the evils of nineteenth-century industrialization and urbanization.
- William Wordsworth, the leading nature poet of the nineteenth century, embraced the redemptive power of nature. Exalting the natural landscape as the source of sublime inspiration and moral truth, Wordsworth and his English contemporaries initiated the Romantic movement.
- The Romantics stressed the free exercise of the imagination, the liberation of the senses, and the cultivation of a more natural language of poetic expression.
- Shelley compared the elemental forces of nature with the creative powers of the poet, while Keats rejoiced that nature's fleeting beauty might forever dwell in art. Blake's deeply spiritual poems reflect a visionary and moral perception of nature.

Nature and the Natural in Asian Literature

- The Romantic embrace of nature and natural imagery was not confined to the West: in Chinese literature, as reflected in Shen Fu's confessional prose, nature became a source of inspiration and personal solace.
- Chinese poets and painters described the natural landscape by way of a few carefully chosen words and images.

Romantic Landscape Painting

- It was among Western Romantics that the landscape became a major vehicle for the expression of the artist's moods and emotions.
- Constable's contemplative scenes of English country life and Turner's sublime vistas are the visual counterparts of the poems of Wordsworth.
- The elegiac landscapes of Friedrich in Germany and Corot in France reflect the efforts of Romantic artists to explore nature's shifting states as metaphors for human feeling.

American Romanticism

- American Romantics endowed the quest for natural simplicity with a robust spirit of individualism. The transcendentalists Emerson and Thoreau sought a union of self with nature; Walt Whitman proclaimed his untamed and "untranslatable" ego in sympathy with nature's energy.
- In the American landscapes of Cole, Bierstadt, and Church, nature becomes symbolic of an unspoiled and rapidly vanishing world; in the art of George Catlin, the native populations and traditions of America are lovingly documented.
- Among Native Americans, yet another (less Romantic but equally mystical) view of nature flourished, as evidenced in magnificent ceremonial objects.
- American folk art, as typified by the paintings of Edward Hicks, made use of natural imagery for decorative and symbolic purposes.

Chapter

28 The Romantic Hero

ca. 1780–1880

*"O hero, with whose bloodied story
Long, long the earth will still resound . . ."*
Pushkin

Figure 28.1 THOMAS PHILLIPS, *Lord Byron Sixth Baron in Albanian Costume*, 1813. Oil on canvas, 29½ × 24½ in. Upon the death of his great-uncle in 1798, Byron became the sixth Baron Byron of Rochdale. Entitled to a seat in the House of Lords when he came of age in 1809, he only attended a few sessions. One of his lovers, Lady Caroline Lamb, characterized Byron as "mad, bad, and dangerous to know."

LOOKING AHEAD

As the Romantics embraced nature, so they exalted the creative individual in the person of the hero. Heroes, whether mortal or divine, symbolize humanity at its best, most powerful and godlike. Like the literary heroes of the past—Gilgamesh, Achilles, and Roland—the Romantic hero was a larger-than-life figure with extraordinary expectations, abilities, and goals. But whereas the literary hero defended the traditions and moral values of a society, the Romantic hero might challenge or seek to reform them.

The Romantics saw themselves as the visionaries of their time: as champions of a cult of the senses and of the heart. *"Exister, pour nous, c'est sentir"* ("For us, to exist is to feel"), proclaimed Rousseau, the late eighteenth-century prophet of Romanticism. The spirit of the heroic self was anticipated in Rousseau's declaration: "I am made unlike anyone I have ever met; I will even venture to say that I am like no one in the whole world. I may be no better, but at least I am different." Working to fulfill their own personal vision, Romantic poets, painters, and composers freed themselves from dependence on the patronage of the Church and state. At the same time, they defended the ideals of liberty and brotherhood associated with emerging nationalism. They opposed entrenched systems of slavery and institutional limitations to personal freedom. The nineteenth century did not produce more heroes than other centuries, but it celebrated the heroic personality as representative of the Romantic sensibility.

Nationalism and the Hero

Nationalism—the exaltation of the sovereign state—was one of the shaping forces of nineteenth-century culture. While the beginnings of the modern nation-state go back at least to the fourteenth century (see chapter 15), nationalism, an ideology (or belief system) grounded in a people's sense of cultural and political unity, did not gain widespread acceptance until roughly 1815. Modern nationalism flourished in the wake of the French Revolution and, thereafter, in resistance to the imperialistic expansion of Napoleonic France. One after another, European states, as well as some in Africa and in Latin America, rose up against foreign rulers. Love of nation and love of liberty became synonymous with the ideals of self-determination and political freedom. In its positive aspects, nationalism cultivated the revival and celebration of a common language, common customs, and a shared history, as expressed in poetry, music, and art. The collection of German fairy tales (1812–1815) by the brothers Jacob and Wilhelm Grimm serves as an example. But nationalism also manifested a malignant aspect: well into the twentieth century, nationalism and patriotic chauvinism motivated policies of imperialism and ignited warfare, not only between nations, but among the ethnic populations of various regions. Indeed, as these chapters reveal, much of the art of the nineteenth century is a visceral response to brutal events associated with nascent nationalism.

Nineteenth-century intellectuals celebrated the heroic personality, especially in its dedication to the causes of liberty and equality. The British historian and essayist Thomas Carlyle (1795–1881) published a series of lectures, *On Heroes and Hero-Worship*, in which he glorified hero-gods, prophets, poets, priests, men of letters, and the quasi-legendary Napoleon Bonaparte. Walter Scott (1771–1832) and Alexandre Dumas (1802–1870) wrote historical novels that described the heroic adventures of swashbuckling soldiers and maidens in distress, while Victor Hugo (1802–1885) made sentimental heroes out of egalitarian patriots in the novel *Les Misérables*. Real-life heroes challenged literary heroes in courage and daring. The Zulu warrior Shaka (1787–1828) changed the destiny of the southern region of Africa by leading aggressive campaigns that united the local clans, thus forming the Zulu nation.

In America, heroic themes occupied the attention of the novelists Nathaniel Hawthorne (1804–1864) and Herman Melville (1819–1891). Each created brooding, melancholic fictional heroes whose moral strength was tested by the forces of evil. The two leading figures (Ishmael and Ahab) in Melville's great sea novel *Moby Dick* are semiautobiographical characterizations, inspired by Melville's adventures as the foremast hand on a whaling ship and as a sailor in the United States Navy. Then too, the Americas produced some notable real-life heroes and champions of political freedom, such as Simón Bolívar (1783–1830)—whose victories over the Spanish forces in South America won independence for Bolivia, Colombia, Ecuador, Peru, and Venezuela—and Frederick Douglass (1817–1895), the leading antislavery spokesman, whose autobiography details a heroic life of oppression and struggle.

Napoleon as a Romantic Hero

In 1799 the thirty-year-old Corsican army general Napoleon Bonaparte (1769–1821) seized control of the government of France. He ended civil strife, reorganized the educational system, and institutionalized the system of civil law known as the *Code Napoléon*. "The Revolution is ended," announced Napoleon as he proclaimed himself emperor in 1804. In the following ten years, he pursued a policy of conquest that brought continental Western Europe to his feet. Throughout much of the West he abolished serfdom, expropriated Church possessions, curtailed feudal privileges, and introduced French laws, institutions, and influence. Spreading the revolutionary ideals of liberty, fraternity, and equality throughout his empire (Map 28.1), he championed popular sovereignty and kindled sentiments of nationalism.

If Napoleon's ambitions were heroic, his military campaigns were stunning. Having conquered Italy, Egypt,

The Promethean Hero

The Promethean Myth in Literature

If Napoleon was nineteenth-century Europe's favorite real-life hero, Prometheus was its favorite fictional hero. Prometheus (the name means "forethought") was one of the primordial deities of Greek mythology. According to legend, Prometheus challenged Zeus by stealing from his home on Mount Olympus the sacred fire (source of divine wisdom and creative inspiration) and bestowing this great gift upon humankind. As punishment, Zeus chained him to a lonely rock, where an eagle fed daily on his liver, miraculously restored each night. A second, less dramatic aspect of the Prometheus story, more popular among the Romans than the Greeks, credited the hero with having fashioned human beings out of clay, in the manner of the Babylonian hero-god Marduk (see chapter 1).

Romantic poets embraced the figure of Prometheus as the suffering champion of humanity—a symbol of freedom and a deliverer whose noble ambitions had incurred the wrath of the gods. Percy Bysshe Shelley, whom we met in chapter 27, made Prometheus the savior-hero of his four-act play *Prometheus Unbound* (1820). In this drama, Prometheus frees the universe from the tyranny of the gods. Two years earlier, in 1818, Shelley's second wife, Mary Godwin Shelley (1797–1851), explored the Promethean legend in her novel *Frankenstein; or, The Modern Prometheus*. The daughter of William Godwin and the feminist writer Mary Wollstonecraft (see chapter 24), Mary Shelley began writing *Frankenstein* at the age of eighteen. Framed as a series of letters, the novel relates the astonishing tale of the scientist–philosopher Victor Frankenstein, who, having discovered the secret of imparting life to inanimate matter, produces a monster endowed with supernatural strength (Figure **28.3**). A modern Prometheus, Frankenstein suffers the punishment for his ambitious designs when the creature, excluded from the normal life of ordinary mortals, betrays his creator: "I was benevolent and good," he protests, "misery made me a fiend." Like the fallen Lucifer, Frankenstein's creation ultimately becomes a figure of heroic evil.

Frankenstein belongs to a literary genre known as the Gothic novel, a type of entertainment that features elements of horror and the supernatural cast in a medieval ("Gothic") setting. Such novels, the earliest of which was Horace Walpole's *The Castle of Otranto* (1764), reflect the rising tide of antirationalism and a revived interest in the medieval past. Shelley's novel—actually a scientific horror tale—has become a modern classic. The first literary work to question the human impact of scientific research, it has inspired numerous science fiction "spinoffs," as well as cinematic and stage renderings. Ironically, however, it is not the scientist but the monster that has captured the modern imagination, even to the point of usurping the name of his creator.

Figure 28.3 The first illustration of the *Frankenstein* monster, frontispiece from the 1831 Standards Novel edition.

READING 28.2 From Mary Shelley's *Frankenstein* (Chapters 4 and 5) (1818)

... One of the phenomena which had peculiarly attracted my 1
attention was the structure of the human frame, and, indeed,
any animal endued with life. Whence, I often asked myself, did
the principle of life proceed? It was a bold question, and one
which has ever been considered as a mystery: yet with how
many things are we upon the brink of becoming acquainted,
if cowardice or carelessness did not restrain our enquiries.
I revolved these circumstances in my mind and determined
thenceforth to apply myself more particularly to those branches
of natural philosophy which relate to physiology. Unless I had 10
been animated by an almost supernatural enthusiasm, my
application to this study would have been irksome and almost
intolerable. To examine the causes of life, we must first have
recourse to death. I became acquainted with the science of
anatomy, but this was not sufficient; I must also observe the
natural decay and corruption of the human body. In my
education my father had taken the greatest precautions that my
mind should be impressed with no supernatural horrors. I do not
ever remember to have trembled at a tale of superstition or to
have feared the apparition of a spirit. Darkness had no effect 20
upon my fancy, and a churchyard was to be merely the
receptacle of bodies deprived of life, which, from being the seat
of beauty and strength, had become food for the worm. Now I
was led to examine the cause and progress of this decay and
forced to spend days and nights in vaults and charnel-houses.
My attention was fixed upon every object the most

insupportable to the delicacy of the human feelings. I saw how the fine form of man was degraded and wasted; I beheld the corruption of death succeed to the blooming cheek of life; I saw how the worm inherited the wonders of the eye and brain. I **30** paused, examining and analysing all the minutiae of causation, as exemplified in the change from life to death, and death to life, until from the midst of this darkness a sudden light broke in upon me—a light so brilliant and wondrous, yet so simple, that while I became dizzy with the immensity of the prospect which it illustrated, I was surprized that among so many men of genius who had directed their enquiries towards the same science, that I alone should be reserved to discover so astonishing a secret.

Remember, I am not recording the vision of a madman. The sun does not more certainly shine in the heavens than that **40** which I now affirm is true. Some miracle might have produced it, yet the stages of the discovery were distinct and probable. After days and nights of incredible labour and fatigue, I succeeded in discovering the cause of generation and life; nay, more, I became myself capable of bestowing animation upon lifeless matter.

The astonishment which I had at first experienced on this discovery soon gave place to delight and rapture. After so much time spent in painful labour, to arrive at once at the summit of my desires was the most gratifying consummation of my toils. **50** But this discovery was so great and overwhelming that all the steps by which I had been progressively led to it were obliterated, and I beheld only the result. What had been the study and desire of the wisest men since the creation of the world was now within my grasp. . . .

. . . Learn from me, if not by my precepts, at least by my example, how dangerous is the acquirement of knowledge and how much happier that man is who believes his native town to be the world, than he who aspires to become greater than his nature will allow. **60**

When I found so astonishing a power placed within my hands, I hesitated a long time concerning the manner in which I should employ it. Although I possessed the capacity of bestowing animation, yet to prepare a frame for the reception of it, with all its intricacies of fibres, muscles, and veins, still remained a work of inconceivable difficulty and labour. I doubted at first whether I should attempt the creation of a being like myself, or one of simpler organization; but my imagination was too much exalted by my first success to permit me to doubt of my ability to give life to an animal as complex **70** and wonderful as man. The materials at present within my command hardly appeared adequate to so arduous an undertaking, but I doubted not that I should ultimately succeed. I prepared myself for a multitude of reverses; my operations might be incessantly baffled, and at last my work be imperfect; yet when I considered the improvement which every day takes place in science and mechanics, I was encouraged to hope my present attempts would at least lay the foundations of future success. Nor could I consider the magnitude and complexity of my plan as any argument of its impracticability. It was with **80** these feelings that I began the creation of a human being. As the minuteness of the parts formed a great hindrance to my speed, I resolved, contrary to my first intention, to make the being of a gigantic stature; that is to say, about eight feet in height, and proportionately large. After having formed this determination and having spent some months in successfully collecting and arranging my materials, I began.

No one can conceive the variety of feelings which bore me onwards, like a hurricane, in the first enthusiasm of success. Life and death appeared to be ideal bounds, which I should first **90** break through, and pour a torrent of light into our dark world. A new species would bless me as its creator and source; many happy and excellent natures would owe their being to me. No father could claim the gratitude of his child so completely as I should deserve theirs. Pursuing these reflections, I thought that if I could bestow animation upon lifeless matter, I might in process of time (although I now found it impossible) renew life where death had apparently devoted the body to corruption.

These thoughts supported my spirits, while I pursued my undertaking with unremitting ardour. My cheek had grown **100** pale with study, and my person had become emaciated with confinement. Sometimes, on the very brink of certainty, I failed; yet still I clung to the hope which the next day or the next hour might realize. One secret which I alone possessed was the hope to which I had dedicated myself; and the moon gazed on my midnight labours, while, with unrelaxed and breathless eagerness, I pursued nature to her hiding-places. Who shall conceive the horrors of my secret toil as I dabbled among the unhallowed damps of the grave or tortured the living animal to animate the lifeless clay? My limbs now tremble, and my eyes **110** swim with the remembrance; but then a resistless and almost frantic impulse urged me forward; I seemed to have lost all soul or sensation but for this one pursuit. It was indeed but a passing trance, that only made me feel with renewed acuteness so soon as, the unnatural stimulus ceasing to operate, I had returned to my old habits. I collected bones from charnel-houses and disturbed, with profane fingers, the tremendous secrets of the human frame. In a solitary chamber, or rather cell, at the top of the house, and separated from all the other apartments by a gallery and staircase, I kept my workshop of filthy creation: my **120** eyeballs were starting from their sockets in attending to the details of my employment. The dissecting room and the slaughter-house furnished many of my materials; and often did my human nature turn with loathing from my occupation, whilst, still urged on by an eagerness which perpetually increased, I brought my work near to a conclusion. . . .

It was on a dreary night of November that I beheld the accomplishment of my toils. With an anxiety that almost amounted to agony, I collected the instruments of life around me, that I might infuse a spark of being into the lifeless thing **130** that lay at my feet. It was already one in the morning; the rain pattered dismally against the panes, and my candle was nearly burnt out, when, by the glimmer of the half-extinguished light, I saw the dull yellow eye of the creation open; it breathed hard, and a convulsive motion agitated its limbs.

How can I describe my emotions at this catastrophe, or how delineate the wretch whom with such infinite pains and care I had endeavoured to form? His limbs were in proportion, and I had selected his features as beautiful. Beautiful! Great God! His yellow skin scarcely covered the work of muscles and **140** arteries beneath; his hair was of a lustrous black, and flowing;

his teeth of pearly whiteness; but these luxuriances only formed a more horrid contrast with his watery eyes, that seemed almost of the same colour as the dun-white sockets in which they were set, his shrivelled complexion and straight black lips.

The different accidents of life are not so changeable as the feelings of human nature. I had worked hard for nearly two years, for the sole purpose of infusing life into an inanimate body. For this I had deprived myself of rest and health. I had desired it with an ardour that far exceeded moderation; but 150 now that I had finished, the beauty of the dream vanished, and breathless horror and disgust filled my heart. Unable to endure the aspect of the being I had created, I rushed out of the room and continued a long time traversing my bedchamber, unable to compose my mind to sleep. At length lassitude succeeded to the tumult I had before endured, and I threw myself on the bed in my clothes, endeavouring to seek a few moments of forgetfulness. But it was in vain; I slept, indeed, but I was disturbed by the wildest dreams. I thought I saw Elizabeth, in the bloom of health, walking in the streets of Ingolstadt. 160 Delighted and surprised, I embraced her, but as I imprinted the first kiss on her lips, they became livid with the hue of death; her features appeared to change, and I thought that I held the corpse of my dead mother in my arms; a shroud enveloped her form, and I saw the grave-worms crawling in the folds of the flannel. I started from my sleep with horror; a cold dew covered my forehead, my teeth chattered, and every limb became convulsed; when, by the dim and yellow light of the moon, as it forced its way through the window shutters, I beheld the wretch—the miserable monster whom I had 170 created. He held up the curtain of the bed; and his eyes, if eyes they may be called, were fixed on me. His jaws opened, and he muttered some inarticulate sounds, while a grin wrinkled his cheeks. He might have spoken, but I did not hear; one hand was stretched out, seemingly to detain me, but I escaped and rushed downstairs. I took refuge in the courtyard belonging to the house which I inhabited, where I remained during the rest of the night, walking up and down in the greatest agitation, listening attentively, catching and fearing each sound as if it were to announce the approach of the daemoniacal corpse to 180 which I had so miserably given life. . . .

Q What are the dangers of "the acquirement of knowledge," according to Dr. Frankenstein?

Q Why does he ultimately experience "breathless horror and disgust"?

Byron and the Promethean Myth

The Promethean myth found its most passionate champion in the life and works of the English poet George Gordon, Lord Byron (1788–1824). Byron was one of the most flamboyant personalities of the age (see Figure 28.1). Dedicated to pleasures of the senses, he was equally impassioned by the ideals of liberty and brotherhood. In his brief, mercurial life, he established the prototype of the Romantic hero, often called the Byronic hero.

As a young man, Byron traveled restlessly throughout Europe and the Mediterranean, devouring the landscape

and the major sites. A physically attractive man (despite the handicap of a club foot) with dark, brooding eyes, he engaged in numerous love affairs, including one with his half-sister. In 1816, Byron abandoned an unsuccessful marriage and left England for good. He lived in Italy for a time with the Shelleys and a string of mistresses. By this time, he had earned such a reputation of dangerous nonconformity that an English woman, catching sight of the poet in Rome, warned her daughter: "Do not look at him! He is dangerous to look at." In 1824, Byron sailed to Greece to aid the Greeks in their war of independence against the Turks—one of the many episodes in the turbulent history of nineteenth-century nationalism. There, in his last heroic role, he died of a fever.

Throughout his life, Byron was given to periodic bouts of creativity and dissipation. A man of violent passions, he once described himself as "half-mad . . . between metaphysics, mountains, lakes, love indistinguishable, and the nightmare of my own delinquencies." Intent on sharing his innermost feelings, he became the hero of his two great poems, *Childe Harold's Pilgrimage* (1812–1818) and *Don Juan*, the latter written in installments between 1819 and 1824, and left unfinished at his death. The first poem narrates the wandering of Childe Harold, Byron's fictional self, whom he describes as "the most unfit /Of men to herd with man; with whom he held /Little in common." The disillusioned hero finds solace, however, in nature, as Byron writes in Canto Three (13):

He had the passion and the power to roam;
The desert, forest, cavern, breaker's foam,
Were unto him companionship; they spake
A mutual language . . .

Begun in Venice, *Don Juan* drew on the legendary, fictional Spanish libertine who had also inspired Mozart's *Don Giovanni* (see chapter 26). Byron's don, however, is not the lustful womanizer of Mozart's opera; rather, he is a figure who stumbles into love in what might be called a romance of roguery, or—in Byron's words—"a satire on the abuses of society." Byron's disdain for the social conventions of his time and place are brilliantly mocked in a work that the author described as an "epic on modern life."

By comparison with the other heroes of his literary career, Prometheus, the god who "stole from Heaven the flame, for which he fell," preoccupied Byron as a symbol of triumphant individualism. For the poet, capturing the imagination in art or in life was comparable to stealing the sacred fire. In a number of his poems, he compares the fallen Napoleon to the mythic Prometheus—symbol of heroic ambition and ungovernable passions. But in the stirring ode called simply "Prometheus," Byron makes of the Promethean myth a parable for the Romantic imagination. He begins by recalling the traditional story of the hero whose "Godlike crime was to be kind." He goes on to identify Prometheus as a "symbol and a sign" to mortals who, although "part divine," are doomed to "funereal destiny." Like Prometheus, says Byron, we must strive to defy that destiny by pursuing the creative projects that will outlive us. Byron's voice sets defiance and hope against melancholy and despair.

READING 28.3 Byron's "Prometheus" (1816)

Titan! to whose immortal eyes   1
   The sufferings of mortality,
   Seen in their sad reality,
Were not as things that gods despise;
What was thy pity's recompense?   5
A silent suffering, and intense;
The rock, the vulture,[1] and the chain,
All that the proud can feel of pain,
The agony they do not show,
The suffocating sense of woe,   10
   Which speaks but in its loneliness,
And then is jealous lest the sky
Should have a listener, nor will sigh
   Until its voice is echoless.

Titan! to thee the strife was given   15
   Between the suffering and the will,
   Which torture where they cannot kill;
And the inexorable Heaven,
And the deaf tyranny of Fate,
The ruling principle of Hate,   20
Which for its pleasure doth create
The things it may annihilate,
Refused thee even the boon to die:
The wretched gift eternity
Was thine—and thou hast borne it well.   25
All that the Thunderer[2] wrung from thee
Was but the menace which flung back
On him the torments of thy rack;
The fate thou didst so well foresee,
But would not to appease him tell;   30
And in thy Silence was his Sentence,
And in his Soul a vain repentance,
And evil dread so ill dissembled,
That in his hand the lightnings trembled.

Thy Godlike crime was to be kind,   35
   To render with thy precepts less
   The sum of human wretchedness,
And strengthen Man with his own mind;
But baffled as thou wert from high,
Still in thy patient energy,   40
In the endurance, and repulse
   Of thine impenetrable Spirit,
Which Earth and Heaven could not convulse,
   A mighty lesson we inherit:
Thou art symbol and a sign   45
   To Mortals of their fate and force;
Like thee, Man is in part divine,
   A troubled stream from a pure source;

And Man in portions can foresee
His own funereal destiny,   50
His wretchedness, and his resistance,
And his sad unallied existence:
To which his Spirit may oppose
Itself—and equal to all woes,
   And a firm will, and a deep sense,   55
Which even in torture can descry
   Its own concenter'd recompense,[3]
Triumphant where it dares defy,
And making Death a Victory.

Q   **How does Byron characterize Prometheus in this poem?**

Q   **What aspects of the Byronic hero are configured in Prometheus?**

Pushkin: The Byron of Russia

Napoleon's invasion of Russia in 1812 was one of the most dramatic events in nineteenth-century history. Sorely outnumbered by the Grand Army of Napoleon, Russian troops resorted to a "scorched earth" policy that produced severe shortages of food for French and Russians alike. As French forces advanced on Moscow, leaving a trail of bloody battles, the Russians burned their own capital city. Napoleon ultimately captured Moscow, but within a few months he and his badly diminished army retreated from Russia, never to return. Deeply moved by Napoleon's role in stirring Russian nationalism, Alexander Pushkin (1799–1837)—Russia's leading lyric poet and dramatist—eulogized the hero who, as he explains in the poem "Napoleon," had "launched the Russian nation/Upon its lofty destinies."

Pushkin, whose maternal great-grandfather was a black African general, came from an old aristocratic family. Nevertheless, he claimed comradery with Russia's humble commoners. He boasted "I am a versewright and a bookman, . . . /No financier, no titled footman,/A commoner: great on his own." Like Byron, Pushkin championed political freedom; he defended liberal causes, which resulted in his banishment to south Russia and ultimately to his dismissal from the foreign service. His agonizing death, at the age of thirty-seven, was the result of wounds suffered in a duel with his wife's alleged lover.

Pushkin's Romantic tragedies and long narrative poems reveal his great admiration for Shakespeare and Byron, and earned him a reputation as "the Byron of Russia." Some of Pushkin's works, such as *Boris Godunov* (1825) and *Eugene Onegin* (1833)—modeled in part on Byron's *Don Juan*—would inspire operas by composers Modest Mussorgsky (1839–1881) and Peter Ilyich Tchaikovsky (see chapter 29) respectively. The lyric poem "Napoleon," part of which follows, conveys Pushkin's gift for buoyant, energetic language and his profound respect for the figure whom he viewed as both oppressor and liberator.

---

[1] Byron replaces the mythological eagle with a vulture.
[2] Zeus, the supreme god of the Greeks.

[3] Catch a glimpse of the Spirit's own sufficient reward.

READING 28.4 From Pushkin's "Napoleon" (1821)

A wondrous fate is now fulfilled,   1
Extinguished a majestic man.
In somber prison night was stilled
Napoleon's grim, tumultuous span.
The outlawed potentate has vanished,   5
Bright Nike's mighty, pampered son;
For him, from all Creation banished,
Posterity has now begun.

O hero, with whose bloodied story
Long, long the earth will still resound,   10
Sleep in the shadow of your glory,
The desert ocean all around . . .
A tomb of rock, in splendor riding!
The urn that holds your mortal clay,
As tribal hatreds are subsiding,   15
Now sends aloft a deathless ray.

How recently your eagles glowered
Atop a disenfranchised world,
And fallen sovereignties cowered
Beneath the thunderbolts you hurled!   20
Your banners at a word would shower
Destruction from their folds and dearth,
Yoke after yoke of ruthless power
You fitted on the tribes of earth.

. . . .

Vainglorious man! Where were you faring,   25
Who blinded that astounding mind?
How came it in designs of daring
The Russian's heart was not divined?
At fiery sacrifice not guessing,
You idly fancied, tempting fate,   30
We would seek peace and count it blessing;
You came to fathom us too late . . .

Fight on, embattled Russia mine,
Recall the rights of ancient days!
The sun of Austerlitz,[1] decline!   35
And Moscow, mighty city, blaze!
Brief be the time of our dishonor,
The auspices are turning now;
Hail Moscow—Russia's blessings on her!
War to extinction, thus our vow!   40

The diadem of iron[2] shaking
In stiffened fingers' feeble clasp,
He stares into a chasm, quaking,
And is undone, undone at last.
Behold all Europe's legions sprawling . . .   45
The wintry fields' encrimsoned glow

Bore testimony to their falling
Till blood-prints melted with the snow.

. . . .

Let us hold up to reprobation
Such petty-minded men as chose   50
With unappeasable damnation
To stir his laurel-dark repose!
Hail him! He launched the Russian nation
Upon its lofty destinies
And augured ultimate salvation   55
For man's long-exiled liberties.

Q **In what ways does this poem reflect
the sentiments of nationalism?**

Q **What, according to Pushkin, did
Napoleon fail to recognize in Russia?**

---

[1] The site of Napoleon's greatest victory where, on December 2,
1805, he defeated the combined Austrian and Russian forces,
acquiring control of European lands north of Rome and making
him king of Italy.

[2] The iron crown of Lombardy, dating back to the fifth century, which
Napoleon had assumed some time after the Italian campaigns.

The Abolitionists: American Prometheans

Among the most fervent champions of liberty in nineteenth-century America were those who crusaded against the institution of slavery. Their efforts initiated a movement for black nationalism that would continue well into the twentieth century (see chapter 36). It is unlikely that the leaders of the abolitionist movement regarded themselves in the image of a Napoleon or the fictional Prometheus but, as historical figures, the abolitionists were the heroes of their time. They fought against the enslavement of Africans (and their descendants), a practice that had prevailed in America since the sixteenth century.* Although the abolitionists constituted only a small minority of America's population, their arguments were emotionally charged and their protests often dramatic and telling.

Antislavery novels—the most famous of which was *Uncle Tom's Cabin* (1852) by Harriet Beecher Stowe (1811–1896)—stirred up public sentiment against the brutality and injustice of the system. Originally serialized in an antislavery newspaper, Stowe's book sold over one million copies within a year of its publication. But the most direct challenge to slavery came from the slaves themselves, and none more so than the slave rebels who—like Prometheus—mounted outright attacks against their owners and masters in their efforts to gain a prized privilege: freedom. While slave rebellions were rare in nineteenth-century America—between 1800 and 1860 only two reached the level of overt insurrection—the threat or rumor of rebellion was terrifying to slave owners.

One of the most notable insurrections of the century took place in Southampton County, Virginia, in 1831. Nat Turner (1800–1831), a slave preacher and mystic, believed that he was divinely appointed to lead the slaves to freedom. The Turner rebellion resulted in the deaths of at least fifty-seven white people (and many more black slaves, killed when the rebellion was suppressed) and the destruction of

---

* The origins and history of the transatlantic slave trade are discussed
in chapters 18 and 25.

several area plantations. Following the defeat of the rebel slaves, the captive Turner explained his motives to a local attorney, who prepared a published version of his personal account in the so-called "Confessions of Nat Turner."

Frederick Douglass A longer, more detailed autobiography, the *Narrative of the Life of Frederick Douglass: An American Slave* (1845), came from the pen of the nineteenth century's leading African-American crusader for black freedom (Figure 28.4). Born a slave on the east coast of Maryland, Douglass (1817–1883) taught himself how to read and write at an early age; he escaped bondage in Baltimore in 1838 and eventually found his way to New England, where he joined the Massachusetts Antislavery Society. A powerful public speaker, who captivated his audiences with accounts of his life, Douglass served as living proof of the potential of black slaves to achieve brilliantly as free persons. He wrote extensively and eloquently in support of abolition, describing the "dehumanizing character of slavery" (that is, its negative effects on both black and white people), and defending the idea that, by abandoning slavelike behavior, even slaves could determine their own lives. On occasion, he employed high irony—contradiction between literal and intended meanings—as is the case with his justification of theft as a moral act if perpetrated by a slave against his master. Though it is unlikely that Douglass had in mind any reference to the Promethean motif of heroic defiance, the parallel is not without significance. "A Slave's Right to Steal" comes from *My Bondage and My Freedom*, the revised and enlarged version of Douglass' autobiography.

Figure 28.4 *Portrait of Frederick Douglass*, 1847. Daguerreotype.

READING 28.5 From Douglass' *My Bondage and My Freedom* (1855)

. . . There were four slaves of us in the kitchen, and four whites **1** in the great house—Thomas Auld, Mrs. Auld, Hadaway Auld (brother of Thomas Auld), and little Amanda. The names of the slaves in the kitchen, were Eliza, my sister; Priscilla, my aunt; Henry, my cousin; and myself. There were eight persons in the family. There was, each week, one half bushel of corn-meal brought from the mill; and in the kitchen, corn-meal was almost our exclusive food, for very little else was allowed us. Out of this half bushel of corn-meal, the family in the great house had a small loaf every morning; thus leaving us, in the **10** kitchen, with not quite a half a peck of meal per week, apiece. This allowance was less than half the allowance of food on Lloyd's plantation. It was not enough to subsist upon; and we were, therefore, reduced to the wretched necessity of living at the expense of our neighbors. We were compelled either to beg, or to steal, and we did both. I frankly confess, that while I hated everything like stealing, *as such*, I nevertheless did not hesitate to take food, when I was hungry, wherever I could find it. Nor was this practice the mere result of an unreasoning instinct; it was, in my case, the result of a clear apprehension **20** of the claims of morality. I weighed and considered the matter closely, before I ventured to satisfy my hunger by such means. Considering that my labor and person were the property of Master Thomas, and that I was by him deprived of the necessaries of life—necessaries obtained by my own labor—it was easy to deduce the right to supply myself with what was my own. It was simply appropriating what was my own to the use of my master, since the health and strength derived from such food were exerted in *his* service. To be sure, this was stealing, according to the law and gospel I heard from St. **30** Michael's pulpit; but I had already begun to attach less importance to what dropped from that quarter, on that point, while, as yet, I retained my reverence for religion. It was not always convenient to steal from master, and the same reason why I might, innocently, steal from him, did not seem to justify me in stealing from others. In the case of my master, it was only a question of *removal*—the taking his meat out of the tub, and putting it into another; the ownership of the meat was not affected by the transaction. At first, he owned it in the *tub*, and last, he owned it in *me*. **40** His meat house was not always open. There was a strict watch kept on that point, and the key was on a large bunch in Rowena's pocket. A great many times have we, poor creatures, been severely pinched with hunger, when meat and bread have been moulding under the lock, while the key was in the pocket of our mistress. This had been so when she *knew* we were nearly half starved; and yet, that mistress, with saintly air, would kneel with her husband, and pray each morning that a merciful God would bless them in basket and in store, and save them, at last, in his kingdom. **50** But I proceed with the argument.

It was necessary that the right to steal from *others* should be established; and this could only rest upon a wider range of generalization than that which supposed the right to steal from my master.

It was sometime before I arrived at this clear right. The reader will get some idea of my train of reasoning, by a brief statement of the case. "I am," thought I, "not only the slave of Master Thomas, but I am the slave of society at large. Society at large has bound itself, in form and in fact, to assist **60** Master Thomas in robbing me of my rightful liberty, and of the just reward of my labor; therefore, whatever rights I have against Master Thomas, I have, equally, against those confederated with him in robbing me of liberty. As society has marked me out as privileged plunder, on the principle of self-preservation I am justified in plundering in turn. Since each slave belongs to all; all must, therefore, belong to each."

I shall here make a profession of faith which may shock some, offend others, and be dissented from by all. It is this: Within the bounds of his just earnings, I hold that the slave is **70** fully justified in helping himself to the *gold and silver, and the best apparel of his master, or that of any other slaveholder; and*

that such taking is not stealing in any just sense of that word.

The morality of *free* society can have no application to *slave* society. Slaveholders have made it almost impossible for the slave to commit any crime, known either to the laws of God or to the laws of man. If he steals, he takes his own; if he kills his master, he imitates only the heroes of the revolution. Slaveholders I hold to be individually and collectively responsible for all the evils which grow out of the horrid **80** relation, and I believe they will be so held at the judgment, in the sight of a just God. Make a man a slave, and you rob him of moral responsibility. . . .

— Q   **With what arguments does Douglass justify stealing?**

— Q   **Does moral responsibility alter according to the status of an individual?**

Sojourner Truth While Frederick Douglass was among the first African-Americans to win international attention through his skills at public speaking, his female contemporary Sojourner Truth (ca. 1797–1883) brought wit and a woman's passion to the fight against slavery. Born to slave parents in Ulster County, New York, Isabella Bomefree was sold four times before the age of thirty, an inauspicious beginning for a woman who would become one of America's most vocal abolitionists, an evangelist, and a champion of women's rights.

After being emancipated in 1828, Bomefree traveled widely in the United States, changing her name to Sojourner Truth in 1843, as she committed her life to "sharing the truth" in matters of human dignity. Although she never learned to read or write, she was determined to have her voice heard across the nation and for future generations. To accomplish the latter, she dictated her story to a friend, Olive Gilbert. The narrative, which was published in 1850, recounts the major events of her life, including the tale of how Isabella engaged in a heroic legal battle to win back her five-year-old son, who was illegally sold into slavery in New York State. Sojourner Truth used her talents as an orator to voice her opposition to slavery,

capital punishment, and the kidnapping and sale of black children (a common practice in some parts of the country). She also supported prison reform, helped to relocate former slaves, and defended the rights of women. Sharp-tongued and outspoken (and a lifelong pipe-smoker), Sojourner Truth won popular notoriety for the short, impromptu speech, "Ain't I a Woman?," delivered in 1851 to the Woman's Convention at Akron, Ohio. While scholars question the authenticity of various versions of the speech (which was published by abolitionists some twelve years later), no such debate clouds Sojourner's narrative, which, even in this short excerpt, captures the spirit of her straightforward rhetoric.

┌─ **READING 28.6** From *The Narrative of Sojourner Truth* (1850)

Isabella's marriage

Subsequently, Isabella was married to a fellow-slave, named   **1** Thomas, who had previously had two wives, one of whom, if not both, had been torn from him and sold far away. And it is more than probable, that he was not only allowed but encouraged to take another at each successive sale. I say it is probable, because the writer of this knows from personal observation, that such is the custom among slaveholders at the present day; and that in a twenty months' residence among them, we never knew any one to open the lip against the practice; and when we severely censured it, the slaveholder   **10** had nothing to say; and the slave pleaded that, under existing circumstances, he could do no better.

Such an abominable state of things is silently tolerated, to say the least, by slaveholders—deny it who may. And what is that religion that sanctions, even by its silence, all that is embraced in the *"Peculiar Institution"*? If there *can* be any thing more diametrically opposed to the religion of Jesus, than the working of this soul-killing system—which is as truly sanctioned by the religion of America as are her ministers and churches—we wish to be shown where it can be found.   **20**

We have said, Isabella was married to Thomas—she was, after the fashion of slavery, one of the slaves performing the ceremony for them; as no true minister of Christ *can* perform, as in the presence of God, what he knows to be a mere *farce*, a *mock* marriage, unrecognised by any civil law, and liable to be annulled at any moment, when the interest or caprice of the master should dictate.

With what feelings must slaveholders expect us to listen to their horror of amalgamation in prospect, while they are well aware that we know how calmly and quietly they contemplate   **30** the present state of licentiousness their own wicked laws have created, not only as it regards the slave, but as it regards the more privileged portion of the population of the South?

Slaveholders appear to me to take the same notice of the vices of the slave, as one does of the vicious disposition of his horse. They are often an inconvenience; further than that, they care not to trouble themselves about the matter. . . .

— Q   **Why does Sojourner Truth claim that slavery is "sanctioned by the religion of America"?**

Slave Songs and Spirituals

The nineteenth century witnessed the flowering of a unique type of folk song that expressed the heroic grief and hopes of the American slave community. Slave songs, sometimes termed "sorrow songs," formed the basis of what later became known as "spirituals." These songs, the most significant musical contribution of America's antebellum population, were a distinctive cultural form that blended the Methodist and Baptist evangelical church music of the eighteenth century with musical traditions brought from Africa to the Americas in the course of 200 years.

A communal vehicle that conveyed the fervent longing for freedom, slave songs and spirituals based their content in Bible stories, usually focused on deliverance—the passage of the "Hebrew children" out of Egyptian bondage, for instance—and the promise of ultimate, triumphant liberation. A typical spiritual, such as "Sometimes I Feel Like a Motherless Child," tempers despair with enduring faith. In form, spirituals embellished typically Protestant melodies and antiphonal structures with the complex, percussive rhythms (such as polymeter and syncopation), overlapping call and response patterns, and improvisational techniques of traditional African music (see chapter 18).

A powerful form of religious music, the spiritual came to public attention only after 1871, when an instructor of vocal music at Fisk University in Tennessee took the school's student choir on a university fundraising tour. A similar group was established by Hampton Institute (now Hampton University in Virginia) in 1873. Beyond the commercial popularity of this song form, spirituals have come to influence the development of numerous musical genres, including jazz, gospel, and blues (see chapter 36).

Goethe's Faust: The Quintessential Romantic Hero

Of all literary heroes of the nineteenth century, perhaps the most compelling is Goethe's Faust. The story of Faust is based on a sixteenth-century German legend: a traveling physician and a practitioner of black magic, Johann or Georg Faust, was reputed to have sold his soul to the Devil in exchange for infinite knowledge. The story became the subject of numerous dramas, the first of which was *The Tragical History of Doctor Faustus* written by the English playwright Christopher Marlowe (1564–1593). Faust was the favorite Renaissance symbol of the lust for knowledge and power balanced against the perils of eternal damnation—a theme that figured largely in literary characterizations of Don Juan as well. In the hands of the German poet Johann Wolfgang von Goethe (1749–1832), Faust became the paradigm of Western man and the quintessential Romantic hero.

One of the literary landmarks of its time, *Faust* was the product of Goethe's entire career: he conceived the piece during the 1770s, published Part One in 1808, but did not complete the play until 1832. Although ostensibly a drama, *Faust* more closely resembles an epic poem. It is written in a lyric German, with a richness of verse forms that is typical of Romantic poetry. As a play, it deliberately ignores the Classical unities of time and place—indeed, its shifting "cinematic" qualities make it more adaptable to modern film than to the traditional stage. Despite a cosmic breadth, which compares with Milton's *Paradise Lost* or Dante's *Divine Comedy*, Goethe's *Faust* focuses more narrowly on the human condition. Goethe neither seeks to justify God's ways to humanity nor to allegorize the Christian ascent to salvation; rather, he uncovers the tragic tension between heroic aspirations and human limitations. A student of law, medicine, theology, theater, biology, optics, and alchemy, Goethe seems to have modeled his hero after himself. Faust is a man of deep learning, a Christian, and a scientist. Having mastered the traditional disciplines, he has turned to magic "to learn what it is that girds/ The world together in its inmost being." While the desire to know and achieve has driven his studies, he feels stale, bored, and deeply dissatisfied: "too old for mere amusement,/ Too young to be without desire." On the verge of suicide, he is enticed by Satan to abandon the world of the intellect for a fuller knowledge of life, a privilege that may cost him dearly.

The Prologue of *Faust* is set in Heaven, where (in a manner reminiscent of the Book of Job) a wager is made between Mephistopheles (Satan) and God. Mephistopheles bets God that he can divert Faust from "the path that is true and fit." God contends that, though "men make mistakes as long as they strive," Faust will never relinquish his soul to Satan. Mephistopheles then proceeds to make a second pact, this one with Faust himself, signed in blood: if he can satisfy Faust's deepest desires and ambitions to the hero's ultimate satisfaction, Mephistopheles will win Faust's soul. Mephistopheles lures the despairing scholar out of his study ("This God-damned dreary hole in the wall") and into the larger world of experience (Figure **28.5**). The newly liberated hero then engages in a passionate love affair with a young woman named Gretchen. Discovering the joys of the sensual life, Faust proclaims the priority of the heart ("Feeling is all!") over the mind. Faust's romance, however, has tragic consequences, including the deaths of Gretchen's mother, her illegitimate child, her brother, and, ultimately, Gretchen herself. Nevertheless, at the close of Part One, Gretchen's pure and selfless love wins her salvation.

In the second part of the drama, the hero travels with Mephistopheles through a netherworld in which he meets an array of witches, sirens, and other fantastic creatures. He encounters the ravishing Helen of Troy, symbol of ideal beauty, who acquaints Faust with the entire history of humankind; but Faust remains unsated. His unquenched thirst for experience now leads him to pursue a life of action for the public good. He undertakes a vast land-reclamation project, which provides habitation for millions of people. In this Promethean effort to benefit humanity, the aged and near-blind Faust finally finds personal fulfillment. He dies, however, before fully realizing his dream, thus never declaring the satisfaction that will doom him to Hell. While Mephistopheles tries to apprehend Faust's soul

Figure 28.5 EUGÈNE DELACROIX, *Mephistopheles Appearing to Faust in His Study*, illustration for Goethe's *Faust*, 1828. Lithograph, 10¾ × 9 in. Dressed in a "suit of scarlet trimmed with gold," a "little cape of stiff brocade," and a stylish hat, Mephistopheles invites Faust to dress up like him and prepare to seek "pleasure and action." Goethe's drama inspired many contemporary visual illustrations, as well as musical settings by Berlioz and other composers (see chapter 29).

as it leaves his body, God's angels, led by Gretchen (Goethe's symbol of the Eternal Female), intervene to shepherd Faust's spirit to Heaven.

The heroic Faust is a timeless symbol of the Western drive for consummate knowledge, experience, and the will to power over nature. Though it is possible to reproduce here only a small portion of Goethe's 12,000-line poem, the following excerpt conveys the powerful lyricism, the verbal subtleties, and the shifts between high seriousness and comedy that make Goethe's *Faust* a literary masterpiece.

┌─ **READING 28.7** From Goethe's *Faust* (1808)
Prologue in Heaven

The Lord. The Heavenly Hosts. Mephistopheles following (the Three Archangels step forward).

  Raphael: The chanting sun, as ever, rivals   1

The chanting of his brother spheres
And marches round his destined circuit—[1]
A march that thunders in our ears.
His aspect cheers the Hosts of Heaven
Though what his essence none can say;
These inconceivable creations
Keep the high state of their first day.
  Gabriel: And swift, with inconceivable swiftness,
The earth's full splendor rolls around,   10
Celestial radiance alternating
With a dread night too deep to sound;
The sea against the rocks' deep bases
Comes foaming up in far-flung force,
And rock and sea go whirling onward

[1] The sun is treated here as one of the planets, all of which, according to Pythagoras, moved harmoniously in crystalline spheres.

In the swift spheres' eternal course.

Michael: And storms in rivalry are raging
From sea to land, from land to sea,
In frenzy forge the world a girdle
From which no inmost part is free   20
The blight of lightning flaming yonder
Marks where the thunder-bolt will play;
And yet Thine envoys, Lord, revere
The gentle movement of Thy day.

Choir of Angels: Thine aspect cheers the Hosts of Heaven
Though what Thine essence none can say,
And all Thy loftiest creations
Keep the high state of their first day.

(Enter Mephistopheles) [2]

Mephistopheles: Since you, O Lord, once more approach and ask
If business down with us be light or heavy—   30
And in the past you've usually welcomed me—
That's why you see me also at your levee.
Excuse me, I can't manage lofty words—
Not though your whole court jeer and find me low;
My pathos certainly would make you laugh
Had you not left off laughing long ago.
Your suns and worlds mean nothing much to me;
How men torment themselves, that's all I see.
The little god of the world, one can't reshape, reshade him;
He is as strange to-day as that first day you made him.   40
His life would be not so bad, not quite,
Had you not granted him a gleam of Heaven's light;
He calls it Reason, uses it not the least
Except to be more beastly than any beast.
He seems to me—if your Honor does not mind—
Like a grasshopper—the long-legged kind—
That's always in flight and leaps as it flies along
And then in the grass strikes up its same old song.
I could only wish he confined himself to the grass!
He thrusts his nose into every filth, alas.   50

Lord: Mephistopheles, have you no other news?
Do you always come here to accuse?
Is nothing ever right in your eyes on earth?

Mephistopheles: No, Lord! I find things there as downright
bad as ever.
I am sorry for men's days of dread and dearth;
Poor things, *my* wish to plague 'em isn't fervent.

Lord: Do you know Faust?

Mephistopheles: The Doctor?

Lord: Aye, my servant.[3]

Mephistopheles: Indeed! He serves you oddly enough,
I think.   60
The fool has no earthly habits in meat and drink.
The ferment in him drives him wide and far,
That he is mad he too has almost guessed;
He demands of heaven each fairest star
And of earth each highest joy and best,
And all that is new and all that is far
Can bring no calm to the deep-sea swell of his breast.

Lord: Now he may serve me only gropingly,
Soon I shall lead him into the light.
The gardener knows when the sapling first turns green   70
That flowers and fruit will make the future bright.

Mephistopheles: What do you wager? You will lose him yet,
Provided *you* give *me* permission
To steer him gently the course I set.

Lord: So long as he walks the earth alive,
So long you may try what enters your head;
Men make mistakes as long as they strive.

Mephistopheles: I thank you for that; as regards the dead,
The dead have never taken my fancy.
I favor cheeks that are full and rosy-red;   80
No corpse is welcome to my house;
I work as the cat does with the mouse.

Lord: Very well; you have my full permission.
Divert this soul from its primal source
And carry it, if you can seize it,
Down with you upon your course—
And stand ashamed when you must needs admit:
A good man with his groping intuitions
Still knows the path that's true and fit.

Mephistopheles: All right—but it won't last for long.   90
I'm not afraid my bet will turn out wrong.
And, if my aim prove true and strong,
Allow me to triumph wholeheartedly.
Dust shall he eat—and greedily—
Like my cousin the Snake renowned in tale and song.[4]

Lord: That too you are free to give a trial;
I have never hated the likes of you.
Of all the spirits of denial
The joker is the last that I eschew.
Man finds relaxation too attractive—   100
Too fond too soon of unconditional rest;
Which is why I am pleased to give him a companion
Who lures and thrusts and must, as devil, be active.
But ye, true sons of Heaven,[5] it is your duty
To take your joy in the living wealth of beauty.
The changing Essence which ever works and lives
Wall you around with love, serene, secure!
And that which floats in flickering appearance
Fix ye it firm in thoughts that must endure.

Choir of Angels: Thine aspect cheers the Hosts of
Heaven   110
Though what Thine essence none can say,
And all Thy loftiest creations
Keep the high state of their first day.

(Heaven closes)

Mephistopheles *(Alone):* I like to see the Old One now and then
And try to keep relations on the level
It's really decent of so great a person
To talk so humanely even to the Devil.

---

[2] The name possibly derives from the Hebrew "Mephistoph," meaning
destroyer of the gods."
[3] Compare the exchange between God and Satan at the beginning of
the Book of Job (see chapter 1).
[4] In Genesis 3: 14, God condemns the serpent to go on its belly and eat
dust for the rest of its days.
[5] The archangels.

The First Part of the Tragedy Night

(In a high-vaulted narrow Gothic room Faust, restless, in a chair at his desk)

    Faust: Here stand I, ach, Philosophy
Behind me and Law and Medicine too
And, to my cost, Theology—[6]   120
All these I have sweated through and through
And now you see me a poor fool
As wise as when I entered school!
They call me Master, they call me Doctor,[7]
Ten years now I have dragged my college
Along by the nose through zig and zag
Through up and down and round and round
And this is all that I have found—
The impossibility of knowledge!
It is this that burns away my heart;   130
Of course I am cleverer than the quacks,
Than master and doctor, than clerk and priest,
I suffer no scruple or doubt in the least,
I have no qualms about devil or burning,
Which is just why all joy is torn from me,
I cannot presume to make use of my learning,
I cannot presume I could open my mind
To proselytize and improve mankind.

Besides, I have neither goods nor gold,
Neither reputation nor rank in the world;   140
No dog would choose to continue so!
Which is why I have given myself to Magic
To see if the Spirit may grant me to know
Through its force and its voice full many a secret,
May spare the sour sweat that I used to pour out
In talking of what I know nothing about,
May grant me to learn what it is that girds
The world together in its inmost being,
That the seeing its whole germination, the seeing
Its workings, may end my traffic in words.   150

O couldst thou, light of the full moon,
Look now thy last upon my pain,
Thou for whom I have sat belated
So many midnights here and waited
Till, over books and papers, thou
Didst shine, sad friend, upon my brow!
O could I but walk to and fro
On mountain heights in thy dear glow
Or float with spirits round mountain eyries
Or weave through fields thy glances glean   160
And freed from all miasmal theories
Bathe in thy dew and wash me clean![8]
Oh! Am I still stuck in this jail?
This God-damned dreary hole in the wall

Where even the lovely light of heaven
Breaks wanly through the painted panes!
Cooped up among these heaps of books
Gnawed by worms, coated with dust,
Round which to the top of the Gothic vault
A smoke-stained paper forms a crust.   170
Retorts and canisters lie pell-mell
And pyramids of instruments,
The junk of centuries, dense and mat—
Your world, man! World? They call it that!

And yet you ask why your poor heart
Cramped in your breast should feel such fear,
Why an unspecified misery
Should throw your life so out of gear?
Instead of the living natural world
For which God made all men his sons   180
You hold a reeking mouldering court
Among assorted skeletons.
Away! There is a world outside!
And this one book of mystic art
Which Nostradamus[9] wrote himself,
Is this not adequate guard and guide?
By this you can tell the course of the stars,
By this, once Nature gives the word,
The soul begins to stir and dawn,
A spirit by a spirit heard,   190
In vain your barren studies here
Construe the signs of sanctity.
You Spirits, you are hovering near;
If you can hear me, answer me!
(He opens the book and perceives the sign of the Macrocosm)[10]
Ha! What a river of wonder at this vision
Bursts upon all my senses in one flood!
And I feel young, the holy joy of life
Glows new, flows fresh, through nerve and blood!
Was it a god designed this hieroglyph to calm
The storm which but now raged inside me,   200
To pour upon my heart such balm,
And by some secret urge to guide me
Where all the powers of Nature stand unveiled around me?
Am I a God? It grows so light!
And through the clear-cut symbol on this page
My soul comes face to face with all creating Nature.
At last I understand the dictum of the sage:
"The spiritual world is always open,
Your mind is closed, your heart is dead;
Rise, young man, and plunge undaunted   210
Your earthly breast in the mourning red."
(He contemplates the sign)
Into one Whole how all things blend,
Function and live within each other!

---

[6] Philosophy, law, medicine, and theology were the four programs of study in medieval universities.

[7] The two advanced degrees beyond the baccalaureate.

[8] Goethe's conception of nature as a source of sublime purification may be compared with similar ideas held by the nature poets and the transcendentalists discussed in chapter 27.

[9] Michel de Notredame or Nostradamus (1503–1566) was a French astrologer famous for his prophecies of future events.

[10] Signs of the universe, such as the pentagram, were especially popular among those who practiced magic and the occult arts.

Passing gold buckets to each other
How heavenly powers ascend, descend!
The odor of grace upon their wings,
They thrust from heaven through earthly things
And as all sing so *the* All sings!
What a fine show! Aye, but only a show!
Infinite Nature, where can I tap thy veins?   220

*[Faust uses a magical sign to call forth the Earth Spirit; it
appears but offers him no solace. He then converses with his
assistant Wagner on the fruitlessness of a life of study. When
Wagner leaves, Faust prepares to commit suicide; but he is
interrupted by the sounds of churchbells and choral music. Still
brooding, he joins Wagner and the townspeople as they
celebrate Easter Sunday. At the city gate, Faust encounters a
black poodle, which he takes back with him to his studio. The
dog is actually Mephistopheles, who soon makes his real self
known to Faust.]*

(The same room. Later)
 Faust: Who's knocking? Come in! *Now* who wants to
annoy me?
 Mephistopheles *(outside door)*: It's I.   290
 Faust: Come in!
 Mephistopheles *(outside door)*: You must say "Come in"
three times.
  Faust: Come in then!
 Mephistopheles *(entering)*: Thank you; you overjoy me.
We two, I hope, we shall be good friends;
To chase those megrims[11] of yours away
I am here like a fine young squire to-day,
In a suit of scarlet trimmed with gold
And a little cape of stiff brocade,
With a cock's feather in my hat   300
And at my side a long sharp blade,
And the most succinct advice I can give
Is that you dress up just like me,
So that uninhibited and free
You may find out what it means to live.
 Faust: The pain of earth's constricted life, I fancy,
Will pierce me still, whatever my attire;
I am too old for mere amusement,
Too young to be without desire.
How can the world dispel my doubt?   310
You must do without, you must do without!
That is the everlasting song
Which rings in every ear, which rings,
And which to us our whole life long
Every hour hoarsely sings.
I wake in the morning only to feel appalled,
My eyes with bitter tears could run
To see the day which in its course
Will not fulfil a wish for me, not one;
The day which whittles away with obstinate carping   320
All pleasures—even those of anticipation,
Which makes a thousand grimaces to obstruct

My heart when it is stirring in creation.
And again, when night comes down, in anguish
I must stretch out upon my bed
And again no rest is granted me,
For wild dreams fill my mind with dread.
The God who dwells within my bosom
Can make my inmost soul react;
The God who sways my every power   330
Is powerless with external fact.
And so existence weighs upon my breast
And I long for death and life—life I detest.
 Mephistopheles: Yet death is never a wholly welcome guest.
 Faust: O happy is he whom death in the dazzle of victory
Crowns with the bloody laurel in the battling swirl!
Or he whom after the mad and breakneck dance
He comes upon in the arms of a girl!
O to have sunk away, delighted, deleted,
Before the Spirit of the Earth,[12] before his might!   340
 Mephistopheles: Yet I know someone who failed to drink
A brown juice on a certain night.[13]
 Faust: Your hobby is espionage—is it not?
 Mephistopheles: Oh I'm not omniscient—but I know a lot.
 Faust: Whereas that tumult in my soul
Was stilled by sweet familiar chimes
Which cozened the child that yet was in me
With echoes of more happy times,
I now curse all things that encompass
The soul with lures and jugglery   350
And bind it in this dungeon of grief
With trickery and flattery.
Cursed in advance be the high opinion
That serves our spirit for a cloak!
Cursed be the dazzle of appearance
Which bows our senses to its yoke!
Cursed be the lying dreams of glory,
The illusion that our name survives!
Cursed be the flattering things we own,
Servants and ploughs, children and wives!   360
Cursed be Mammon[14] when with his treasures
He makes us play the adventurous man
Or when for our luxurious pleasures
He duly spreads the soft divan!
A curse on the balsam of the grape!
A curse on the love that rides for a fall!
A curse on hope! A curse on faith!
And a curse on patience most of all!
(The invisible Spirits sing again)
 Spirits: Woe! Woe!
You have destroyed it,   370
The beautiful world;
By your violent hand
'Tis downward hurled!
A half-god has dashed it asunder!

---

[11] Low or morbid spirits.

[12] The Earth Spirit that Faust called forth earlier.
[13] Mephistopheles alludes to Faust's contemplation of suicide by poison
  earlier in the drama.
[14] Riches or material wealth.

From under
We bear off the rubble to nowhere
And ponder
Sadly the beauty departed.
Magnipotent
One among men,   380
Magnificent
Build it again,
Build it again in your breast!
Let a new course of life
Begin
With vision abounding
And new songs resounding
To welcome it in!
    Mephistopheles: These are the juniors
Of my faction.   390
Hear how precociously they counsel
Pleasure and action.
Out and away
From your lonely day
Which dries your senses and your juices
Their melody seduces.
Stop playing with your grief which battens
Like a vulture on your life, your mind!
The worst of company would make you feel
That you are a man among mankind.   400
Not that it's really my proposition
To shove you among the common men;
Though I'm not one of the Upper Ten.
If you would like a coalition
With me for your career through life,
I am quite ready to fit in,
I'm yours before you can say knife.
I am your comrade;
If you so crave,
I am your servant, I am your slave.   410
    Faust: And what have I to undertake in return?
    Mephistopheles: Oh it's early days to discuss what that is.
    Faust: No, no, the devil is an egoist
And ready to do nothing gratis
Which is to benefit a stranger.
Tell me your terms and don't prevaricate!
A servant like you in the house is a danger.
    Mephistopheles: I will bind myself to your service in this world,
To be at your beck and never rest nor slack;
When we meet again on the other side,   420
In the same coin you shall pay me back.
    Faust: The other side gives me little trouble;
First batter this present world to rubble,
Then the other may rise—if that's the plan.
This earth is where my springs of joy have started.
And this sun shines on me when broken-hearted;
If I can first from them be parted,
Then let happen what will and can!
I wish to hear no more about it—
Whether there too men hate and love   430
Or whether in those spheres too, in the future,
There is a Below or an Above.

    Mephistopheles: With such an outlook you can risk it.
Sign on the line! In these next days you will get
Ravishing samples of my arts;
I am giving you what never man saw yet.
    Faust: Poor devil, can *you* give anything ever?
Was a human spirit in its high endeavor
Even once understood by one of your breed?
Have you got food which fails to feed?   440
Or red gold which, never at rest,
Like mercury runs away through the hand?
A game at which one never wins?
A girl who, even when on my breast,
Pledges herself to my neighbor with her eyes?
The divine and lovely delight of honor
Which falls like a falling star and dies?
Show me the fruits which, before they are plucked, decay
And the trees which day after day renew their green!
    Mephistopheles: Such a commission doesn't alarm me,   450
I have such treasures to purvey.
But, my good friend, the time draws on when we
Should be glad to feast at our ease on something good.
    Faust: If ever I stretch myself on a bed of ease,
Then I am finished! Is that understood?
If ever your flatteries can coax me
To be pleased with myself, if ever you cast
A spell of pleasure that can hoax me—
Then let *that* day be my last!
That's my wager![15]   460
    Mephistopheles: Done!
    Faust: Let's shake!
If ever I say to the passing moment
"Linger for a while! Thou art so fair!"
Then you may cast me into fetters,
I will gladly perish then and there!
Then you may set the death-bell tolling,
Then from my service you are free,
The clock may stop, its hand may fall,
And that be the end of time for me!   470

[Faust agrees to sign the pact with a drop of his blood.]

    Faust: Only do not fear that I shall break this contract.
What I promise is nothing more
Than what all my powers are striving for.
I have puffed myself up too much, it is only
Your sort that really fits my case.   510
The great Earth Spirit has despised me
And Nature shuts the door in my face.
The thread of thought is snapped asunder.
I have long loathed knowledge in all its fashions.
In the depths of sensuality
Let us now quench our glowing passions!
And at once make ready every wonder
Of unpenetrated sorcery!
Let us cast ourselves into the torrent of time,
Into the whirl of eventfulness,   520

---

[15] The wager between Faust and Mephistopheles recalls that between God and Mephistopheles in the Prologue.

Where disappointment and success,
Pleasure and pain may chop and change
As chop and change they will and can;
It is restless action makes the man.
    Mephistopheles: No limit is fixed for you, no bound;
If you'd like to nibble at everything
Or to seize upon something flying round—
Well, may you have a run for your money!
But seize your chance and don't be funny!
    Faust: I've told you, it is no question of happiness.   530
The most painful joy, enamored hate, enlivening
Disgust—I devote myself to all excess.
My breast, now cured of its appetite for knowledge,
From now is open to all and every smart,
And what is allotted to the whole of mankind
That will I sample in my inmost heart,
Grasping the highest and lowest with my spirit,
Piling men's weal and woe upon my neck,
To extend myself to embrace all human selves
And to founder in the end, like them, a wreck.   540
    Mephistopheles: O believe *me*, who have been chewing
These iron rations many a thousand year,
No human being can digest
This stuff, from the cradle to the bier.
This universe—believe a devil—
Was made for no one but a god!
He exists in eternal light
But *us* he has brought into the darkness
While *your* sole portion is day and night.
    Faust: I will all the same!   550
    Mephistopheles: That's very nice.
There's only one thing I find wrong;
Time is short, art is long.[16]
You could do with a little artistic advice.
Confederate with one of the poets
And let him flog his imagination
To heap all virtues on your head,
A head with such a reputation:
Lion's bravery,
Stag's velocity,   560
Fire of Italy,
Northern tenacity.
Let *him* find out the secret art
Of combining craft with a noble heart
And of being in love like a young man,
Hotly, but working to a plan.
Such a person—*I'd* like to meet him;
"Mr. Microcosm" is how I'd greet him.
    Faust: What am I then if fate must bar
My efforts to reach that crown of humanity   570
After which all my senses strive?
    Mephistopheles: You are in the end . . . what you are.
You can put on full-bottomed wigs with a million locks,
You can put on stilts instead of your socks,
You remain for ever what you are.

---

[16] An adaptation of the famous Latin aphorism *Ars longa, vita brevis* ("Art is long-lasting, but life is short").

    Faust: I feel my endeavours have not been worth a pin
When I raked together the treasures of the human mind,
If at the end I but sit down to find
No new force welling up within.
I have not a hair's breadth more of height,   580
I am no nearer the Infinite.
    Mephistopheles: My very good sir, you look at things
Just in the way that people do;
We must be cleverer than that
Or the joys of life will escape from you.
Hell! You have surely hands and feet,
Also a head and you-know-what;
The pleasures I gather on the wing,
Are they less mine? Of course they're not!
Suppose I can afford six stallions,   590
I can add that horse-power to my score
And dash along and be a proper man
As if my legs were twenty-four.
So good-bye to thinking! On your toes!
The world's before us. Quick! Here goes!
I tell you, a chap who's intellectual
Is like a beast on a blasted heath
Driven in circles by a demon
While a fine green meadow lies round beneath.
    Faust: How do we start?   600
    Mephistopheles: We just say go—and skip.
But please get ready for this pleasure trip.
(Exit Faust)
    Only look down on knowledge and reason,
The highest gifts that men can prize,
Only allow the spirit of lies
To confirm you in magic and illusion,
And then I have you body and soul.
Fate has given this man a spirit
Which is always pressing onwards, beyond control,
And whose mad striving overleaps   610
All joys of the earth between pole and pole.
Him shall I drag through the wilds of life
And through the flats of meaninglessness,
I shall make him flounder and gape and stick
And to tease his insatiableness
Hang meat and drink in the air before his watering lips;
In vain he will pray to slake his inner thirst,
And even had he not sold himself to the devil
He would be equally accursed.
(Re-enter Faust)
    Faust: And now, where are we going?   620
    Mephistopheles: Wherever you please.
The small world, then the great for us.
With what pleasure and what profit
You will roister through the syllabus!
    Faust: But I, with this long beard of mine,
I lack the easy social touch,
I know the experiment is doomed;
Out in the world I never could fit in much.
I feel so small in company
I'll be embarrassed constantly.   630
    Mephistopheles: My friend, it will solve itself, any such

misgiving;
Just trust yourself and you'll learn the art of living.
   Faust: Well, then, how do we leave home?
Where are your grooms? Your coach and horses?
   Mephistopheles: We merely spread this mantle wide,
It will bear us off on airy courses.
But do not on this noble voyage
Cumber yourself with heavy baggage.
A little inflammable gas which I'll prepare
Will lift us quickly into the air.   **640**
If we travel light we shall cleave the sky like a knife.
Congratulations on your new course of life!

  Q **Compare the personalities of Faust and Mephistopheles.**

  Q **Why might Faust be considered the quintessential romantic hero?**

Romantic Love and Romantic Stereotypes

Romantic love, the sentimental and all-consuming passion for spiritual as well as sexual union with the opposite sex, was a favorite theme of nineteenth-century writers, painters, and composers. Many Romantics perceived friendship, religious love, and sexual love—both heterosexual and homosexual—as closely related expressions of an ecstatic harmony of souls. Passionate love, and especially unrequited or unfulfilled love, was the subject of numerous literary works. To name but three: Goethe's *Sorrows of Young Werther* (1774) told the story of a lovesick hero whose passion for a married woman leads him to commit suicide—the book was so popular that it made suicide something of a nineteenth-century vogue; Hector Berlioz's *Symphonie fantastique* (1830–1831) described the composer's obsessive infatuation with a flamboyant actress (see chapter 29); and Richard Wagner's opera *Tristan and Isolde* (1859) dramatized the tragic fate of two legendary medieval lovers.

While Romantics generated an image of masculinity that emphasized self-invention, courage, and the quest for knowledge and power, they either glorified the female as chaste, passive, and submissive, or characterized her as dangerous and threatening. Romantic writers inherited the dual view of womankind that had prevailed since the Middle Ages: like Eve, woman was the *femme fatale*, the seducer and destroyer of mankind; like Mary, however, woman was the source of salvation and the symbol of all that was pure and true. The Eve stereotype is readily apparent in such works as Prosper Mérimée's novella *Carmen*, on which the opera by Georges Bizet (1835–1875) was based. Set in Seville, Spain, Bizet's *Carmen* (1875) is a story of seduction, rejection, and fatal revenge. Carmen, a shameless flirt who works in a cigarette factory, lures the enamored Don José into deserting the army in order to follow her. Soon tiring of the soldier, she abandons him in favor of a celebrity toreador, only to meet her end at the hand of her former lover. Bizet's heroine became the late nineteenth-century symbol of faithless and dangerous Womankind.

At the other extreme, the Mary stereotype is present in countless nineteenth-century stories, including *Faust* itself, where Gretchen is cast as the Eternal Female, the source of procreation and personal salvation. The following lines by the German poet Heinrich Heine (1797–1856), which were set to music by his contemporary Robert Schumann (1810–1856), typify the female as angelic, ethereal, and chaste—an object that thrilled and inspired the imaginations of many European Romantics.

READING 28.8 Heine's "You are Just Like a Flower" (1827)

You are just like a flower
So fair and chaste and dear;
Looking at you, sweet sadness
Invades my heart with fear.
I feel I should be folding
My hands upon your hair,
Praying that God may keep you
So dear and chaste and fair.

  Q **What stereotype is established by the simile in this poem?**

  Q **Why does the speaker experience "sweet sadness"?**

The Female Voice

The nineteenth century was the first great age of female writers. Examples include the English novelists George Eliot, a pseudonym for Mary Ann Evans (1819–1880); Emily Brontë (1818–1848), author of the hypnotic novel *Wuthering Heights*; her sister Charlotte Brontë, author of *Jane Eyre* (hailed as a masterpiece only after her death); and Mary Godwin Shelley, whose novel *Frankenstein* is discussed earlier in this chapter. In France, Germaine Necker, known as Madame de Stael (1760–1817), was hailed by her contemporaries as the founder of the Romantic movement; a brilliant woman, if not a brilliant novelist, her writings were widely read and admired in her own time. And in America, the Bostonian Louisa May Alcott (1832–1888) produced the classic novel *Little Women* (1868), a semiautobiographical work inspired by a childhood spent with her three sisters. Some of these writers struck a startling note of personal freedom in their lives. In their novels, however, they tended to perpetuate the Romantic stereotype of the chaste and clinging female. Even the most free-thinking of nineteenth-century women novelists might portray her heroine as a creature who submitted to the will and values of the superior male. In general, the dominant male-generated stereotype of the Romantic hero influenced female literary characterization well into the mid nineteenth century.

The novels of Jane Austen (1775–1817) represent something of an exception. In *Sense and Sensibility* (1811), which the author published at her own expense, Austen wittily attacks sentimental love and Romantic rapture. Here, as in her other novels, *Pride and Prejudice, Mansfield Park, Emma, Northanger Abbey* and *Persuasion*, she turned her attention to the everyday concerns of England's provincial middle-class families. Her heroines, intelligent and generous in spirit, are concerned with reconciling economic security with proper social and moral behavior. Austen's keen eye for the details of family life, and for the comic contradictions between human actions and values, show her to be the first Realist in the English novel-writing tradition.

Among French writers of the Romantic era, the most original female voice was that of Amadine Aurore-Lucile Dupin, who used the pen name George Sand (1804–1876). A woman who assumed the name of a man, Sand self-consciously examined the popular Romantic stereotypes, offering not one, but many different points of view concerning male–female dynamics. Defending the passions of Romantic love, one of Sand's heroines exclaims: "If I give myself up to love, I want it to wound me deeply, to electrify me, to break my heart or to exalt me . . . What I want is to suffer, to go crazy." Sand held that true and complete love involved the union of the heart, mind, and body. She avowed that "Love's ideal is most certainly everlasting fidelity," and most of her more than eighty novels feature themes of Romantic love and deep, undying friendship. But for some of her novels, she created heroines who freely exercised the right to love outside of marriage. These heroines did not, however, physically consummate their love, even when that love was reciprocal.

Sand's heroines were very unlike Sand herself, whose numerous love affairs with leading Romantic figures—including the poet Alfred de Musset, the novelist Prosper Mérimée, and the composer Frédéric Chopin—impassioned her life and work. When Sand's affair with Musset came to an unhappy end, she cut off her hair and sent it to him encased in a skull. Sand defied society not only by adopting a life of bohemianism and free love but also by her notorious habit of wearing men's clothes and smoking cigars (Figure **28.6**). The female counterpart of the Byronic hero, Sand confessed, "My emotions have always been stronger than the arguments of reason, and the restrictions I tried to impose on myself were to no avail."

Sand may have been expressing her own ambiguities concerning matters of love and marriage in her third novel, *Lélia* (1833), the pages of which are filled with musings on the meaning of "true love." At one point in her spiritual odyssey, the disenchanted heroine openly ventures:

Figure 28.6 EUGÈNE DELACROIX, *Portrait of George Sand,* 1830. A prolific writer, Sand produced a body of work—some of which has still not been translated into English—that would fill at least 150 volumes, twenty-five of which, each a thousand pages long, would contain her correspondence with the leading artists and intellectuals of her day.

As I continue to live, I cannot help realizing that youthful ideas about the exclusive passion of love and its eternal rights are false, even fatal. All theories ought to be allowed. I would give that of conjugal fidelity to exceptional souls. The majority have other needs, other strengths. To those others I would grant reciprocal freedom, tolerance, and renunciation of all jealous egotism. To others I would concede mystical ardors, fires brooded over in silence, a long and voluptuous reserve. Finally, to others I would admit the calm of angels, fraternal chastity, and an eternal virginity.—Are all souls alike? Do all men have the same abilities? Are not some born for the austerity of religious faith, others for voluptuousness, others for work and passionate struggle, and others, finally, for the vague reveries of the imagination? Nothing is more arbitrary than the understanding of *true love.* All loves are true, whether they be fiery or peaceful, sensual or ascetic, lasting or transient, whether they lead men to suicide or pleasure. The loves *of the mind* lead to actions just as noble as the loves *of the heart.* They have as much violence and power, if not as much duration.

Sand's writings explore a variety of contradictory ideas concerning the fragile relationship between men and women; they also provide a wealth of information about nineteenth-century European life and culture. In addition to her novels and letters, Sand also left an autobiography and dozens of essays and articles championing socialism, women, and the working classes. She explained the power of Romantic creativity with these words: "The writer's trade is a violent, almost indestructible passion. Once it has entered a poor head, nothing can stop it . . . long live the artist's life! Our motto is freedom."

Chronology

ca. 1804	Napoleon is crowned emperor
1812	Napoleon invades Russia
1814	Napoleon is exiled to Elba
1815	Battle of Waterloo
1829	Greece achieves independence from Turkey
1832	Goethe completes *Faust*

LOOKING BACK

Nationalism and the Hero

- For nineteenth-century Romantics, the hero was an expression of the expansive subjectivity of the individual. Characterized by superhuman ambition and talents, the hero, whether a historical figure or a fictional personality, experienced life with self-destructive intensity.
- Napoleon Bonaparte's remarkable career became a model for heroic action propelled by an unbounded imagination and ambition.
- To a great extent, Western literature of the early nineteenth century resembles a personal diary recording the moods and passions of the hero as a larger-than-life personality.

The Promethean Hero

- Prometheus, a Greek deity who selflessly imparted wisdom to humanity, influenced the Romantics as a symbol of heroic freedom. Mary Shelley, Byron, and other Romantics found in Prometheus an apt metaphor for the creative and daring human spirit. Byron in England and Pushkin in Russia took Napoleon as their source of inspiration.
- In America, Frederick Douglass, champion of the abolitionist movement, served as a prime example of Promethean defiance of authority and defense of human liberty.

Goethe's Faust: The Quintessential Romantic Hero

- Faust, the literary hero who symbolizes the quest to exceed the limits of knowledge and power, became the quintessential figure for Romantic writers, painters, and composers (discussed in chapter 29).
- Goethe envisioned the legendary Faust as a symbol of the ever-striving human will to master all forms of experience, at the risk of imperiling his eternal soul.

Romantic Love and Romantic Stereotypes

- Romantic love was a popular theme among nineteenth-century writers, many of whom tended to stereotype females as either angels or *femmes fatales.*
- The nineteenth century, the first great age of female novelists, produced such outstanding writers as George Eliot, Mary Shelley, and Jane Austen.
- In the novels of George Sand, the Romantic heroine might be a self-directed creature whose passions incite her to contemplate (if not actually exercise) sexual freedom.

Chapter

The Romantic Style in Art and Music

ca. 1780–1880

"Success is impossible for me if I cannot write as my heart dictates."
Verdi

Figure 29.1 FRANCISCO GOYA, *The Third of May, 1808: The Execution of the Defenders of Madrid*, 1814. Oil on canvas, 8 ft. 8 in. × 10 ft. 4 in. Six years after the French were ousted, the Spanish government commissioned Goya to commemorate the massacre of May 8, 1808. Goya maintained that the work warned against future acts of brutality.

LOOKING AHEAD

As with literature, so in the visual arts and music the Romantics favored subjects that gave free rein to the imagination. Nature and the natural landscape, the hero and heroism, and nationalist struggles for political independence—the very themes that intrigued Romantic writers—also inspired much of the art and music of the nineteenth century. Romantic artists abandoned the intellectual discipline of the Neoclassical style in favor of emotion and spontaneity. In place of the cool rationality and order of a Neoclassical composition, the Romantics introduced a studied irregularity and disorder.

Even the most superficial comparison of Neoclassical and Romantic paintings reveals essential differences in style: Neoclassical artists usually defined form by means of line (an artificial or "intellectual" boundary between the object and the space it occupied); Romantics preferred to model form by way of color. Neoclassicists generally used shades of a single color for each individual object, while Romantics might use touches of complementary colors to heighten the intensity of the painted object. And whereas Neoclassical painters smoothed out brushstrokes to leave an even and polished surface finish, Romantics often left their brushstrokes visible, as if to underline the immediacy of the creative act. They might deliberately blur details and exaggerate the sensuous aspects of texture and tone. Rejecting the Neoclassical rules of propriety and decorum, they made room for temperament, accident, and individual genius. Romantic composers shared with the artists of their time the development of a more personal and unconstrained style. They tended to modify the "rules" of classical composition in order to increase expressive effect. They abandoned the clarity and precision of the classical composition, expanding and loosening form and introducing unexpected shifts of meter and tempo. Just as Romantic painters made free use of color to heighten the emotional impact of a subject, so composers gave **tone color**—the distinctive quality of musical sound made by a voice, a musical instrument, or a combination of instruments—a status equal to melody, harmony, and rhythm. During the nineteenth century, the symphony orchestra reached heroic proportions, while smaller, more intimate musical forms became vehicles for the expression of longing, nostalgia, and love. Program music, music-drama, and virtuoso instrumental forms added to the wide range of Romantic music.

Finally, the period saw the emergence of grand opera and the Romantic ballet, artforms that (as with the other arts of the nineteenth century) attracted the growing middle class. The exchange of ideas and themes among the artists of this era encouraged a new and lively synthesis of the arts.

Heroic Themes in Art

Gros and the Glorification of the Hero

Among the principal themes of Romantic art were those that glorified creative individualism, patriotism, and nationalism. Napoleon Bonaparte, the foremost living hero of the age and the symbol of French nationalism, was the favorite subject of many early nineteenth-century French painters. His imperial status was celebrated in the official portraits executed by his "first painter," Jacques-Louis David (see Figure 28.2); but the heroic dimension of his career was publicized by yet another member of his staff, Antoine-Jean Gros (1775–1835). Gros' representations of Napoleon's military campaigns became powerful vehicles of political propaganda.

Gros was a pupil of David, but, unlike David, he rejected the formal austerity of Neoclassicism. In his monumental canvas, *Napoleon Visiting the Plague Victims at Jaffa* (Figure 29.2), Gros converted a minor historical event—Napoleon's tour of his plague-ridden troops in Jaffa (in Palestine)—into an exotic allegorical drama that cast Napoleon in the guise of Christ as healer. He enhanced the theatricality of the scene by means of atmospheric contrasts of light and dark. Vivid details draw the eye from the foreground, filled with the bodies of the diseased and dying, into the background with its distant cityscape.

In its content, the painting manifested the Romantic taste for themes of personal heroism, suffering, and death. When it was first exhibited in Paris, an awed public adorned it with palm branches and wreaths. But the inspiration for Gros' success was also the source of his undoing: after Napoleon was sent into exile, Gros' career declined, and he committed suicide by throwing himself into the River Seine.

Popular Heroism in Goya and Géricault

Throughout most of Western history, the heroic image in art was bound up with Classical lore and Christian legend. But with Gros, we see one of the earliest efforts to glorify contemporary heroes and heroic events. The Spanish master Francisco Goya (1746–1828) helped to advance this phenomenon. He began his career as a Rococo-style tapestry designer and came into prominence as court painter to the Spanish king Charles IV. But following the invasion of Spain by Napoleon's armies in 1808, Goya's art took a new turn. Horrified by the guerrilla violence of the French occupation, he became a bitter social critic, producing some of the most memorable records of human warfare and savagery in the history of Western art.

The Third of May, 1808: The Execution of the Defenders of Madrid (see Figure 29.1) was Goya's nationalistic response to the events ensuing from an uprising of Spanish

Figure 29.2 ANTOINE-JEAN GROS, *Napoleon Visiting the Plague Victims at Jaffa*, 1804. Oil on canvas, 17 ft. 5 in. × 23 ft. 7 in.

citizens against the French army of occupation. In a puni-
tive measure, the French troops rounded up Spanish sus-
pects in the streets of Madrid, and brutally executed them
in the city outskirts. Goya recreated the episode with imaginative force, setting it against a dark sky and an ominous
urban skyline. In the foreground, an off-center lantern
emits a triangular beam of light that illuminates the
Spanish rebels: some lie dead in pools of blood, while others cover their faces in fear and horror. Among the victims
is a young man whose arms are flung upward in a final,
Christlike gesture of terror and defiance. Goya deliberately
spotlights this wide-eyed and bewildered figure as he confronts imminent death. On the right, in the shadows, the
hulking executioners are lined up as anonymously as pieces
of artillery. Emphatic contrasts of light and dark and the
theatrical attention to graphic details heighten the intensity of a contemporary political event.

An indictment of butchery in the name of war, *The Third
of May, 1808* is itself restrained compared to "The Disasters
of War," a series of etchings and **aquatints** that Goya produced in the years of the French occupation of Spain. "The
Disasters of War" have their source in historical fact as well
as in Goya's imagination. *Brave Deeds Against the Dead*
(Figure **29.3**) is a shocking record of the inhuman cruelty
of Napoleon's troops, as well as a reminder that the heroes
of modern warfare are often its innocent victims.

Goya's French contemporary, Théodore Géricault
(1791–1824), broadened the range of Romantic subjects.
He found inspiration in the restless vitality of untamed
horses and the ravaged faces of the clinically insane. Such
subjects, uncommon in academic art, reflect the Romantic
fascination with the life lying beyond the bounds of reason.
The painting that brought Géricault instant fame was *The
Raft of the "Medusa."* It immortalized a controversial event
that made headlines in Géricault's own time: the wreck of
a government frigate called the *Medusa* and the ghastly fate
of its passengers (Figure **29.4**). When the ship hit a reef fifty
miles off the coast of West Africa, the inexperienced captain, a political appointee, tried ignobly to save himself and
his crew, who filled the few available lifeboats. Over a hundred passengers piled onto a makeshift raft, which was to be
towed by the lifeboats. Cruelly, the crew set the raft adrift.
With almost no food and supplies, chances of survival were
scant; after almost two weeks, in which most died and several resorted to cannibalism, the raft was sighted and the
fifteen survivors were rescued.

Géricault (a staunch opponent of the regime that
appointed the captain of the *Medusa*) was so fired by newspaper reports of the tragedy that he resolved to immortalize
it in paint. He interviewed the few survivors, made drawings
of the mutilated corpses in the Paris morgue, and even had
a model of the raft constructed in his studio. The result was

Figure 29.3 FRANCISCO GOYA, *Brave Deeds Against the Dead*, from the "Disasters of War" series, ca. 1814. Etching, 6 × 8¼ in. Goya himself wrote the biting captions for these etchings. Because some of the prints satirized the Church and other bastions of authority, they were not published until thirty-five years after the artist's death.

Figure 29.4 THÉODORE GÉRICAULT, *The Raft of the "Medusa,"* 1818. Oil on canvas, 16 ft. 1 in. × 23 ft. 6 in. Much like the panoramic landscapes of Frederic Church, Géricault's painting became an object of popular display and entertainment. Exhibited in London, it drew some 40,000 visitors between June and December 1820.

enormous, both in size (the canvas measures 16 feet 1 inch × 23 feet 6 inches) and in dramatic impact. In the decade immediately preceding the invention of photography, Géricault provided the public with a powerful visual record of a sensational contemporary event. He organized the composition on the basis of a double triangle: one triangle is formed by the two lines that stay the mast and is bisected by the mast itself, the other by the mass of agitated figures, culminating in the magnificently painted torso of a black man who signals the distant vessel that will make the rescue. Sharp diagonals, vivid contrasts of light and dark (reminiscent of Caravaggio), and muscular nudes (inspired by Michelangelo and Rubens) heighten the dramatic impact of the piece.

Géricault's *Raft* elevated ordinary men to the position of heroic combatants in the eternal struggle against the forces of nature. It celebrated their collective heroism in confronting deadly danger, a theme equally popular in Romantic literature, and, as with Turner's *Slave Ship* and Goya's *Third of May*, it publicly protested an aspect of contemporary political injustice. In essence, it brought together the reality of a man-made disaster and the more abstract theme of the Romantic *sublime*: the terror experienced by ordinary human beings in the face of nature's overpowering might.

Delacroix and Revolutionary Heroism

While Goya and Géricault democratized the image of the hero, Géricault's pupil and follower Eugène Delacroix (1798–1863) raised that image to Byronic proportions. A melancholic and an intellectual, Delacroix shared Byron's hatred of tyranny, his sense of alienation, and his self-glorifying egotism—features readily discernible in the pages of his journal. Delacroix prized the imagination as "paramount" in the life of the artist. "Strange as it may seem," he observed, "the great majority of people are devoid of imagination. Not only do they lack the keen, penetrating imagination which would allow them to see objects in a vivid way—which would lead them, as it were, to the very root of things—but they are equally incapable of any clear understanding of works in which imagination predominates."

Delacroix loved dramatic narrative. He drew sensuous and violent subjects from contemporary life, popular literature, and ancient and medieval history. A six-month visit in 1831 to Morocco, neighbor of France's newly conquered colony of Algeria, provoked a lifelong interest in exotic subjects and a love of light and color. He depicted the harem women of Islamic Africa, recorded the poignant and shocking results of the Turkish massacres in Greece, brought to life Dante's *Inferno*, and made memorable illustrations for Goethe's *Faust* (see Figure 28.5). His paintings of human and animal combat, such as *Arabs Skirmishing in the Mountains* (Figure **29.5**), are filled with fierce vitality. Such works are faithful to his declaration, "I have no love for reasonable painting." In his journal, Delacroix defended the artist's freedom to Romanticize form and content: "The most sublime effects of every master," he wrote, "are often the result of *pictorial licence*; for example, the lack of finish in Rembrandt's work, the exaggeration in Rubens. Mediocre painters never have sufficient daring, they never get beyond themselves."

Delacroix's landmark work, *Liberty Leading the People*, transformed a contemporary event (the revolution of 1830) into a heroic allegory of the struggle for human freedom (see Figure 29.6). When King Charles X (1757–1836) dissolved the French legislature and took measures to

Figure 29.5 EUGÈNE DELACROIX, *Arabs Skirmishing in the Mountains*, 1863. Oil on linen, 36⅜ × 29⅜ in. The composition is built on a series of diagonals that lead the eye from foreground to background so as to take in each aspect of the skirmish. Note how Delacroix has used the color red to reinforce dramatic movement.

MAKING CONNECTIONS

Figure 29.6 EUGÈNE DELACROIX, *Liberty Leading the People*, 1830. Oil on canvas, 8 ft. 6 in. × 10 ft. 7 in.

Delacroix's painting *Liberty Leading the People* (Figure **29.6**) is often compared with David's *The Oath of the Horatii* (Figure **29.7**) because both paintings are clear calls to heroic action. But in conception and in style, the two paintings are totally different. While David looked to the Roman past for his theme, Delacroix drew on the issues of his time, allegorizing *real* events in order to increase their dramatic impact. Whereas David's appeal was essentially elitist, Delacroix celebrated the collective heroism of ordinary people.

Delacroix was never a slave to the facts: although, for instance, the nudity of the fallen rebel in the left foreground (clearly related to the nudes of Géricault's *Raft*) has no basis in fact—it is uncommon to lose one's trousers in combat. The detail serves, however, to emphasize vulnerability and the imminence of death in battle. Stylistically, Delacroix's *Liberty* explodes with romantic passion. Surging rhythms link the smoke-filled background with the figures of the advancing rebels and the bodies of the fallen heroes heaped in the foreground. By comparison, David's Neoclassical *Oath* is cool and restrained, his composition gridlike, and his figures defined with linear clarity. Where Delacroix's canvas resonates with dense textures and loose, tactile brushstrokes, David's surfaces are slick and finished.

Figure 29.7 JACQUES-LOUIS DAVID, *The Oath of the Horatii*, 1785. Oil on canvas, 10 ft. 10 in. × 14 ft.

repress voting rights and freedom of the press, liberal leaders, radicals, and journalists rose in rebellion. Delacroix envisioned this rebellion as a monumental allegory. Its central figure, a handsome, bare-breasted female—the personification of Liberty—leads a group of French rebels through the narrow streets of Paris and over barricades strewn with corpses. A bayonet in one hand and the tricolor flag of France in the other, she presses forward to challenge the forces of tyranny. She is champion of "the people": the middle class, as represented by the gentleman in a frock coat; the lower class, as symbolized by the scruffy youth carrying pistols; and racial minorities, as conceived in the black saber-bearer at the left. She is, moreover, France itself, the banner-bearer of the spirit of nationalism that infused nineteenth-century European history.

Delacroix's *Liberty* instantly became a symbol of democratic aspirations. In 1884 France sent as a gift of friendship to the young American nation a monumental copper and cast-iron statue of an idealized female bearing a tablet and a flaming torch (Figure **29.8**). Designed by Frédéric-Auguste Bartholdi (1834–1904), the Statue of Liberty (Liberty Enlightening the World) is the "sister" of Delacroix's painted heroine; it has become a classic image of freedom for oppressed people everywhere.

Heroic Themes in Sculpture

In sculpture as in painting, heroic subjects served the cause of nationalism. *The Departure of the Volunteers of 1792* (Figure **29.9**) by François Rude (1784–1855) embodied the dynamic heroism of the Napoleonic Era. Installed at the foot of the Arc de Triomphe (see Figure 26.31), which stands at the end of the Champs Elysées in Paris, the 42-foot-high stone sculpture commemorates the patriotism of a band of French volunteers—presumably the battalion of Marseilles, who marched to Paris in 1792 to defend the republic. Young and old, nude or clothed in ancient or medieval garb (a convention that augmented dramatic effect while universalizing the heroic theme), the spirited members of this small citizen army are led by the allegorical figure of Bellona, the Roman goddess of war. Like Delacroix's Liberty, Rude's Classical goddess urges the patriots onward. The vitality of the piece is enhanced by deep undercutting that achieves dramatic contrasts of light and dark. In this richly textured work, Rude captured the revolutionary spirit and emotional fervor of this battalion's marching song, *La Marseillaise*, which the French later adopted as their national anthem.

In America, the passage of the Thirteenth Amendment to the Constitution, which outlawed the practice of slavery

Figure 29.8 FRÉDÉRIC-AUGUSTE BARTHOLDI, Statue of Liberty (Liberty Enlightening the World), Liberty Island (Bedloe's Island), New York, 1871–1884. Framework constructed by A. G. Eiffel. Copper sheets mounted on steel frame, height 152 ft. While France gave America the statue, it did not provide the pedestal. To assist in raising for the latter, the poet Emma Lazarus was commissioned to write a poem. Her concern for the 2000 Russian-Jewish immigrants arriving monthly in New York inspired the famous lines that begin "Give me your tired, your poor,/ Your huddled masses yearning to breathe free."

in the United States, was met with a similar outburst of heroic celebration. In the commemorative marble sculpture, *Forever Free* (1867), a young slave who has broken his chains raises his arm in victory, while his female companion kneels in grateful prayer (Figure **29.10**). The artist who conceived this remarkable work of art, Edmonia Lewis (1845–ca. 1885) was the daughter of an African-American father and a Chippawa mother. Like most talented young American artists of this era, Lewis made her way to Europe for academic training. She remained in Rome to pursue her career and gained great notoriety for her skillfully carved portrait busts and allegorical statues, some of which exalted heroic women in biblical and ancient history. Many of her works are now lost and almost nothing is known of her life after 1885.

Science and Technology

1836	Samuel Colt produces a six-cylinder revolver
1841	the breech-loading rifle known as the "needlegun" is introduced
1847	an Italian chemist develops explosive nitroglycerin

Figure 29.9 FRANÇOIS RUDE, *La Marseillaise (The Departure of the Volunteers of 1792)*, 1833–1836. Stone, approx. 42 ft. × 26 ft.

Nineteenth-century nationalism stimulated an interest in the cultural heritage of ethnic groups beyond the European West. Just as Catlin found in the American West a wealth of fascinating visual resources, so Europeans turned to Africa and the East for exotic subjects. Napoleon's invasion of Egypt (1798–1801) had started a virtual craze for things North African, and such interests were further stimulated by the French presence in Algeria beginning in the 1830s. In 1848, the French government abolished slavery in France and all of its colonies.

Charles-Henri-Joseph Cordier (1827–1905), a member of Rude's studio and a favorite exhibitor in the academic Salon of Paris, requested a governmental assignment in Africa in order to make a record of its peoples. The result of Cordier's ethnological studies was a series of twelve busts of Africans and Asians, executed by means of innovative polychrome techniques that combined bronze or colored marble with porphyry, jasper, and onyx from Algerian quarries (Figure **29.11**). Cordier's portrait heads reveal a sensitivity to individual personality and a commitment to capturing the dignity of his models. Rather than perceiving his subject as an exotic "other," he regarded each as a racial type "at the point," as he explained, "of merging into one and the same people."

Figure 29.11 **CHARLES-HENRI-JOSEPH CORDIER**, *African in Algerian Costume*, ca. 1856–1857. Bronze and onyx, 37¾ × 26 × 14 in. Rich details and sensuous materials characterize Cordier's portraits, which became famous as examples of a new visual anthropology focused on the physical appearance of what he called "the different indigenous types of the human race."

Trends in Mid Nineteenth-Century Architecture

Neomedievalism in the West

Architects of the early to mid nineteenth century regarded the past as a source of inspiration and moral instruction. Classical Greek and republican Roman buildings embodied the political and aesthetic ideals of nation-builders like Napoleon and Jefferson (see chapter 26); but the austere dignity of Neoclassicism did not appeal to all tastes. More typical of the Romantic imagination was a nostalgic affection for the medieval world, with its brooding castles and towering cathedrals. No less than Neoclassicism, *Neomedievalism*—the revival of medieval culture—served the cause of nationalism. It exalted the state by recapturing its unique historical and cultural past. On the eve of the unification of Germany (1848), and for decades thereafter, German craftsmen restored many of its most notable Gothic monuments, including its great cathedrals.

In England, where the Christian heritage of the Middle Ages was closely associated with national identity, writers embraced the medieval past: Alfred Lord Tennyson

Figure 29.10 **EDMONIA LEWIS**, *Forever Free*, 1867. Marble, height 40½ in.

Figure 29.12 CHARLES BARRY and **A. W. N. PUGIN**, (above) Houses of Parliament, London, 1840–1860. Length 940 ft. Following the fire of 1834, which destroyed the earlier structure (also known as the Palace of Westminster), a royal commission directed Barry to design a Neo-Gothic replacement. Pugin was largely responsible for the interior details. His designs seem to have coincided with his conversion to Roman Catholicism. He perceived purity of structure and the meaningful application of details as equivalent to the Catholic faith, but equally appropriate to the ideals of the largely Protestant nation.

Figure 29.13 JAMES RENWICK and **WILLIAM BODRIGUE**, (below) Saint Patrick's Cathedral, Fifth Avenue and 50th Street, New York, 1853–1858.

(1802–1892), poet laureate of Great Britain, for example, fused early British legend with the Christian mission in a cycle of Arthurian poems entitled *Idylls of the King*; while Sir Walter Scott immortalized medieval heroes and heroines in avidly read historical novels and Romantic poems.

The revival of the Gothic style was equally distinctive in architecture. The British Houses of Parliament, conceived by Charles Barry (1795–1860) and Augustus Welby Northmore Pugin (1812–1852) and begun in 1836, are among the most aesthetically successful large-scale Neo-Gothic public buildings. The picturesque combination of spires and towers fronting on the River Thames in London was the product of Pugin's conviction that the Gothic style best expressed the dignity befitting the official architecture of a Christian nation (Figure **29.12**). Moreover, the Gothic style was symbolically appropriate for the building that epitomized the principles of parliamentary rule, pioneered in England with the signing of the Magna Carta in 1215. The Houses of Parliament might be said to reflect the importance of medieval historical tradition—both religious and political—in shaping England's self-image.

Neomedievalism gave rise to a movement for the archeological restoration of churches and castles throughout Europe: it also inspired some extraordinary new architectural activity in North America. Colleges and universities (such as Harvard and Yale), museums (such as the Smithsonian in Washington D.C.), and numerous churches and cathedrals were modeled on medieval prototypes. One of the most elegant examples of the Gothic revival in the United States is Saint Patrick's Cathedral in New York City (Figure **29.13**), which (along with Grace

Figure 29.14 JOHN NASH, The Royal Pavilion, Brighton, from the northeast, 1815–1821.

Church in Manhattan and the Smithsonian) was designed by James Renwick (1818–1895).

Exoticism in Western Architecture

Romantic architecture also drew inspiration from the "exotic" East, and especially those parts of the world in which the European powers were building colonial empires. The most intriguing Western pastiche of non-Western styles is the Royal Pavilion at Brighton, on the south coast of England. Designed by the English architect John Nash (1752–1835) between 1815 and 1821 as a seaside resort for the Prince Regent, it combines a fanciful assortment of Chinese, Indian, and Islamic motifs (Figure **29.14**). Nash raised bulbous domes and slender minarets over a hidden frame of cast iron, the structural medium that would soon come to dominate modern architecture (see chapter 30). The bizarre interior decor, which includes waterlily chandeliers and cast-iron palm trees with copper leaves, produced an eclectic style that Nash's critics called "Indian Gothic."

The Romantic Style in Music

"Music is the most romantic of all the arts—one might almost say, the only genuine romantic one—for its sole subject is the infinite." Thus wrote the German novelist and musician E. T. A. Hoffmann (1776–1822). Like many Romantic composers, Hoffmann believed that music held a privileged position in its capacity to express what he called "an inexpressible longing." For the Romantics, music—the most abstract and elusive of the arts—was capable of freeing the intellect and speaking directly to the heart.

The nineteenth century produced an enormous amount of music in all genres—a phenomenon that is reflected in the fact that audiences today listen to more nineteenth-century music than to the music of any previous time period. Its hallmark is personalized expression, a feature as apparent in large orchestral works as it is in small, intimate pieces.

During the Romantic era, the orchestra grew to grand proportions. Mid nineteenth-century orchestras were often five times larger than those used by Haydn and Mozart. While the volume of sound expanded, the varieties of instrumental possibilities also grew larger, in part because of technical improvements made in the instruments themselves. Brass instruments (such as the trumpet and the tuba) gained new pitches and a wider range with the addition of valves; woodwind instruments (such as the flute and the clarinet) underwent structural changes that greatly facilitated fingering and tuning. Modifications to the violin lent the instrument greater power; and the early nineteenth-century piano, which acquired an iron frame, two or three pedals, and thicker strings, was capable of increased brilliance in tone and greater expressiveness—features that made it the most popular musical instrument of the century. Such mechanical improvements expanded the tonal potential of musical instruments and produced a virtual revolution in orchestral textures.

In terms of musical composition, the symphony and the concerto were the most important of the large orchestral forms. Equally significant, however, were song forms, especially songs that dealt with themes of love and death or nature and nature's moods. Composers found inspiration in heroic subjects, in contemporary events, and in the legends and histories of their native lands. Like the Romantic painters and writers, they embraced exotic themes. In both small musical forms and in large operatic compositions, they made every effort to achieve an ideal union of poetry and music. The close association between the arts is seen in the many operas and symphonic pieces based on nineteenth-century plays, novels, and poems. The Faust legend and Goethe's *Faust* in particular inspired numerous musical settings. Bizet's *Carmen*, discussed in chapter 28, was based on a novella that was influenced in turn by Pushkin's narrative poem, *The Gypsies* (1824); and Pushkin's verse poem *Eugene Onegin* (1832) inspired Peter Ilyich Tchaikovsky's opera of the same name. But it was Sir Walter Scott's historical novels that were the favorite source for at least a dozen operas by French, British, and Italian composers.

As in the eighteenth century, nineteenth-century composers were often also performers. They drew attention to their own technical abilities by writing **virtuoso** pieces (usually for piano or violin) that only highly accomplished musicians like themselves could perform with facility. No longer completely at the mercy of the patronage system, they indulged, often publicly, in bouts of euphoria, melancholy, and petty jealousy. The talented Genoese composer and violinist, Niccolò Paganini (1782–1840), for instance, refused to publish his own pieces, which he performed with such astounding technical agility that rumor had it he had come by his virtuosity through a pact with the Devil.

The Genius of Beethoven

The leading composer of the early nineteenth century and one of the greatest musicians of all time was the German-born Ludwig van Beethoven (1770–1827). Beethoven's lifelong residency in Vienna brought him in contact with the music of Mozart and Haydn; he studied briefly with the latter. It also provided the composer with the fundamentals of the classical style. His indebtedness to classical composition, especially evident in his early works, makes him something of a bridge between the classical and Romantic eras.

Beethoven was a gifted pianist, organist, and violinist. While he composed works in almost every musical form, his thirty-two piano sonatas reflect a lifelong love for the expressive potential of that instrument. His nine symphonies, which critics claim as his greatest achievement, generally adhere to the classical format, but they move beyond the bounds of classical structure. The Third Symphony, which he subtitled the *Eroica* ("Heroic") is a case in point. It is longer and more complex than any previous orchestral work. While it follows the standard number and order of movements found in the classical symphony, it is almost twice as long as its typical twenty-

to twenty-five-minute predecessors. The first movement, which one French critic called "the Grand Army of the soul," engages six (rather than the traditional two) themes dictated by the sonata form (see chapter 26). The movement begins with two commanding hammer strikes of the French horn—symbolic of the hero throughout the symphony. The second movement is a somber and solemn funeral march. For the third movement, instead of the traditional minuet, Beethoven introduces a vigorous **scherzo** ("joke"), which replaces the elegant courtly dance form with a melody that is fast and varied in tempo—a joke in that it is essentially undanceable! The last movement, a victory finale, brings the themes and variations of the first movement together with a long coda that again features the majestic horn section. It is worth noting that for the triumphant last movement of this stirring symphony, Beethoven included musical passages originally written for a ballet on the subject of Prometheus.

Beethoven had originally intended to dedicate the Third Symphony to Napoleon, whom he admired as a popular hero and a champion of liberty. But when Napoleon crowned himself emperor in 1804, Beethoven angrily scratched out the name "Buonaparte" and replaced it with a generalized dedication: "Heroic symphony, dedicated to the memory of a great man." "So, he is no more than a common mortal!" Beethoven is said to have exclaimed. "Now he will trample on all the rights of man and…become a tyrant." Ultimately, the symphony was dedicated and presented to a minor nobleman, Prince Franz Joseph Maximillian Lobkowitz.

Beethoven's genius lay in his use of compositional elements that gave his music unprecedented expressive power. He introduced into his compositions a new rhythmic vitality, strong and sudden contrasts of sound, and an expanded range of instrumental textures. By adding piccolo, bass clarinet, trombone, bass drum, and cymbals to the scoring and doubling the number of flutes, oboes, clarinets, and bassoons, he vastly broadened the expressive range and dramatic power of orchestral sound.

In his use of musical **dynamics** (gradations of loudness and softness), Beethoven was more explicit and varied than his classical predecessors. Prior to 1812 Beethoven made use of only five terms to indicate the softness or loudness of piano performance; increasingly, however, he expanded the classical vocabulary with such words as *dolente* ("sorrowful") and *teneramente* ("tenderly") to indicate nuances. Like other Romantic artists—Delacroix, in particular, comes to mind—Beethoven blurred the divisions between the structural units of a composition, exploiting textural contrasts for expressive effect. He often broke with classical form, adding, for example, a fifth movement to his Sixth (or "Pastoral") Symphony and embellishing the finale of his Ninth Symphony with a chorus and solo voices. Beethoven's daring use of dissonances, his sudden pauses and silences, and his brilliance of thematic and rhythmic

---

🎼 See Music Listening Selections at end of chapter.

invention reflect his preference for dramatic spontaneity over measured regularity. The powerful opening notes of the Fifth Symphony—a motif that Beethoven is said to have called "fate knocking at the door"—exemplify his affection for inventive repetitions and surging rhythms that propel the music toward a powerful climax.

Difficult as it is to imagine, Beethoven wrote much of his greatest music when he was functionally deaf. From the age of twenty-nine, when he became aware of a progressive degeneration of his hearing, he labored against depression and despair. Temperamental and defiant, he scorned the patronage system that had weighed heavily upon both Mozart and Haydn, and often sold his musical compositions as an independent artist. He declared contempt for the nobility and ignored their demands. In 1802 he confided to his family, "I am bound to be misunderstood; for me

there can be no relaxation with my fellow men, no refined conversations, no mutual exchange of ideas. I must live alone like one who has been banished." In retreat from society, the alienated composer turned to nature (Figure 29.15).

In the woods outside of Vienna, Beethoven roamed with his musical sketchbook under one arm, often singing to himself in a loud voice. "Woods, trees and rock," he wrote in his diary, "give the response that man requires." His discovery that nature mirrored his deepest emotions inspired his programmatic Sixth Symphony (1808), which he subtitled "A recollection of country life." Each of the five movements of the "Pastoral" is labeled with a specific reference to nature: "Awakening of happy feelings on arriving in the country"; "By the brook"; "Joyous gatherings of country folk"; "Storm"; and "Shepherd's Song, happy and thankful feelings after the storm." In the tradition of

Figure 29.15 *Beethoven Composing the "Pastoral" by a Brook*, from the Twenty-Second Almanac of the Zürich Musikgesellschaft for 1834: Biography of Ludwig van Beethoven. Colored lithograph, 6½ × 5⅞ in. In 1802, as his hearing became increasingly worse, Beethoven moved to the small village of Heiligenstadt, outside of Vienna. His sense of isolation and his heroic struggle to overcome despair are reflected in his music.

Vivaldi's *Four Seasons* (see chapter 23), Beethoven occasionally imitated the sounds of nature. For example, at the end of the second movement, flute, oboe, and clarinet join to create bird calls; and a quavering *tremolo* (the rapid repetition of a tone to produce a trembling effect) on the lower strings suggests the sounds of a murmuring brook.

Some critics regard Beethoven's last symphony, the Ninth Symphony (1824), as his greatest work. It is the first example of a symphony that uses the human voice as a component of the instrumentation: In the last movement Beethoven took the unprecedented step of including four solo voices and a large chorus. The inspiration for the "Choral Symphony" was a poem by Friedrich Schiller (see chapter 27): *An die Freude* ("To Joy"), an ode that celebrates the joy of universal brotherhood. The final, choral movement of this long, ambitious symphony is a brilliant exposition of Beethoven's imaginative power and his defense of a humanistic ideal. At the premier performance of the symphony in Vienna, the aging composer shared the stage with the conductor, beating out the tempo for music he could hear only in his head.

Art Songs

The art songs of Beethoven's Austrian contemporary Franz Schubert (1797–1828) aptly reflect the nineteenth-century composer's ambition to unite poetry and music. Schubert is credited with originating the Romantic **lied** (German for "song," pl. *lieder*), an independent song for solo voice and piano. The *lied* is not a song in the traditional sense but, rather, a poem recreated in musical terms. Its lyric qualities, like those of simple folk songs, are generated by the poem itself. The *lieder* of Schubert, Robert Schumann (1810–1856), and Johannes Brahms (1833–1897), which set to music the poetry of Heine and Goethe, among others, are intimate evocations of personal feelings and moods. They recount tales of love and longing, describe nature and its moods (some forty songs are related to water or to fish), or lament the transience of human happiness.

Among Schubert's 1000 or so works (which include nine symphonies, five operas, and numerous chamber pieces) are 600 *lieder*. Of these, his musical settings for Goethe's ballads rank as landmark expressions of the Romantic spirit of music. *Gretchen am Spinnrade* ("Gretchen at the Spinning Wheel"), written when the composer was only seventeen years old, is based on a poem by Goethe which occurs near the end of Part One of *Faust*. In the piece, Gretchen laments the absence of her lover Faust and anticipates the sorrows that their love will bring. Repeated three times are the poignant lines with which the song opens: "My peace is gone, my heart is sore:/I shall find it never and never more." While the melody and tone color of the voice line convey the sadness expressed in the words of the poem, the propelling piano line captures the rhythms of the spinning wheel.

Yet another of Schubert's finest art songs is *Erlkönig* ("The Erlking"), which combines elements of the natural (a raging storm), the supernatural (the figure of death in the person of the legendary king of the elves), and the heroic

(a father's desperate effort to save the life of his ailing son). Here, Schubert's music mingles the rhythms of the stormy ride on horseback, the struggle for survival, and the threatening lure of death. Schubert himself died of syphilis at the age of thirty-one.

The Programmatic Symphonies of Berlioz

The French composer Hector Berlioz (1803–1869) began his first symphony in 1830. An imaginative combination of the story of Faust and Berlioz's own life, the *Symphonie fantastique* tells the dramatic tale of Berlioz's "interminable and inextinguishable passion"—as he described it—for the captivating Irish actress Harriet Smithson. Berlioz wrote the symphony in the first flush of his passion, when he was only twenty-seven years old. Following an intense courtship, he married Harriet, only to discover that he and the woman he idolized were dreadfully mismatched—the marriage turned Smithson into an alcoholic and Berlioz into an adulterer.

The *Symphonie fantastique* belongs to the genre known as **program music**, that is, instrumental music endowed with a specific literary or pictorial content indicated by the composer. Berlioz was not the first to write music that was programmatic: in *The Four Seasons*, Vivaldi had linked music to poetic phrases, as had Beethoven in his "Pastoral" Symphony. But Berlioz was the first to build an entire symphony around a musical motif that tells a story. The popularity of program music during the nineteenth century testifies to the powerful influence of literature upon the other arts. Berlioz, whose second symphony, *Harold in Italy*, was inspired by Byron's *Childe Harold* (see chapter 28), was not alone in his attraction to literary subjects. The Hungarian composer Franz Liszt (1811–1886) wrote symphonic poems based on the myth of Prometheus and Shakespeare's *Hamlet*. He also composed the *Faust Symphony*, which he dedicated to Berlioz. The Russian composer Peter Ilyich Tchaikovsky (1840–1893) wrote many programmatic pieces, including the tone poem *Romeo and Juliet*. European political events inspired the composition of nationalistic program music, such as Beethoven's *Battle Symphony* of 1813 (also known as "Wellington's Victory") and Tchaikovsky's colorful *1812 Overture* (1880), which, commemorating Napoleon's retreat from Moscow, incorporated portions of the national anthems of both France and tzarist Russia.

In the *Symphonie fantastique*, Berlioz links a specific mood or event to a musical phrase, or **idée fixe** ("fixed idea"). This recurring motif, becomes the means by which the composer binds together the individual parts of his dramatic narrative. Subtitled "Episode in the Life of an Artist," the *Symphonie fantastique* is an account of the young musician's opium-induced dream, in which, according to Berlioz's program notes, "the Beloved One takes the form of a melody in his mind, like a fixed idea which is ever returning and which he hears everywhere."

See Music Listening Selections at end of chapter.

Figure 29.16 ANDREW GEIGER, *A Concert of Hector Berlioz in 1846*, 1846. Engraving.

Unified by the *idée fixe*, the symphony consists of a sequence of five parts, each distinguished by a particular mood: the lover's "reveries and passions"; a ball at which the hero meets his beloved; a stormy scene in the country; a "March to the Scaffold" (marking the hero's dream of murdering his lover and his subsequent execution); and a final and feverishly orchestrated "Dream of a Witches' Sabbath" inspired by Goethe's *Faust*. (Berlioz's *Damnation of Faust*, a piece for soloists, chorus, and orchestra, likewise drew on Goethe's great drama.) The "plot" of the *Symphonie fantastique*, published along with the musical score, was (and usually still is) printed in program notes available to listeners. But the written narrative is *not* essential to the enjoyment of the music, for, as Berlioz himself explained, the music holds authority as absolute sound, above and beyond its programmatic associations.

The spiritual heir to Beethoven, Berlioz took liberties with traditional symphonic form. He composed the *Symphonie fantastique* in five movements instead of the usual four and combined instruments inventively so as to create unusual mixes of sound. In the third movement, for example, a solo English horn and four kettledrums produce the effect of "distant thunder." He also expanded tone color, stretching the register of clarinets to screeching highs, for instance, and playing the strings of the violin with the wood of the bow instead of with the hair. Berlioz's favorite medium was the full symphony orchestra, which he enlarged to include 150 musicians. Called "the apostle of bigness," Berlioz conceived an ideal orchestra that consisted of over 400 musicians, including 242 string instruments, 30 pianos, 30 harps, and a chorus of 360 voices. The monumental proportions of Berlioz's orchestras

and choirs, and the volume of sound they produced, inspired spoofs in contemporary French and German journals. Cartoons showed the maestro, also spoofed for his extravagant hairstyles, beating time with an electric telegraph pole, recruiting orchestra members from the artillery of a garrison, and conducting a sea of instrumentalists (Figure **29.16**). But Berlioz, who was also a talented writer and a music critic for Parisian newspapers, thumbed his nose at the critics in lively essays that defended his own musical philosophy.

The Piano Music of Chopin

If the nineteenth century was the age of Romantic individualism, it was also the age of the virtuoso: composers wrote music that might be performed gracefully and accurately only by individuals with extraordinary technical skills. The quintessential example of this phenomenon is the Polish-born composer Frédéric Chopin (1810–1849). At the age of seven, Chopin gave his first piano concert in Warsaw. Slight in build even as an adult, Chopin had small hands that nevertheless could reach across the keys of the piano like "the jaws of a snake" (as one of his peers observed). After leaving Warsaw, Chopin became the acclaimed pianist of the Paris *salons* and a close friend of Delacroix (who painted the portrait in Figure **29.17**), Berlioz, and many of the leading novelists of his time, including George Sand (see chapter 28), with whom he had a stormy seven-year love affair.

Figure 29.17 EUGÈNE DELACROIX, *Frédéric Chopin*, 1838. Oil on canvas, 18 × 15 in. This unfinished portrait was originally part of a larger double portrait that showed George Sand listening to the virtuoso pianist at the keyboard.

In his brief lifetime—he died of tuberculosis at the age of thirty-nine—Chopin created an entirely personal musical idiom linked to the expressive potential of the modern piano. For the piano, Chopin wrote over 200 pieces, most of which were short keyboard works, such as dances, *préludes*, **nocturnes** (slow, songlike pieces), **impromptus** (pieces that sound improvised), and *études* (instrumental studies designed to improve a player's technique). His Etude in G-flat Major, **Opus** 10, No. 5, is a breathtaking piece that challenges the performer to play very rapidly on the black keys, which are less than half the width of the white ones.

Much like Delacroix, Chopin was given to violent mood swings. And, as with Delacroix's paintings, which though carefully contrived give the impression of spontaneity, much of Chopin's music seems improvised—the impetuous record of fleeting feeling, rather than the studied product of diligent construction. The most engaging of his compositions are marked by fresh turns of harmony and free tempos and rhythms. Chopin might embellish a melodic line with unusual and flamboyant devices, such as a rolling **arpeggio** (the sounding of the notes of a chord in rapid succession). His *préludes* provide bold contrasts of calm meditation and bravura, while his nocturnes—like the Romantic landscapes of Friedrich and Corot (see Figures 27.7 and 27.11)—are often dreamy and wistful. Of his dance forms, the polonaise and the mazurka preserve the robustness of the folk tunes of his native Poland, while the waltz mirrors the Romantic taste for a new type of dance, more sensuous

See Music Listening Selections at end of chapter.

and physically expressive than the courtly and formal minuet. Considered vulgar and lewd when it was introduced in the late eighteenth century, the waltz, with its freedom of movement and intoxicating rhythms, became the most popular of all nineteenth-century dances.

The Romantic Ballet

The theatrical artform known as "ballet" gained immense popularity in the Romantic era. While the great ballets of Tchaikovsky—*Swan Lake*, *The Nutcracker*, and *Sleeping Beauty*—brought fame to Russia toward the end of the 1800s, it was in early nineteenth-century Paris that Romantic ballet was born. By the year 1800, ballet had moved from the court to the theater, where it was enjoyed as a middle-class entertainment. Magnificent theaters, such as the Paris Opéra (Figure **29.18**), designed by Jean-Louis Charles Garnier (1825–1878), became showplaces for public entertainment.

The Neobaroque polychrome façade of the Paris opera house reflects Garnier's awareness that Greek architects had painted parts of their buildings; but the glory of the structure is its interior, which takes as its focus a sumptuous grand staircase (Figure **29.19**). Luxuriously appointed, and illuminated by means of the latest technological invention,

Figure 29.18 JEAN-LOUIS CHARLES GARNIER, the façade of the Opéra, Paris, 1860–1875. The 2200-seat theater is now used primarily for the production of ballets. Both in its exterior design and in its lavish interior, it recalls the palace of Versailles. The swampy foundation and underground lake that had to be pumped out during the building's construction were made famous in the French novel *The Phantom of the Opera* (1909) by Gaston Leroux.

Figure 29.19 JEAN-LOUIS CHARLES GARNIER, the Grand Staircase in the Opéra, Paris, 1860–1875. Engraving from Charles Garnier, *Le Nouvel Opéra de Paris*, 1880, Vol. 2, plate 8. The Paris Opéra ruled that all works presented there must be in French, thus requiring foreign composers to translate their librettos. Also required was a second-act ballet, which became a standard device in French operas.

gaslight, the Paris Opéra became the model for public theaters throughout Europe. For the façade, Jean-Baptiste Carpeaux (1827–1875) created a 15-foot-high sculpture whose exuberant rhythms capture the spirit of the dance as the physical expression of human joy (Figure **29.20**).

The ballets performed on the stage of the Paris Opéra were the culmination of a golden age in European dance. In Paris in 1830, the Italian-born **prima ballerina** (the first, or leading, female dancer in a ballet company) Maria Taglioni (1804–1884) perfected the art of dancing *sur les*

Figure 29.20 JEAN-BAPTISTE CARPEAUX, *The Dance*, 1868. Stone, height 13⁷⁄₁₀ × length 9⁷⁄₁₀ × depth 4⁴⁄₁₀ ft. Created for the façade of the Opéra, Paris, now in Musée d'Orsay, Paris. Between 1854 and 1861, Carpeaux worked in Rome where he studied the sculptures of the Renaissance masters. He broke with Classical and Renaissance traditions, however, in creating sculptures that incorporate spontaneous movement.

points ("on the toes") in ballet shoes that were no more than flimsy slippers made from woven strips of silk ribbon and padded with cotton wool (Figure **29.21**). Taglioni's landmark performance in the ballet *La sylphide* (choreographed by her father) was hailed as nothing less than virtuoso. Clothed in a diaphanous dress with a fitted bodice and a bell-shaped skirt (the prototype of the *tutu*), Taglioni performed perfect **arabesques**—a ballet position in which the dancer stands on one leg with the other extended behind her, and one or both arms held to create the longest line possible from one extremity to the other. She also astonished audiences by crossing the stage in three magnificent, floating leaps. While faithful to the exact steps of classical ballet, she brought to formal dance the new, more sensuous spirit of nineteenth-century Romanticism.

Popular legends and fairy tales inspired many of the ballets of the Romantic era, including *La sylphide*, *Giselle*, and Tchaikovsky's more widely known *Swan Lake* and *Sleeping Beauty*. The central figure of each ballet is usually some version of the angelic female—a fictional creature drawn from fable, fairy tale, and fantasy. In *La sylphide*, a sylph (a mythical nature deity) enchants the hero and lures him away from his bride-to-be. Pursued by the hero, she nevertheless eludes his grasp and dies—the victim of a malevolent witch—before their love is consummated. The heroine of this and other Romantic ballets symbolized the elusive ideals of love and beauty that were a favorite subject of the Romantic poets. She conformed as well to the stereotype of the pure and virtuous female found in the pages of many Romantic novels. The traditional equation of beauty and innocence in the person of the idealized female is well illustrated in the comments of one French critic, who, describing "the aerial and virginal grace of Taglioni," exulted, "She flies like a spirit in the midst of transparent clouds of white muslin—she resembles a happy angel." Clearly, the nineteenth-century ballerina was the Romantic realization of the Eternal Female, a figure that fitted the stereotype of the angelic woman.

Romantic Opera

Verdi and Italian Grand Opera

Romantic opera, designed to appeal to a growing middle-class audience, came into existence after 1820. The culmination of Baroque theatricality, Romantic opera was grand both in size and in spirit. It was a flamboyant spectacle that united all aspects of theatrical production: music, dance, stage sets, and costumes. While Paris was the operatic capital of Europe in the first half of the nineteenth century, Italy ultimately took the lead in seducing the public with hundreds of wonderfully tuneful and melodramatic Romantic operas.

The art of singing, as it flourished in Italy through the first decades of the nineteenth century, established the **bel canto** tradition. Literally, "beautiful singing" ("or "beautiful song,") bel canto-style opera emphasizes the melodic line, and the vocalist's ability to execute such florid embellishments as rapid-fire runs and trills. Two of the early nineteenth century's most famous *bel canto* operas are Gaetano Donizetti's *Lucia di Lammermoor* (1835), which is based on a novel by Sir Walter Scott, and Gioachino Rossini's *Il barbiere de Siviglia* (*The Barber of Seville*, 1816). In these works, showpiece arias with long, winding melodic lines (usually sung in the upper register) demand stunning vocal agility.

The shift to operatic drama, marked by more intense and powerful singing, is evident in the music of the Italian composer Giuseppe Verdi (1813–1901). In his twenty-six operas, the long Italian operatic tradition that had begun with Monteverdi (see chapter 20) came to its peak. Reflecting on his gift for capturing high drama in music, Verdi exclaimed, "Success is impossible for me if I cannot write as my heart dictates." The heroines of Verdi's most beloved operas—*Rigoletto* (1851), *La Traviata* (1853), and *Aïda* (1870)—are also creatures of the heart, who all die for love.

Perhaps the most famous of Verdi's operas is *Aïda*, which was commissioned by the Turkish viceroy of Egypt to mark the opening of the Suez Canal. *Aïda* made a nationalistic plea for unity against foreign domination—one critic called the opera "agitator's music." Indeed, the aria "O patria mia" ("O my country") is an expression of Verdi's ardent love for the newly unified Italy. But *Aïda* is also the passionate love story of an Egyptian prince and an Ethiopian princess held as a captive slave. Verdi's stirring arias, vigorous choruses, and richly colored orchestral passages can be enjoyed by listening alone. But the dramatic force of this opera can only be appreciated by witnessing firsthand a theatrical performance—especially one that engages such traditional paraphernalia as horses, chariots, and, of course, elephants.

Wagner and the Birth of Music-Drama

In Germany, the master of opera and one of the most formidable composers of the century was Richard Wagner (1813–1883). The stepson of a gifted actor, he spent much of his childhood composing poems and plays and setting them to music. This union of music and literature culminated in the birth of what Wagner called **music-drama**—a continuous fabric of sound and story that replaced the

Figure 29.21 Maria Taglioni in her London debut of 1830. Color lithograph. In romantic ballet, grace, delicacy, and flamboyant technique were paramount. Taglioni is shown here dancing *en pointe*, a talent that brought her fame as a prima ballerina.

traditional divisions of the opera into arias, duets, choruses, and instrumental passages. Wagner's conception of opera shattered long-standing Western theatrical traditions. He aimed, as he explained, "to force the listener, for the first time in the history of opera, to take an interest in a poetic idea by making him follow all its developments" as dramatized in music. While earlier composers generally told the story by way of the vocal line, Wagner made the orchestra an equal component in the drama. Heroic in size, Wagner's orchestra generally engulfs the listener in a maelstrom of uninterrupted melody. Characters and events emerge by way of the application of the **leitmotif**, a short musical phrase that—like the *idée fixe*—signifies a particular person, thing, or idea in the story.

Deeply nationalistic, Wagner based his music-dramas almost exclusively on heroic themes from Germany's medieval past. His librettos, which he himself wrote, brought to life the fabulous events and personalities of German folk tales and legends. Among his recurring themes are two he shared with Goethe: the redeeming love of the Eternal Female and the Faustian lust for power. Magical devices—the ring, the sword, or the chalice—like the individual characters in the opera, might each assume its own musical phrase or *leitmotif*.

Of his nine principal operas, the most ambitious is a monumental fifteen-hour cycle of four music-dramas collectively titled *Der Ring des Nibelungen* (*The Ring of the Nibelung*). Based on Norse and Germanic mythology, *The Ring* involves the quest for a magical but accursed golden ring, whose power would provide its possessor with the potential to control the universe (Figure **29.22**). Out of a struggle between the gods of Valhalla and an assortment of giants, dragons, and dwarfs emerges the hero, Siegfried, whose valorous deeds secure the ring for his lover Brünnhilde. In the end Siegfried loses both his love and his life, and Valhalla crumbles in flames, destroying the gods and eliciting the birth of a new order. Like Goethe, whose *Faust* was a lifetime effort and a tribute to his nation's past, Wagner toiled on the monumental *Ring* for over twenty-five years, from 1848 to 1874.

While *The Ring* gives imaginative breadth to the hero myths of Germanic literary tradition, its music matches its poetry in scope and drama. Wagner's orchestra for the cycle called for 115 pieces, including 64 string instruments. No fewer than twenty individual *leitmotifs* weave a complex web of dramatic musical density. "Every bar of dramatic music," proclaimed Wagner, "is justified only by the fact that it explains something in the action or in the character of the actor." In harmonic style, some Wagnerian passages anticipate the more radical experiments of twentieth-century music, such as dissonance and the dissolution of classical tonality (see chapter 32). Orchestral interludes that "describe" raging floods and rings of fire capture the Romantic sublime in musical form. The artist's mission, Wagner insisted, is to communicate "the necessary spontaneous emotional mood." In music-drama he not only fulfilled that mission, but brought Romantic music to the threshold of modernity.

Figure 29.22 Metropolitan Opera production of Wagner's *The Rhinegold* from *The Ring of the Nibelung*. In scene four of *Das Rheingold* *(The Gold of the Rhine)*, the giants Fasolt and Fafner refuse to relinquish their hostage Freia unless they are given enough gold to hide her body from view. Wotan (on the right) negotiates with them. Critics compare Wagner's story to J. R. R. Tolkien's fantasy trilogy, *The Lord of the Rings* (1937–1949), which shares the mythical themes of loss and recovery and the epic quest for magical power.

LOOKING BACK

Heroic Themes in Art

- Romantic artists generally elevated the heart over the mind and the emotions over the intellect. They favored subjects that gave free rein to the imagination, the mysteries of the spirit, and the cult of the ego.
- Increasingly independent of the official sources of patronage, Romantic artists saw themselves as the heroes of their age. They favored heroic themes and personalities, especially those illustrating the struggle for political independence.
- Gros, Géricault, Goya, and Delacroix stretched the bounds of traditional subject matter to include controversial contemporary events, exotic subjects, and medieval legends. Their paintings gave substance to the spirit of nationalism that swept through nineteenth-century Europe.
- The Romantic turn to heroic themes was matched by new freedoms in composition and technique. Neoclassical principles of pictorial balance, clarity, and restraint gave way to dynamic composition, bold color, and vigorous brushwork.

Trends in Mid Nineteenth-Century Architecture

- The search for national identity is also evident in the Gothic revival in Western architecture. Neomedievalism challenged Neoclassicism in paying homage to Europe's historic past.
- Increasing familiarity with the cultures of Asia and Islam inspired exotic architecture, such as the Royal Pavilion of Brighton.

The Romantic Style in Music

- Romantic music found inspiration in heroic and nationalistic themes, as well as in nature's moods and the vagaries of human love. In their desire to express strong personal emotions, composers often abandoned classical models and stretched musical forms.

- The enlargement of the symphony orchestra in size and expressive range is apparent in the works of Beethoven, Berlioz, and Wagner. The creative giant of the age, Beethoven composed nine symphonies and numerous instrumental works. Berlioz's *idée fixe* and Wagner's *leitmotif* tied sound to story, evidence of the Romantic search for an ideal union of poetry and music.
- Lyrical melody and tone color became as important to Romantic music as the free use of line and color was to Romantic painters.
- Schubert united poetry and music in the intimate form of the *lied*, while Chopin captured a vast range of moods and emotions in virtuoso piano pieces.

The Romantic Ballet

- Romantic ballet, which featured themes drawn from fantasy and legend, flowered in France and, later, in Russia.
- The ballets performed on the stage of the Paris Opéra were the culmination of a golden age in European dance. In Paris in 1830, Maria Taglioni perfected the art of dancing *sur les points*.
- Tchaikovsky heightened the importance of fantasy and story in his legendary ballets *Swan Lake*, *The Nutcracker*, and *Sleeping Beauty*.

Romantic Opera

- Romantic opera, designed to appeal to a growing middle-class audience, came into existence after 1820. The culmination of Baroque theatricality, Romantic opera was grand both in size and spirit. It was a flamboyant spectacle that united all aspects of theatrical production: music, dance, stage sets, and costumes.
- Grand opera was brought to its peak in Italy by Verdi and in Germany by Wagner, both of whom exploited nationalistic themes.

Music Listening Selections

CD Two Selection 12 Beethoven, Symphony No. 3 in E-flat Major, "The Eroica," first movement, excerpt, 1803–1804.
CD Two Selection 13 Schubert, *Erlkönig*, 1815.
CD Two Selection 14 Berlioz, *Symphonie fantastique*, Op. 14, "March to the Scaffold," fourth movement, excerpt, 1830.
CD Two Selection 15 Chopin, Etude in G-flat Major, Op. 10, No. 5, 1833.

Glossary

aquatint a type of print produced by an engraving method similar to etching but involving finely granulated tonal areas rather than line alone

arabesque in ballet, a position in which the dancer stands on one leg with the other extended behind and one or both arms held to create the longest line possible from one extremity of the body to the other

arpeggio the sounding of the notes of a chord in rapid succession

bel canto (Italian, "beautiful singing" or "beautiful song") an operatic style characterized by lyricism and florid vocal embellishment

dynamics the gradations of loudness or softness with which music is performed

étude (French, "study") an instrumental study designed to improve a player's performance technique

idée fixe (French, "fixed idea") a term used by Berlioz for a recurring theme in his symphonic works

impromptu (French, "improvised") a short keyboard composition that sounds as if it were improvised

leitmotif (German, "leading motif") a short musical theme that designates a person, object, place, or idea and that reappears throughout a musical composition

lied (German, "song," pl. *lieder*) an independent song for solo voice and piano; also known as "art song"

music-drama a unique synthesis of sound and story in which both are developed simultaneously and continuously; a term used to describe Wagner's later operas

nocturne a slow, songlike piece, usually written for piano; the melody is played by the right hand, and a steady, soft accompaniment is played by the left

opus (Latin, "work") a musical composition; followed by a number, it designates either the chronological place of a musical composition in the composer's total musical output or the order of its publication; often abbreviated "op."

prima ballerina the first, or leading, female dancer in a ballet company

program music instrumental music endowed with specific literary or pictorial content that is indicated by the composer

scherzo (Italian, "joke") in Beethoven's music, a sprightly, lively movement

tone color the distinctive quality of musical sound made by a voice, a musical instrument, or a combination of instruments; also called "timbre"

tremolo in music, the rapid repetition of a single pitch or two pitches alternately, producing a trembling effect

virtuoso one who exhibits great technical ability, especially in musical performance; also used to describe a musical composition demanding (or a performance demonstrating) great technical skill

Chapter

30

Industry, Empire, and the Realist Style

ca. 1850–1900

"Show me an angel and I'll paint one."
Courbet

Figure 30.1 HONORÉ DAUMIER, *The Third-Class Carriage*, ca. 1862. Oil on canvas, 25¾ × 35½ in. A lower-class family, consisting of a grandmother, her daughter, and two children, are depicted with the candor and immediacy that typifies Daumier's on-the-spot visual records of Parisian life.

LOOKING AHEAD

Nations have long drawn their strength and identity from their economic and military superiority over other nations. But during the late nineteenth century, nationalism and the quest for economic supremacy took on a more aggressive form. Fueled by advancing industrialization, Western nations not only competed among themselves for economic and political pre-eminence, but also sought control of markets throughout the world. The combined effects of nationalism, industrialization, and the consequent phenomena of imperialism and colonialism influenced the materialist direction of modern Western history and that of the world beyond the West as well.

It was in this climate that Realism emerged. As a cultural movement, Realism reflected popular demands for greater access to material wealth and well-being. In place of nostalgia and the sentimental embrace of the Romantic past, Realists manifested a renewed sense of social consciousness and a commitment to contemporary issues of class and gender. Unlike the Romantics, whose passionate subjectivity often alienated them from society, Realists regarded themselves as men and woman "of their time."

As a style, Realism called for an objective and unidealized assessment of everyday life. Artists, writers, and composers attacked the reigning stereotypes and pursued scientifically based fidelity to nature. Lithography and photography encouraged the Realist sensibility. Advances in science and technology facilitated increased mobility and transformed urban life. The city, with its monumental skyscrapers and its bustling mix of people, became the site of new ideas and cultural norms that propelled the West toward Modernism.

The Global Dominion of the West

Advancing Industrialization

Industrialization provided the economic and military basis for the West's rise to dominion over the rest of the world. This process is well illustrated in the history of the railroad, the most important technological phenomenon of the early nineteenth century because it facilitated economic and political expansion. It was made possible by the combined technologies of steam power, coal, and iron.

The first all-iron rails were forged in Britain in 1789, but it was not until 1804 that the British built their first steam railway locomotive, and several more decades until "iron horses" became a major mode of transportation. The drive to build national railways spread, encompassing Europe and the vast continent of North America. By 1850, 23,000 miles of railway track crisscrossed Europe, linking the sources of raw materials—such as the coal mines of northern Germany's Ruhr valley—to factories and markets. The second half of the nineteenth century saw the unification of both Italy and Germany, the modernization of Russia, and the transformation of the United States into an economic powerhouse, fueled by abundant resources of iron ore and coal. Across the vast continent of North America railroads facilitated rapid economic and political expansion. As Western nations colonized other parts of the globe, they took with them the railroad and other agents of industrialization.

Before the end of the nineteenth century, Western technology included the internal combustion engine, the telegraph, the telephone, the camera, and—perhaps most significant for the everyday life of human beings—electricity. Processed steel, aluminum, the steam turbine, and the pneumatic tire—all products of the 1880s—further altered the texture of life in the industrialized world. These technologies, along with such lethal instruments of war as the fully automatic "machine gun," gave Europe clear advantages over other parts of the globe and facilitated Western imperialism in less industrially developed areas. In the enterprise of empire building, the industrialized nations of Britain, France, Belgium, Germany, Italy, and the United States took the lead.

Colonialism and the New Imperialism

The history of European expansion into Asia, Africa, and other parts of the globe dates back at least to the Renaissance. Between approximately 1500 and 1800, Europeans established trading outposts in Africa, China, and India. But not until after 1800, in the wake of the Industrial Revolution, did European imperialism transform the territories of foreign peoples into outright colonial possessions. Driven by the need for raw materials and markets for their manufactured goods, and aided immeasurably by their advanced military technology, the industrial nations quickly colonized or controlled vast parts of Asia, Africa, and Latin America. So massive was this effort that, by the end of the nineteenth century, the West had established economic, political, and cultural dominion over much of the world.

European imperialists defended the economic exploitation of weaker countries with the view, inspired by social Darwinism, that in politics, as in nature, the strongest or "most fit" prevailed in the "struggle for survival." Since Caucasians had proved themselves the "most fit," they argued, it was the white population's "burden" to care for, protect, and rule over the "less fit" nonwhite peoples of the earth. Britain, the leader in European industrialization, spearheaded the thrust of colonization.

The self-appointed mission of Western rule in less technologically developed countries is best expressed in a poem by one of the most popular British writers of his time, Rudyard Kipling (1864–1936). Three verses of his poem "The White Man's Burden" sum up two of the key imperialist notions: racial superiority and the spirit of paternal and heroic deliverance.

READING 30.1 From Kipling's "The White Man's Burden" (1899)

Take up the White Man's burden—   1
  Send forth the best ye breed—
Go bind your sons to exile
  To serve your captive's need;
To wait in heavy harness,   5
  On fluttered folk and wide—
Your new-caught, sullen peoples,
  Half-devil and half-child.

    . . . .

Take up the White Man's Burden—
  Ye dare not stoop to less—   10
Nor call too loud on Freedom
  To cloak your weariness;
By all ye cry or whisper,
  By all ye leave to do,
The silent, sullen peoples   15
  Shall weigh your Gods and you.

Take up the White Man's burden—
  Have done with childish days—
The lightly proffered laurel,
  The easy, ungrudged praise.   20
Comes now, to search your manhood

Through all the thankless years,
Cold, edged with dear-bought wisdom,
  The judgment of your peers!

Q To whom might the terms "half-devil" and "half-child" apply?

Q How is the "White Man" in this poem described?

Kipling dedicated "The White Man's Burden" to the United States to commemorate the American annexation of the Philippines in 1899, but the pattern for colonialism had been fixed by the British. In the race for overseas colonies, Britain led the way. The first major landmass to be subjugated was India, where commercial imperialism led to conquest, and finally, to British rule, in 1858. In less than a century, the nation had established control over so much territory across the globe that it could legitimately claim that "the sun never set" on the British Empire (Map **30.1**).

The most dramatic example of the new imperialism was in Africa. In 1880, European nations controlled only 10 percent of the continent; but by 1900 all of Africa, save Ethiopia and Liberia, had been carved up by European powers, who introduced new models of political and economic authority, often with little regard for native

Map 30.1 European Colonies and Independent Nations in 1900. For many of the "independent states," such as Persia and China, the political and economic influence of the West presented an often destabilizing threat.

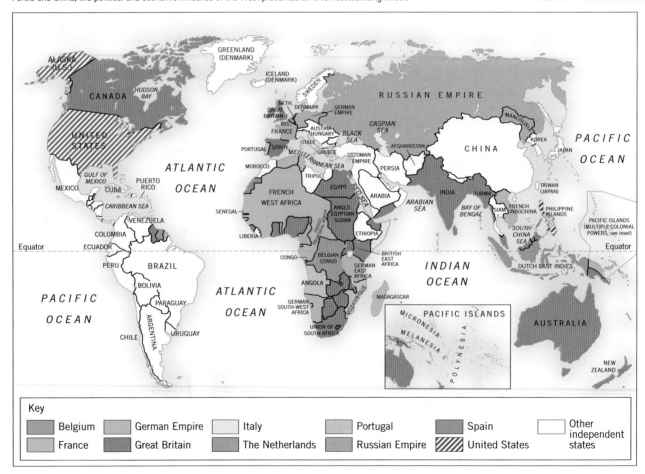

populations. The partitioning of Africa began in 1830 with the French conquest of Algeria (in the north). In the decades thereafter, Belgium laid claim to the Congo, and the Dutch and the British fought each other for control of South Africa—both nations savagely wresting land from the Zulu and other African peoples.

A century-long series of brutal wars with the Asante Empire in West Africa left the British in control of the Gold Coast, while the conquest of the Sudan in 1898 saw 11,000 Muslims killed by British machine guns (the British themselves lost twenty-eight men). Profit-seeking European companies leased large tracts of African land from which native goods such as rubber, diamonds, and gold might be extracted; and increasingly Africans were forced to work on white-owned plantations and mines. The seeds of racism and mutual contempt were sown in this troubled era, an era that predictably spawned modern liberation movements, such as those calling for pan-Islamic opposition to colonialism (see chapter 36).

By the mid nineteenth century, the United States (itself a colony of Britain until 1776) had joined the scramble for economic control. America forced Japan to open its doors to Western trade in 1853. This event, which marked the end of Japan's seclusion, ushered in the overthrow of the Tokugawa regime (see chapter 21) and marked the beginning of Japanese modernization under Meiji rule (1858–1912). In the Western hemisphere, the United States established its own overseas empire.

North Americans used the phrase "manifest destiny" to describe and justify a policy of unlimited expansion into the American West, Mexico, and elsewhere. The end result was the United States' acquisition of more than half of Mexico, control of the Philippines and Cuba, and a dominant position in the economies of the politically unstable nations of Latin America. Although Westerners rationalized their militant expansionism by contending that they were "civilizing" the backward peoples of the globe, in fact their diplomatic policies contributed to undermining cultural traditions, to humiliating and often enfeebling the civilizations they dominated, and to creating conditions of economic dependency that would last well into the twentieth century (see chapter 36).

China and the West

The nineteenth century marked the end of China's long history as an independent civilization. The European powers, along with Russia and Japan, carved out trade concessions in China. Subsequent trade policies, which took advantage of China's traditionally negative view of profit-taking, delayed any potential Chinese initiative toward industrialization.

More devastating still was the triangular trade pattern in opium and tea between India, China, and Britain. Established by Britain in the early nineteenth century, trade policy worked to stem the tide of British gold and silver that flowed to China to buy tea, a favorite British

Science and Technology

1844	Samuel Morse (American) transmits the first telegraph message
1866	the first successful transatlantic telegraph cable is laid
1869	the first American transcontinental railroad is completed
1875	Alexander Graham Bell (Scottish) produces the first functional telephone in America

beverage. The Chinese had used narcotic opium for centuries, but as a result of the new arrangement large quantities of the drug—harvested in India—were exported directly to China. In exchange, the Chinese shipped tea to Britain. Opium addiction became an increasingly severe social problem in China. Following the opium-related death of the Chinese emperor's son, the Chinese made every effort to restrict the importation of the drug and stem the activities of opium smugglers (Figure 30.2). British merchants refused to cooperate. The result was a series of wars between Britain and China (the Opium Wars, 1839– 1850) that brought China to its knees. In 1839, just prior to the first of these wars, the Chinese commissioner Lin Zexu (1785–1850) sent a detailed communication to the British queen pleading for Britain's assistance in ending opium smuggling and trade. Whether or not Queen Victoria ever read Lin's letter is unknown, but the document remains a literary tribute to the futile efforts of a great Asian civilization to achieve peace through diplomacy in the age of imperialism.

READING 30.2 From Lin Zexu's *Letter of Advice to Queen Victoria* (1839)

. . .The kings of your honorable country by a tradition handed   1
down from generation to generation have always been noted
for their politeness and submissiveness. We have read your
successive tributary memorials saying, "In general our
countrymen who go to trade in China have always received His
Majesty the Emperor's gracious treatment and equal justice,"
and so on. Privately we are delighted with the way in which the
honorable rulers of your country deeply understand the grand
principles and are grateful for the Celestial grace. For this
reason the Celestial Court in soothing those from afar has   10
redoubled its polite and kind treatment. The profit from trade
has been enjoyed by them continuously for two hundred years.
This is the source from which your country has become known
for its wealth.

But after a long period of commercial intercourse, there
appear among the crowd of barbarians both good persons and
bad, unevenly. Consequently there are those who smuggle
opium to seduce the Chinese people and so cause the spread of
the poison to all provinces. Such persons who only care to profit
themselves, and disregard their harm to others, are not   20

Zè vos dis qu'il faut, qué vo ach'lè ce poisonne to d'suite, no vollons qué vo empposonniéz vo véritéblement, pou queno avions du thé bocoupe pou dègerer conforteblement nos Beef-SteaKs!..

Figure 30.2 Cartoon from a Paris newspaper, date unknown. The inscription reads: "I tell you that you have to buy this opium immediately so that you can poison yourself; and then you will buy a lot of tea to digest our beefsteaks in a comfortable manner."

tolerated by the laws of heaven and are unanimously hated by human beings. His Majesty the Emperor, upon hearing of this, is in a towering rage. He has especially sent me, his commissioner, to come to Kwangtung, and together with the governor-general and governor jointly to investigate and settle this matter. . . .

We find that your country is [some 20,000 miles] from China. Yet there are barbarian ships that strive to come here for trade for the purpose of making a great profit. The wealth of China is used to profit the barbarians. That is to say, the great profit 30 made by barbarians is all taken from the rightful share of China. By what right do they then in return use the poisonous drug to injure the Chinese people? Even though the barbarians may not necessarily intend to do us harm, yet in coveting profit to an extreme, they have no regard for injuring others. Let us ask, where is your conscience? I have heard that the smoking of opium is very strictly forbidden by your country; that is because the harm caused by opium is clearly understood. Since it is not permitted to do harm to your own country, then even less should you let it be passed on to the harm of other 40 countries—how much less to China! Of all that China exports to foreign countries, there is not a single thing which is not beneficial to people: they are of benefit when eaten, or of benefit when used, or of benefit when resold: all are beneficial. Is there a single article from China which has done any harm to foreign countries? Take tea and rhubarb, for example; the foreign countries cannot get along for a single day without them. If China cuts off these benefits with no sympathy for those who are to suffer, then what can the

barbarians rely upon to keep themselves alive? Moreover the 50 [textiles] of foreign countries cannot be woven unless they obtain Chinese silk. If China, again, cuts off this beneficial export, what profit can the barbarians expect to make? As for other foodstuffs, beginning with candy, ginger, cinnamon, and so forth, and articles for use, beginning with silk, satin, chinaware, and so on, all the things that must be had by foreign countries are innumerable. On the other hand, articles coming from the outside to China can only be used as toys. We can take them or get along without them. Since they are not needed by China, what difficulty would there be if we closed 60 the frontier and stopped the trade? Nevertheless our Celestial Court lets tea, silk, and other goods be shipped without limit and circulated everywhere without begrudging it in the slightest. This is for no other reason but to share the benefit with the people of the whole world.

The goods from China carried away by your country not only supply your own consumption and use, but also can be divided up and sold to other countries, producing a triple profit. Even if you do not sell opium, you still have this threefold profit. How can you bear to go further, selling products injurious to others 70 in order to fulfil your insatiable desire?

Suppose there were people from another country who carried opium for sale to England and seduced your people into buying and smoking it; certainly your honorable ruler would deeply hate it and be bitterly aroused. We have heard heretofore that your honorable ruler is kind and benevolent. Naturally you would not wish to give unto others what you yourself do not want. We have also heard that the ships coming to Canton have all had regulations promulgated and given to them in which it is stated that it is not permitted to carry contraband 80 goods. This indicates that the administrative orders of your honorable rule have been originally strict and clear. Only because the trading ships are numerous, heretofore perhaps they have not been examined with care. Now after this communication has been dispatched and you have clearly understood the strictness of the prohibitory laws of the Celestial Court, certainly you will not let your subjects dare again to violate the law. . . .

Now we have set up regulations governing the Chinese people. He who sells opium shall receive the death penalty and 90 he who smokes it also the death penalty. Now consider this: if the barbarians do not bring opium, then how can the Chinese people resell it, and how can they smoke it? The fact is that the wicked barbarians beguile the Chinese people into a death trap. How then can we grant life only to these barbarians? He who takes the life of even one person still has to atone for it with his own life; yet is the harm done by opium limited to the taking of one life only? Therefore in the new regulations, in regard to those barbarians who bring opium to China, the penalty is fixed at decapitation or strangulation. This is what is 100 called getting rid of a harmful thing on behalf of mankind. . . .

Q What "balance of trade" is described in this letter?

Q To what extent is Lin's letter an appeal to conscience?

The process of colonization had dramatic effects on the Islamic world. Muslims in the Middle East, India, Arabia, Malaya, and much of Africa regarded the European efforts at colonization as an assault on their cultures and their religious faith. Europeans, who tended to see premodern agrarian societies as backward, looked upon "Orientals" (a term that lumped together all Eastern people) as inherently inferior. Unlike Japan or China, which had never been colonized, and were therefore able to retain many of their economic and political traditions, Islamic states were often debilitated and humiliated by dependency on the West.

European colonization of the Islamic world began in the late eighteenth-century. Napoleon had invaded the Near East in 1798, bringing with him a corpus of European literature and a printing press with Arabic type. Despite the failure of Napoleon's campaign in Egypt, the country made ambitious efforts to modernize. The failure of these efforts, however, which left Egypt bankrupt, led ultimately to British occupation.

A second instance of the Western presence in Islamic lands occurred in Persia (renamed Iran in 1935). Strategically located in the Middle East, Persia was forced into wars with Britain and Russia, whose rival interests in Middle Eastern territory threatened the autonomy of the Qajar dynasty (1794–1925). In the late nineteenth century the Persian reformer Aqa Khan Kirmani (1853–1896) urged Muslims to adopt a program of Western-style modernization, to replace the *sharia* with a modern secular code of law and to institute parliamentary representation. Iran's first modern college system would emerge in 1848. Others throughout the Islamic world, however, opposed the intrusion of the West and Western ways of life as a threat to Muslim traditions and religious ideals (see chapter 36). One of the most significant differences involved the political gulf between time-honored Islamic theocracy and Western representative democracy. Such issues have continued to trouble the world well into our own time.

To the European mind, the benefits of Western science, technology, and religion far outweighed the negative impact of colonialism. But the "gift" of progress was received in China with extreme caution and increasing isolationism. No dramatically new developments took place in the arts of China (nor, for that matter, in India) during the nineteenth century; in general, there was a marked decline in both productivity and originality. The full consequences of Western colonialism in Asia and elsewhere, however, would not become clear until the twentieth century.

Social and Economic Realities

In global terms, advancing industrialization polarized the nations of the world into the technologically advanced—the "haves"—and the technologically backward—the "have-nots." But industrialization had an equally profound impact within the industrialized nations themselves: it changed the nature and character of human work, altered relationships between human beings, and affected the natural environment.

Prior to 1800, the practice of accumulating capital for industrial production and commercial profit played only a limited role in European societies. But after this date, industrial production, enhanced by advances in machine technology, came to be controlled by a relatively small group of middle-class **entrepreneurs** (those who organize, manage, and assume the risks of a business) and by an even smaller number of **capitalists** (those who provide money to finance business).

Industrialization created wealth, but that wealth was concentrated in the hands of a small minority of the population.

The vast majority of men and women lived hard lives supported by meager wages—the only thing they had to sell was their labor. Factory laborers, including women and children, worked under dirty and dangerous conditions for long hours—sometimes up to sixteen hours per day (Figure **30.3**). In the 1830s almost half of London's funerals were for children under ten years old. Mass production brought more (and cheaper) goods to more people more rapidly, ultimately raising the standard of living for industrialized nations. But European industrialization and the unequal distribution of wealth contributed to a widening gap between capitalist entrepreneurs—the "haves" of society—and the working classes—the "have-nots." In 1846, the British statesman Benjamin Disraeli (1804–1881) described Britain under the rule of Queen Victoria (1819–1901) as two nations: the nation of the poor and the nation of the rich.

Beginning in 1848, the lower classes protested against these conditions with sporadic revolts. Economic unrest prevailed not only in the cities but in rural areas as well. The French population was two-thirds rural, largely poor, and often reduced to backbreaking labor (see Figure 30.11). Wealthy landowners in some parts of Europe treated their agricultural laborers as slaves. In America, until after the Civil War (1861–1865), most of those who worked the great Southern plantations were, in fact, African-American slaves. Between 1855 and 1861, there were almost 500 peasant uprisings across Europe (Figure **30.4**). Reform, however, was slow in coming. Outside of England—in Germany, for instance—trade unions and social legislation to benefit the working classes did not appear until 1880 or later, while in Russia economic reform would require nothing less than a full-scale revolution (see chapter 34).

Figure 30.3 ADOLPH FRIEDRICH ERDMANN VON MENZEL,
Iron Mill (Das Eisenwalzwerk—Moderne Zyklopen), 1875.
Oil on canvas, 5 ft. ¼ in. × 8 ft. 3⅝ in.

Figure 30.4 KATHE KOLLWITZ, *March of the Weavers*, from "The Weavers
Cycle," 1897. Etching, 8⅜ × 11⅝ in. Kollwitz (1867–1945) was a German
social realist, a pacifist, and a feminist. The series of prints known as "The
Weavers" illustrates a play by Gerhart Hauptmann that dramatized the failed
revolt of Silesian weavers in 1842. A sculptor as well as a printmaker,
Kollwitz went on to create searing protest images of the two world wars.

Nineteenth-Century Social Theory

Among nineteenth-century European intellectuals there developed a serious debate over how to address the social results of industrial capitalism. Matters of social reform were central to the development of ideologies that dictated specific policies of political and economic action. Traditional *conservatives* stressed the importance of maintaining order and perpetuating conventional power structures and religious authority. *Liberals*, on the other hand, whose ideas were rooted in Enlightenment theories of human progress and perfectibility (see chapter 24), supported gradual reform through enlightened legal systems, constitutional guarantees, and a generally equitable distribution of material benefits. The British liberal Jeremy Bentham (1748–1832) advanced the doctrine of *utilitarianism*, which held that governments should work to secure "the greatest happiness for the greatest number of people"; while Bentham's student, John Stuart Mill (1806–1873), expounded the ideology of social liberalism.

Mill emphasized freedom of thought over equality and personal happiness. He held that individuals must be free to direct their own lives,

EXPLORING ISSUES

The Limits of Authority

In *On Liberty*, John Stuart Mill examined the nature of freedom, advocating individual rights over those of the state. He argued, however, that it was the legitimate duty of government to limit the exercise of any freedom that might harm other members of the community. Wrestling with key issues concerning limits to the authority of the state with regard to the individual, he asked, "What, then, is the rightful limit to the sovereignty of the individual over himself? Where does the authority of society begin? How much of human life should be assigned to individuality, and how much to society?"

Enlarging more generally on these questions, Mill's American contemporary Abraham Lincoln (1809–1865) observed, "The legitimate object of government is to do for a community of people whatever they need to have done, but can not do at all, or can not

so well do for themselves in their separate and individual capacities." Is providing for the *needs* of the community—much like providing *protection* for its citizens—the function of the government? Suppose the political process of providing for these needs (like the obligation to protect the individual) comes at the cost of limiting the absolute freedom of others?

To one degree or another, most of the great political divisions emerging from nineteenth-century social thought proceeded from these questions. They are still debated today, mainly in the opposing political ideologies of *liberalism* and *conservatism*. Contemporary liberals would incline toward a relatively greater use of government authority in serving the needs of society. Conservatives would incline toward a relatively lesser exercise of such control.

---

but, recognizing the disadvantages that might result from free competition, he argued that the state must protect its weaker members by acting to regulate the economy where private initiative failed to do so. Mill feared that the general will—the will of unenlightened, propertyless masses—might itself prove tyrannical and oppressive. In his classic statement of the liberal creed, *On Liberty* (1859), he concluded that "as soon as any part of a person's conduct affects prejudicially the interests of others, society has jurisdiction over it." For Mill, as for most nineteenth-century liberals, government was obliged to intervene to safeguard and protect the wider interests of society.

Such theories met with strenuous opposition from European *socialists*. For the latter, neither conservatism nor liberalism responded adequately to current social and economic inequities. Socialists attacked capitalism as unjust; they called for the common ownership and administration of the means of production and distribution in the interest of a public good. Society, according to the socialists, should operate entirely in the interest of the needs of the people, communally and cooperatively, rather than competitively. The utopian socialist Pierre Joseph Proudhon (1809–1865) envisioned a society free of state control, while the more extreme *anarchists* favored the complete dissolution of the state and the elimination of the force of law.

The Radical Views of Marx and Engels

The German theorist Karl Marx (1818–1883) agreed with the socialists that bourgeois capitalism corrupted humanity, but his theory of social reform was even more radical, for it preached violent revolution that would both destroy the old order and usher in a new society. Marx began his career by studying law and philosophy at the university of Berlin. Moving to Paris, he became a lifelong friend of the social

scientist and journalist Friedrich Engels (1820–1895). Marx and Engels shared a similar critical attitude in respect of the effects of European industrial capitalism. By 1848 they completed the *Communist Manifesto*, a short treatise published as the platform of a workers' association called the Communist League. The *Manifesto*, which still remains the "guidebook" of Marxist socialism, demanded the "forcible overthrow of all existing social conditions" and the liberation of the **proletariat**, or working class. Marx offered an even more detailed criticism of the free enterprise system in *Das Kapital*, a work on which he toiled for thirty years.

The *Communist Manifesto* is a sweeping condemnation of the effects of capitalism on the individual and society at large. It opens with a dramatic claim: "The history of all hitherto existing society is the history of class struggles." It further contends that capitalism concentrates wealth in the hands of the few, providing great luxuries for some, while creating an oppressed and impoverished proletariat. The psychological effects of such circumstances, it holds, are devastating: bourgeois capitalism alienates workers from their own productive efforts and robs individuals of their basic humanity. Finally, the *Manifesto* calls for revolution by which workers will seize the instruments of capitalistic production and abolish private ownership.

The social theories of Marx and Engels had enormous practical and theoretical influence. They not only supplied a justification for lower-class revolt, but they brought attention to the role of economics in the larger life of a society. Marx perceived human history in exclusively materialistic terms, arguing that the conditions under which one earned a living determined all other aspects of life: social, political, and cultural. A student of Hegel (see chapter 27), he viewed history as a struggle between "haves" (thesis) and

Science and Technology

1839	Charles Goodyear (American) produces industrial-strength rubber
1846	Elias Howe (American) patents an interlocking-stitch sewing machine
1866	the first dynamo, capable of generating massive quantities of electricity, is produced
1876	Nikolaus Otto (German) produces a workable internal-combustion engine

"have-nots" (antithesis) that would resolve in the synthesis of a classless society. From Hegel, Marx also derived the utopian idea of the perfectibility of the state. The end product of dialectical change, argued Marx, was a society free of class antagonisms and the ultimate dissolution of the state itself.

Although Marx and Engels failed to anticipate capitalism's potential to spread rather than to limit wealth, their manifesto gave sharp focus to prevailing class differences and to the actual condition of the European economy of their time. Despite the fact that they provided no explanation of *how their classless society* might function, their apocalyptic call to revolution would be heeded in the decades to come. Oddly enough, communist revolutions would occur in some of the least industrialized countries of the world, such as Russia and China, rather than in the most industrialized countries, as Marx and Engels expected. Elsewhere, communists would operate largely through *nonrevolutionary* vehicles, such as labor unions and political organizations, to initiate better working conditions, higher wages, and greater social equality. But the anticommunist revolutions and the collapse of the communist government in the Soviet Union in the late twentieth century reveal mounting frustration with the failure of most Communist regimes to raise economic standards among the masses. Although the *Manifesto* did not accurately predict the economic destiny of the modern world, the treatise remains a classic expression of nineteenth-century social consciousness.

READING 30.3 From Marx's and Engels' *Communist Manifesto* (1848)

I Bourgeois and Proletarians[1]

The history of all hitherto existing society is the history of class struggles.　　**1**

Freeman and slave, patrician and plebeian, lord and serf, guild-master[2] and journeyman, in a word, oppressor and oppressed, stood in constant opposition to one another, carried on an uninterrupted, now hidden, now open fight, a fight that each time ended either in a revolutionary reconstitution of society at large or in the common ruin of the contending classes.

In the earlier epochs of history we find almost everywhere a complicated arrangement of society into various orders, a　　**10**

manifold gradation of social rank. In ancient Rome we have patricians, knights, plebeians, slaves; in the Middle Ages, feudal lords, vassals, guild-masters, journeymen, apprentices, serfs; in almost all of these classes, again, subordinate gradations.

The modern bourgeois society that has sprouted from the ruins of feudal society has not done away with class antagonisms. It has but established new classes, new conditions of oppression, new forms of struggle in place of the old ones.　　**20**

Our epoch, the epoch of the bourgeoisie, possesses, however, this distinctive feature: it has simplified the class antagonisms. Society as a whole is splitting up more and more into two great hostile camps, into two great classes directly facing each other: Bourgeoisie and Proletariat.

From the serfs of the Middle Ages sprang the chartered burghers of the earliest towns. From these burgesses the first elements of the bourgeoisie were developed.

The discovery of America, the rounding of the Cape, opened up fresh ground for the rising bourgeoisie. The East Indian and　　**30** Chinese markets, the colonization of America, trade with the colonies, the increase in the means of exchange and in commodities generally, gave to commerce, to navigation, to industry, an impulse never before known, and thereby, to the revolutionary element in the tottering feudal society, a rapid development.

The feudal system of industry, under which industrial production was monopolized by closed guilds, now no longer sufficed for the growing wants of the new markets. The manufacturing system took its place. The guild-masters were　　**40** pushed on one side by the manufacturing middle class; division of labor between the different corporate guilds vanished in the face of division of labor in each single workshop.

Meantime the markets kept ever growing, the demand ever rising. Even manufacture no longer sufficed. Thereupon, steam and machinery revolutionized industrial production. The place of manufacture was taken by the giant, Modern Industry, the place of the industrial middle class by industrial millionaires—the leaders of whole industrial armies, the modern bourgeois.

Modern industry has established the world market, for which　　**50** the discovery of America paved the way. This market has given an immense development to commerce, to navigation, to communication by land. This development has, in its turn, reacted on the extension of industry; and in proportion as industry, commerce, navigation, railways extended, in the same proportion the bourgeoisie developed, increased its capital, and pushed into the background every class handed down from the Middle Ages.

---

[1] By bourgeoisie is meant the class of modern capitalists, owners of the means of social production and employers of wage labor. By proletariat, the class of modern wage-laborers who, having no means of production of their own, are reduced to selling their labor power in order to live. [1888.]

[2] Guild-master, that is, a full member of a guild, a master within, not a head of a guild. [1888.]

We see, therefore, how the modern bourgeoisie is itself the product of a long course of development, of a series of revolutions in the modes of production and of exchange. 60

Each step in the development of the bourgeoisie was accompanied by a corresponding political advance of that class. An oppressed class under the sway of the feudal nobility, an armed and self-governing association in the medieval commune,[3] here independent urban republic (as in Italy and Germany), there taxable "third estate" of the monarchy (as in France), afterward, in the period of manufacture proper, serving either the semi-feudal or the absolute monarchy as a counterpoise against the nobility, and, in fact, cornerstone of 70 the great monarchies in general, the bourgeoisie has at last, since the establishment of Modern Industry and of the world market, conquered for itself, in the modern representative State, exclusive political sway. The executive of the modern State is but a committee for managing the common affairs of the whole bourgeoisie.

The bourgeoisie, historically, has played a most revolutionary part.

The bourgeoisie, wherever it has got the upper hand, has put an end to all feudal, patriarchal, idyllic relations. It has 80 pitilessly torn asunder the motley feudal ties that bound man to his "natural superiors," and has left remaining no other nexus between man and man than naked self-interest, than callous "cash payment." It has drowned the most heavenly ecstasies of religious fervor, of chivalrous enthusiasm, of philistine sentimentalism, in the icy water of egotistical calculation. It has resolved personal worth into exchange value, and in place of the numberless indefeasible chartered freedoms has set up that single, unconscionable freedom— Free Trade. In one word, for exploitation, veiled by religious 90 and political illusions, it has substituted naked, shameless, direct, brutal exploitation.

The bourgeoisie has stripped of its halo every occupation hitherto honored and looked up to with reverent awe. It has converted the physician, the lawyer, the priest, the poet, the man of science, into its paid wage-laborers.

The bourgeoisie has torn away from the family its sentimental veil, and has reduced the family relation to a mere money relation. . . .

The bourgeoisie, by the rapid improvement of all instruments 100 of production, by the immensely facilitated means of communication, draws all, even the most barbarian, nations into civilization. The cheap prices of its commodities are the heavy artillery with which it batters down all Chinese walls, with which it forces the barbarians' intensely obstinate hatred of foreigners to capitulate. It compels all nations, on pain of extinction, to adopt the bourgeois mode of production; it compels them to introduce what it calls civilization into their midst, i.e., to become bourgeois themselves. In a word, it

creates a world after its own image. 110

The bourgeoisie has subjected the country to the rule of the towns. It has created enormous cities, has greatly increased the urban population as compared with the rural, and has thus rescued a considerable part of the population from the idiocy of rural life. Just as it has made the country dependent on the towns, so it has made barbarian and semi-barbarian countries dependent on the civilized ones, nations of peasants on nations of bourgeois, the East on the West.

The bourgeoisie keeps doing away more and more with the scattered state of the population, of the means of production, 120 and of property. It has agglomerated population, centralized means of production, and has concentrated property in a few hands. The necessary consequence of this was political centralization. Independent or but loosely connected provinces with separate interests, laws, governments and systems of taxation became lumped together into one nation, with one government, one code of laws, one national class interest, one frontier and one customs tariff.

The bourgeoisie during its rule of scarce one hundred years has created more massive and more colossal productive forces 130 than have all preceding generations together. Subjection of nature's forces to man, machinery, application of chemistry to industry and agriculture, steam navigation, railways, electric telegraphs, clearing of whole continents for cultivation, canalization of rivers, whole populations conjured out of the ground—what earlier century had even a presentiment that such productive forces slumbered in the lap of social labor? . . .

But not only has the bourgeoisie forged the weapons that bring death to itself; it has also called into existence the men who are to wield those weapons—the modern working class, 140 the proletarians.

In proportion as the bourgeoisie, i.e., capital, is developed, in the same proportion is the proletariat, the modern working class, developed—a class of laborers who live only as long as they find work, and who find work only as long as their labor increases capital. These laborers, who must sell themselves piecemeal, are a commodity like every other article of commerce, and are consequently exposed to all the vicissitudes of competition, to all the fluctuations of the market.

Owing to the extensive use of machinery and to division of 150 labor, the work of the proletarians has lost all individual character and, consequently, all charm for the workman. He becomes an appendage of the machine, and it is only the most simple, most monotonous, and most easily acquired knack that is required of him. . . .

Modern industry has converted the little workshop of the patriarchal master into the great factory of the industrial capitalist. Masses of laborers, crowded into the factory, are organized like soldiers. As privates of the industrial army they are placed under the command of a perfect hierarchy of 160 officers and sergeants. Not only are they slaves of the bourgeois class and of the bourgeois State; they are daily and hourly enslaved by the machine, by the overseer and, above all, by the individual bourgeois manufacturer himself. The more openly this despotism proclaims gain to be its end and aim, the more petty, the more hateful and the more embittering it is.

The less the skill and exertion of strength implied in manual

[3] "Commune" was the name taken in France by the nascent towns even before they had conquered from their feudal lords and masters local self-government and political rights as the "Third Estate." Generally speaking, for the economic development of the bourgeoisie, England is here taken as the typical country; for its political development, France. [1888.]

labor, in other words, the more modern industry becomes developed, the more is the labor of men superseded by that of women. Differences of age and sex no longer have any distinctive social validity for the working class. All are instruments of labor, more or less expensive to use, according to their age and sex. 170

No sooner is the exploitation of the laborer by the manufacturer so far at an end that he receives his wages in cash, than he is set upon by the other portions of the bourgeoisie, the landlord, and shopkeeper, the pawnkeeper, etc...

II Proletarians and Communists

...The Communist revolution is the most radical rupture with traditional property relations; no wonder that its development 180 involves the most radical rupture with traditional ideas.

But let us have done with the bourgeois objections to Communism.

We have seen above that the first step in the revolution by the working class is to raise the proletariat to the position of ruling class, to win the battle of democracy.

The proletariat will use its political supremacy to wrest, by degrees, all capital from the bourgeoisie, to centralize all instruments of production in the hands of the State, i.e., of the proletariat organized as the ruling class; and to increase the 190 total of productive forces as rapidly as possible. . . .

III Position of the Communists

...The Communists disdain to conceal their views and aims. They openly declare that their ends can be attained only by the forcible overthrow of all existing social conditions. Let the ruling classes tremble at a Communistic revolution. The proletarians have nothing to lose but their chains. They have a world to win.

WORKING MEN OF ALL COUNTRIES, UNITE!

Q Which of the *Manifesto's* arguments are the strongest? Which are the weakest?

Mill and Women's Rights

While Marx and Engels criticized a society that made middle-class women "mere instrument[s] of production," Mill described women of all classes as the unwilling subjects of more powerful males. In the treatise *The Subjection of Women*, Mill condemned the legal subordination of one sex to the other as objectively "wrong in itself, and . . . one of the chief hindrances to human improvement." Mill's optimism concerning the unbounded potential for social change—a hallmark of liberalism—may have been shortsighted, for women would not obtain voting rights in Britain until 1928.

In the United States, the first women's college—Mount Holyoke—was founded at South Hadley, Massachusetts, in 1836; and in 1848, at Seneca Falls in upstate New York, American feminists, led by Elizabeth Cady Stanton (1815–1902) and Susan B. Anthony (1820–1906), issued the first of many declarations that demanded female equality in all areas of life.

The rights of women had been an issue addressed in the literature of feminists from Christine de Pisan to Condorcet and Mary Wollstonecraft (see chapter 24), but nowhere was the plight of women more eloquently treated than in Mill's essay. Mill compared the subjection of women to that of other subject classes in the history of culture. But his most original contribution was his analysis of the male/female relationship and his explanation of how that relationship differed from that of master and slave.

READING 30.4 From Mill's *The Subjection of Women* (1869)

All causes, social and natural, combine to make it unlikely that 1 women should be collectively rebellious to the power of men. They are so far in a position different from all other subject classes that their masters require something more from them than actual service. Men do not want solely the obedience of women, they want their sentiments. All men, except the most brutish, desire to have, in the woman most nearly connected with them, not a forced slave but a willing one, not a slave merely, but a favorite. They have therefore put everything in practice to enslave their minds. The masters of all other slaves 10 rely, for maintaining obedience, on fear, either fear of themselves, or religious fears. The masters of women wanted more than simple obedience, and they turned the whole force of education to effect their purpose. All women are brought up from the very earliest years in the belief that their ideal of character is the very opposite to that of men; not self-will and government by self-control, but submission and yielding to the control of others. All the moralities tell them that it is the duty of women and all the current sentimentalities that it is their nature to live for others, to make complete abnegation of 20 themselves, and to have no life but in their affections. And by their affections are meant the only ones they are allowed to have—those to the men with whom they are connected, or to the children who constitute an additional and indefeasible tie between them and a man. When we put together three things—first, the natural attraction between opposite sexes; secondly, the wife's entire dependence on the husband, every privilege or pleasure she has being either his gift, or depending entirely on his will; and lastly, that the principal object of human pursuit, consideration, and all objects of social ambition 30 can in general be sought or obtained by her only through him, it would be a miracle if the object of being attractive to men had not become the polar star of feminine education and formation of character. And this great means of influence over the minds of women having been acquired, an instinct of selfishness made men avail themselves of it to the utmost as a means of holding women in subjection, by representing to them meekness, submissiveness, and resignation of all individual will into the hands of a man, as an essential part of sexual attractiveness. . . . 40

The preceding considerations are amply sufficient to show that custom, however universal it may be, affords in this case no presumption and ought not to create any prejudice in favor of the arrangements which place women in social and political subjection to men. But I may go further, and maintain that the course of history, and the tendencies of progressive human society afford not only no presumption in favor of this system of inequality of rights, but a strong one against it; and that, so far as the whole course of human improvement up to this time, the whole stream of modern tendencies warrants any 50 inference on the subject, it is that this relic of the past is discordant with the future and must necessarily disappear.

For, what is the peculiar character of the modern world—the difference which chiefly distinguishes modern institutions, modern social ideas, modern life itself, from those of times long past? It is, that human beings are no longer born to their place in life and chained down by an inexorable bond to the place they are born to, but are free to employ their faculties and such favorable chances as offer, to achieve the lot which may appear to them most desirable. Human society of old was 60 constituted on a very different principle. All were born to a fixed social position and were mostly kept in it by law or interdicted from any means by which they could emerge from it. As some men are born white and others black, so some were born slaves and others freemen and citizens; some were born patricians, others plebeians; some were born feudal nobles, others commoners. . . .

The old theory was that the least possible should be left to the choice of the individual agent; that all he had to do should, as far as practicable, be laid down for him by superior wisdom. 70 Left to himself he was sure to go wrong. The modern conviction, the fruit of a thousand years of experience, is that things in which the individual is the person directly interested never go right but as they are left to his own discretion; and that any regulation of them by authority, except to protect the rights of others, is sure to be mischievous. . . .

Q How, in Mill's view, does the relationship between male and female differ from that of master and slave?

Q What does Mill consider to be the "peculiar character" of modernism?

The New Historicism

While issues of class and gender preoccupied some of the finest minds of the nineteenth century, so too did matters surrounding the interpretation of the historical past. For many centuries, history was regarded as a branch of literature rather than a social science. The Romantic histories, such as those of Thomas Carlyle (see chapter 28), served to emphasize the role of great men in shaping the destinies of nations. At the same time, the spirit of high patriotism inspired nineteenth-century historians such as Thomas Babington Macaulay (1800–1859) in Britain and Fustel de Coulanges (1830–1889) in France to write nationalistic histories that brought attention to the greatness of their own people and culture.

Patriotism, however, also led historians to renew their efforts to retrieve the evidence of the past. Scholars compiled vast collections of primary source materials; and, enamored of the new, positivist zeal for objective measurement and recording, they applied scientific methods to the

writing of history. The result was an effort to recreate history "as it actually was," a movement later called *historicism*. Led by the German historian Leopold von Ranke (1795–1886), historians produced historical works that depended on the objective interpretation of eyewitness reports and authentic documents. Von Ranke himself wrote sixty volumes on modern European history that rested on the critical study of sources that he had gleaned from numerous archives. This method of writing history came to dominate modern-day historiography.

The new historicism that scholars brought to the critical study of religious history stirred great controversy. Rejecting all forms of supernaturalism, some nineteenth-century scholars disputed the literal interpretation of the Bible, especially where its contents conflicted with scientific evidence (as in the case of the Virgin Birth). Since the facts of Jesus' life are so few, some also questioned the historicity of Jesus (that is, whether or not he had ever actually lived), while still others—such as the eminent French scholar Ernest Renan, author of the *Life of Jesus* (1863)— questioned his divinity. Renan and his followers offered a rationalist reconstruction of religious history that worked to separate personal belief and moral conduct from conventional religious history and dogma. As universal education spread throughout the literate world, Church and state moved further apart, and education became increasingly secularized.

Realism in Literature
The Novels of Dickens and Twain

Inequities of class and gender had existed throughout the course of history, but in an age that pitted the progressive effects of industrial capitalism against the realities of poverty and inequality, social criticism was inevitable. Many writers pointed to these conditions and described them with unembellished objectivity. This unblinking attention to contemporary life and experience was the basis for the style known as *literary realism*.

More than any other genre, the nineteenth-century novel—by its capacity to detail characters and conditions—fulfilled the Realist credo of depicting life with complete candor. In place of heroic and exotic subjects, the Realist novel portrayed men and women in actual, everyday, and often demoralizing situations. It examined the social consequences of middle-class materialism, the plight of the working class, and the subjugation of women, among other matters.

While Realism did not totally displace Romanticism as the dominant literary mode of the nineteenth century, it often appeared alongside the Romantic—indeed, Romantic and sentimental elements can be found in generally realistic narratives. Such is the case in the novels of Charles Dickens (1812–1870) in England and Mark Twain, the pseudonym of Samuel Langhorne Clemens (1835–1910), in America. Twain's writings, including his greatest achievement, *The Adventures of Huckleberry Finn*, reveal a blend of humor and irony that is not generally characteristic of Dickens. But both writers employ a masterful use of dialect, sensitivity to pictorial detail, and a humanitarian sympathy in their descriptions of nineteenth-century life in specific locales—for Twain, the rural farmlands along the Mississippi River, and for Dickens, the streets of England's industrial cities.

The most popular English novelist of his time, Dickens came from a poor family who provided him with little formal education. His early experiences supplied some of the themes for his most famous novels: *Oliver Twist* (1838) vividly portrays the slums, orphanages, and boarding schools of London; *Nicholas Nickleby* (1839) is a bitter indictment of England's brutal rural schools; and *David Copperfield* (1850) condemns debtors' prisons and the conditions that produced them.

Dickens' novels are frequently theatrical, his characters may be drawn to the point of caricature, and his themes often suggest a sentimental faith in kindness and good cheer as the best antidotes to the bitterness of contemporary life. But, as the following excerpt illustrates, Dickens' evocation of realistic detail was acute, and his portrayal of physical ugliness was unflinching. In this passage from *The Old Curiosity Shop*, he painted an unforgettable picture of the horrifying urban conditions that gave rise to the despair of the laboring classes and inspired their cries for social reform (Figure 30.5). His description of the English mill town of Birmingham, as first viewed by the novel's heroine, little Nell, and her grandfather, finds striking parallels in nineteenth-century visual representations of Europe's laboring poor; it also calls to mind the popular conceptions of Hell found in medieval art and literature (see chapter 12).

Figure 30.5 **THOMAS ANNAN**, *Close No. 193 High Street*, 1868–1877, print ca. 1877. Carbon print, 27.3 × 23 cm. While Annan spent most of his life in Glasgow, Scotland, his photographs of disease-ridden slums are representative of similar circumstances in late nineteenth-century industrial centers. Annan's photographs were instrumental in the eventual demolition of Glasgow's slum areas.

READING 30.5 *From Dickens' The Old Curiosity Shop* (1841)

. . . A long suburb of red-brick houses—some with patches of 1
garden-ground, where coal-dust and factory smoke darkened
the shrinking leaves and coarse, rank flowers; and where the
struggling vegetation sickened and sank under the hot breath
of kiln and furnace, making them by its presence seem yet
more blighting and unwholesome than in the town itself—a
long, flat, straggling suburb passed, they came by slow
degrees upon a cheerless region, where not a blade of grass
was seen to grow; where not a bud put forth its promise in the
spring; where nothing green could live but on the surface of   10
the stagnant pools, which here and there lay idly sweltering by
the black roadside.

Advancing more and more into the shadow of this mournful
place, its dark depressing influence stole upon their spirits, and
filled them with a dismal gloom. On every side, as far as the eye
could see into the heavy distance, tall chimneys, crowding on

each other, and presenting that endless repetition of the same
dull, ugly form, which is the horror of oppressive dreams,
poured out their plague of smoke, obscured the light, and made
foul the melancholy air. On mounds of ashes by the wayside,   20
sheltered only by a few rough boards, or rotten pent-house
roofs, strange engines spun and writhed like tortured creatures;
clanking their iron chains, shrieking in their rapid whirl from
time to time as though in torment unendurable, and making the
ground tremble with their agonies. Dismantled houses here and
there appeared, tottering to the earth, propped up by fragments
of others that had fallen down, unroofed, windowless,
blackened, desolate, but yet inhabited. Men, women, children,
wan in their looks and ragged in attire, tended the engines, fed
their tributary fires, begged upon the road, or scowled half   30
naked from the doorless houses. Then came more of the
wrathful monsters, whose like they almost seemed to be in
their wildness and their untamed air, screeching and turning
round and round again; and still, before, behind, and to the
right and left, was the same interminable perspective of brick
towers, never ceasing in their black vomit, blasting all things
living or inanimate, shutting out the face of day, and closing in
on all these horrors with a dense dark cloud.

But night-time in this dreadful spot!—night, when the smoke
was changed to fire; when every chimney spirited up its flame;   40

and places, that had been dark vaults all day, now shone red-hot, with figures moving to and fro within their blazing jaws, and calling to one another with hoarse cries—night, when the noise of every strange machine was aggravated by the darkness; when the people near them looked wilder and more savage; when bands of unemployed laborers paraded in the roads, or clustered by torch-light round their leaders, who told them in stern language of their wrongs, and urged them on to frightful cries and threats; when maddened men, armed with sword and firebrand, spurning the tears and prayers of women **50** who would restrain them, rushed forth on errands of terror and destruction, to work no ruin half so surely as their own—night, when carts came rumbling by, filled with rude coffins (for contagious disease and death had been busy with the living crops); when orphans cried, and distracted women shrieked and followed in their wake—night, when some called for bread, and some for drink to drown their cares; and some with tears, and some with staggering feet, and some with bloodshot eyes, went brooding home—night, which, unlike the night that Heaven sends on earth, brought with it no peace, nor quiet, nor signs of **60** blessed sleep—who shall tell the terrors of the night to that young wandering child!

Q **Which descriptive details are most effective in setting the tone of this novel?**

Mark Twain's literary classic, *The Adventures of Huckleberry Finn*, is the most widely taught book in American literature. Published as a sequel to the popular "boys' book" *The Adventures of Tom Sawyer* (1876), which, like Dickens' novels, appeared in serial format, the book recounts the exploits of the young narrator, Huck Finn, and the runaway slave, Jim, as the two make their way down the Mississippi River on a ramshackle raft. As humorist, journalist, and social critic, Twain offered his contemporaries a blend of entertainment and vivid insight into the dynamics of a unique time and place: the American South just prior to the Civil War. More generally, he conveys the innocence of youthful boyhood as it wrestles with the realities of greed, hypocrisy, and the moral issues arising from the troubled relations between black and white Americans in the mid nineteenth century. These he captures in an exotic blend of dialects—the vernacular rhythms and idioms of local, untutored speech.

In the excerpt that follows, Huck, a poor, ignorant, but good-hearted Southern boy, experiences a crisis of conscience when he must choose between aiding and abetting a fugitive slave—a felony offense in the slave states of the South—and obeying the law, by turning over his older companion and friend to the local authorities. Huck's moral dilemma, the theme of this excerpt, was central to the whole system of chattel slavery. Historically, slaves were considered property (chattel), that is, goods that could be bought, sold, or stolen. Clearly, however, they were also human beings. In opting to help Jim escape, Huck is, in effect, an accomplice to a crime. Nevertheless, Huck chooses to aid Jim the *man*, even as he violates the law in harboring Jim the *slave*.

READING 30.6 From Twain's *The Adventures of Huckleberry Finn* (1884)

Chapter 16

We slept most all day, and started out at night, a little ways **1** behind a monstrous long raft that was as long going by as a procession. She had four long sweeps[1] at each end, so we judged she carried as many as thirty men, likely. She had five big wigwams aboard, wide apart, and an open camp fire in the middle, and a tall flag-pole at each end. There was a power of style about her. It *amounted* to something being a raftsman on such a craft as that.

We went drifting down into a big bend, and the night clouded up and got hot. The river was very wide, and was walled with **10** solid timber on both sides; you couldn't see a break in it hardly ever, or a light. We talked about Cairo,[2] and wondered whether we would know it when we got to it. I said likely we wouldn't, because I had heard say there warn't but about a dozen houses there, and if they didn't happen to have them lit up, how was we going to know we was passing a town? Jim said if the two big rivers joined together there, that would show. But I said maybe we might think we was passing the foot of an island and coming into the same old river again. That disturbed Jim—and me too. So the question was, what to do? I said, paddle ashore **20** the first time a light showed, and tell them pap was behind, coming along with a trading-scow, and was a green hand at the business, and wanted to know how far it was to Cairo. Jim thought it was a good idea, so we took a smoke on it and waited.

There warn't nothing to do, now, but to look out sharp for the town, and not pass it without seeing it. He said he'd be mighty sure to see it, because he'd be a free man the minute he seen it, but if he missed it he'd be in the slave country again and no more show for freedom. Every little while he jumps up and says: **30**

"Dah she is!"

But it warn't. It was Jack-o-lanterns, or lightning-bugs;[3] so he set down again, and went to watching, same as before. Jim said it made him all over trembly and feverish to be so close to freedom. Well, I can tell you it made me all over trembly and feverish, too, to hear him, because I begun to get it through my head that he *was* most free—and who was to blame for it? Why, *me*. I couldn't get that out of my conscience, no how nor no way. It got to troubling me so I couldn't rest; I couldn't stay still in one place. It hadn't ever come home to me before, what **40** this thing was that I was doing. But now it did; and it staid with me, and scorched me more and more. I tried to make out to myself that I warn't to blame, because I didn't run Jim off from his rightful owner; but it warn't no use, conscience up and says, every time, "But you knowed he was running for his freedom, and you could a paddled ashore and told somebody." That was so—I couldn't get around that, noway. That was where it pinched. Conscience says to me, "What had poor Miss Watson done to you, that you could see her nigger go off right under your eyes and never say one single word? What did **50**

---

[1] Long oars.
[2] A city in Illinois.
[3] Fireflies.

that poor old woman do to you, that you could treat her so mean? Why, she tried to learn you your book, she tried to learn you your manners, she tried to be good to you every way she knowed how. *That's* what she done."

I got to feeling so mean and so miserable I most wished I was dead. I fidgeted up and down the raft, abusing myself to myself, and Jim was fidgeting up and down past me. We neither of us could keep still. Every time he danced around and says, "Dah's Cairo!" it went through me like a shot, and I thought if it *was* Cairo I reckoned I would die of miserableness. 60

Jim talked out loud all the time while I was talking to myself. He was saying how the first thing he would do when he got to a free State he would go to saving up money and never spend a single cent, and when he got enough he would buy his wife, which was owned on a farm close to where Miss Watson lived; and then they would both work to buy the two children, and if their master wouldn't sell them, they'd get an Ab'litionist to go and steal them.

It most froze me to hear such talk. He wouldn't ever dared to talk such talk in his life before. Just see what a difference it 70 made in him the minute he judged he was about free. It was according to the old saying, "give a nigger and inch and he'll take an ell."[4] Thinks I, this is what comes of my not thinking. Here was this nigger which I had as good as helped to run away, coming right out flat-footed and saying he would steal his children—children that belonged to a man I didn't even know; a man that hadn't ever done me no harm.

I was sorry to hear Jim say that, it was such a lowering of him. My conscience got to stirring me up hotter than ever, until at last I says to it, "Let up on me—it ain't too late, yet—I'll 80 paddle ashore at the first light, and tell." I felt easy, and happy, and light as a feather, right off. All my troubles was gone. I went to looking out sharp for a light, and sort of singing to myself. By-and-by one showed. Jim sings out:

"We's safe, Huck, we's safe! Jump up and crack yo' heels, dat's de good ole Cairo at las', I jis knows it!"

I says:

"I'll take the canoe and go see, Jim. It mightn't be, you know."

He jumped and got the canoe ready, and put his old coat in 90 the bottom for me to set on, and give me the paddle; and as I shoved off, he says:

"Pooty soon I'll be a-shout'n for joy, en I'll say, it's all on accounts o' Huck; I's a free man, en I couldn't ever ben free ef it hadn' ben for Huck; Huck done it. Jim won't ever forgit you, Huck; you's de bes' fren' Jim's ever had; en you's de *only* fren' ole Jim's got now."

I was paddling off, all in a sweat to tell on him; but when he says this, it seemed to kind of take the tuck all out of me. I went along slow then, and I warn't right down certain whether 100 I was glad I started or whether I warn't. When I was fifty yards off, Jim says:

"Dah you goes, de ole true Huck; de on'y white genlman dat ever kep' his promise to old Jim."

Well, I just felt sick. But I says, I *got* to do it—I can't get *out* of it. Right then, along comes a skiff with two men in it, with

guns, and they stopped and I stopped. One of them says:

"What's that, yonder?"

"A piece of a raft," I says.

"Do you belong on it?" 110

"Yes, sir."

"Any men on it?"

"Only one, sir."

"Well, there's five niggers run off to-night, up yonder above the head of the bend. Is you man white or black?"

I didn't answer up prompt. I tried to, but the words wouldn't come. I tried, for a second or two, to brace up and out with it, but I warn't man enough—hadn't the spunk of a rabbit. I see I was weakening; so I just give up trying, and up and says—

"He's white." 120

"I reckon we'll go and see for ourselves."

"I wish you would," says I, "because it's pap that's there, and maybe you'd help me tow the raft ashore where the light is. He's sick—and so is mam and Mary Ann."

"Oh, the devil! we're in a hurry, boy. But I s'pose we've got to. Come—buckle to your paddle, and let's get along."

I buckled to my paddle and they laid to their oars. When we had made a stroke or two, I says:

"Pap'll be mighty much obleeged to you, I can tell you. Everybody goes away when I want them to help me tow the 130 raft ashore, and I can't do it by myself."

"Well, that's infernal mean. Odd, too. Say, boy, what's the matter with your father?"

"It's the—a—the—well, it ain't anything, much."

They stopped pulling. It warn't but a mighty little ways to the raft, now. One says:

"Boy, that's a lie. What *is* the matter with your pap? Answer up square, now, and it'll be the better for you."

"I will, sir, I will, honest—but don't leave us, please. It's the—the—gentlemen, if you'll only pull ahead, and let me 140 heave you the head-line, you won't have to come a-near the raft—please do."

"Set her back, John, set her back!" says one. They backed water. "Keep away, boy—keep to looard.[5] Confound it, I just expect the wind has blowed it to us. Your pap's got the smallpox, and you know it precious well. Why didn't you come out and say so? Do you want to spread it all over?"

"Well," says I, a-blubbering, "I've told everybody before, and then they just went away and left us."

"Poor devil, there's something in that. We are right down 150 sorry for you, but we—well, hang it, we don't want the smallpox, you see. Look here, I'll tell you what to do. Don't you try to land by yourself, or you'll smash everything to pieces. You float along down about twenty miles and you'll come to a town on the left-hand side of the river. It will be long after sun-up, then, and when you ask for help, you tell them your folks are all down with chills and fever. Don't be a fool again, and let people guess what is the matter. Now we're trying to do you a kindness; so you just put twenty miles between us, that's a good boy. It wouldn't do any good to land yonder where the 160 light is—it's only a wood-yard. Say—I reckon your father's poor, and I'm bound to say he's in pretty hard luck. Here—I'll

---

[4] An English measure equal to 45 inches.

[5] Leeward; away from the wind.

put a twenty dollar gold piece on this board, and you get it when it floats by. I feel mighty mean to leave you, but my kingdom! it won't do to fool with small-pox, don't you see?"

"Hold on, Parker," says the other man, "here's a twenty to put on the board for me. Good-bye, boy, you do as Mr. Parker told you, and you'll be all right."

"That's so, my boy—good-bye, good-bye. If you see any runaway niggers, you get help and nab them, and you can   170 make some money by it."

"Good-bye, sir," says I, "I won't let no runaway niggers get by me if I can help it."

They went off, and I got aboard the raft, feeling bad and low, because I knowed very well I had done wrong, and I see it warn't no use for me to try to learn to do right; a body that don't get *started* right when he's little, ain't got no show[6]—when the pinch comes there ain't nothing to back him up and keep him to his work, and so he gets beat. Then I thought a minute, and says to myself, hold on,—s'pose you'd a done right and give   180 Jim up; would you felt better than what you do now? No, says I, I'd feel bad—I'd feel just the same way I do now. Well, then, says I, what's the use you learning to do right, when it's troublesome to do right and ain't no trouble to do wrong, and the wages is just the same? I was stuck. I couldn't answer that. So I reckoned I wouldn't bother no more about it, but after this always do whichever come handiest at the time. . . .

Q **How does Twain bring to life the personalities of Huck and Jim?**

Q **How does Huck resolve his moral dilemma?**

Russian Realism: Dostoevsky and Tolstoy

More pessimistic than Dickens or Twain, and more profoundly analytic of the universal human condition, were the Russian novelists Fyodor Dostoevsky (1821–1881) and Leo Tolstoy (1828–1910). Both men were born and bred in wealth, but both turned against upper-class Russian society and sympathized with the plight of the lower classes.

Tolstoy ultimately renounced his wealth and property and went to live and work among the peasants. His historical novel *War and Peace* (1869), often hailed as the greatest example of realistic Russian fiction, traces the progress of five families whose destinies unroll against the background of Napoleon's invasion of Russia in 1812. In this sprawling narrative, as in many of his other novels, Tolstoy exposes the privileged position of the nobility and the cruel exploitation of the great masses of Russian people. This task, along with sympathy for the cause of Russian nationalism in general, was shared by Tolstoy's friend and admirer, Ilya Repin (1844–1930), whose portrait of Tolstoy brings the writer to life with skillful candor (Figure **30.6**). Russia's preeminent Realist painter, Repin rendered with detailed accuracy the miserable lives of ordinary Russians—peasants, laborers, and beggars—in genre paintings that might well serve as illustrations for the novels of Tolstoy and Dostoevsky.

---

[6] Has no chance.

Figure 30.6 ILYA REPIN, *Portrait of Leo Tolstoy*, 1887. Oil on canvas. Repin was celebrated for his realistic depictions of contemporary Russian life and for the psychological insight he brought to his portraits of notable Russian writers and composers.

Dostoevsky paid greater attention than Tolstoy to philosophical and psychological issues. His characters are often victims of a dual plight: poverty and conscience. Their energies are foiled by bitter efforts to resolve their own contradictory passions. Dostoevsky's personal life contributed to his bleak outlook: associated with a group of proletarian revolutionaries, he was arrested and deported to Siberia, where he spent five years at hard labor. The necessity of suffering is a central theme in his writing, as is the hope of salvation through suffering.

The novels *Crime and Punishment* (1866), *The Possessed* (1871), and *The Brothers Karamazov* (1880) feature protagonists whose irrational behavior and its psychological consequences form the central theme of the novel. In *Crime and Punishment*, Raskolnikov, a young, poor student, murders an old woman and her younger sister; his crime goes undetected. Thereafter, he struggles with guilt—the self-punishment for his criminal act. He also explores the problems arising from one's freedom to commit evil. In the following excerpt, the protagonist addresses the moral question of whether extraordinary individuals, by dint of their uniqueness, have the right to commit immoral acts. The conversation, which takes place between Raskolnikov and his friends, is spurred by an article on crime that Raskolnikov had published in a journal shortly after dropping out of university. This excerpt is typical of Dostoevsky's fondness for developing character through monologue and dialogue, rather than through descriptive detail.

Dostoevsky's Realism (and his genius) lie in the way in which he forces the reader to understand the character as that character tries to understand himself.

READING 30.7 From Dostoevsky's *Crime and Punishment* (1866)

"... the 'extraordinary' man has the right ... I don't mean a   1
formal, official right, but he has the right in himself, to permit
his conscience to overstep ... certain obstacles, but only in
the event that his ideas (which may sometimes be salutary for
all mankind) require it for their fulfilment. You are pleased to
say that my article is not clear; I am ready to elucidate it for
you, as far as possible. Perhaps I am not mistaken in supposing
that is what you want. Well, then. In my opinion, if the
discoveries of Kepler and Newton, by some combination of
circumstances, could not have become known to the world
in any other way than by sacrificing the lives of one, or ten,   10
or more people, who might have hampered or in some way
been obstacles in the path of those discoveries, then Newton
would have had the right, or might even have been under an
obligation
... to *remove* those ten or a hundred people, so that his
discoveries might be revealed to all mankind. It does not follow
from this, of course, that Newton had the right to kill any Tom,
Dick, or Harry he fancied, or go out stealing from market-stalls
every day. I remember further that in my article I developed the
idea that all the ... well, for example, the law-givers and   20
regulators of human society, beginning with the most ancient,
and going on to Lycurgus, Solon, Mahomet, Napoleon and so
on, were without exception transgressors,[1] by the very fact that
in making a new law they *ipso facto* broke an old one, handed
down from their fathers and held sacred by society; and, of
course, they did not stop short of shedding blood, provided only
that the blood (however innocent and however heroically shed
in defence of the ancient law) was shed to their advantage. It
is remarkable that the greater part of these benefactors and law-
givers of humanity were particularly blood-thirsty. In a word, I   30
deduce that all of them, not only the great ones, but also those
who diverge ever so slightly from the beaten track, those, that
is, who are just barely capable of saying something new, must,
by their nature, inevitably be criminals—in a greater or less
degree, naturally. Otherwise they would find it too hard to leave
their rut, and they cannot, of course, consent to remain in the
rut, again by the very fact of their nature; and in my opinion they
ought not to consent. In short, you see that up to this point
there is nothing specially new here. It has all been printed, and
read, a thousand times before. As for my division of people into   40

ordinary and extraordinary, that I agree was a little arbitrary, but
I do not insist on exact figures. Only I do believe in the main
principle of my idea. That consists in people being, by the law
of nature, divided *in general* into two categories: into a lower
(of ordinary people), that is, into material serving only for the
reproduction of its own kind, and into people properly speaking,
that is, those who have the gift or talent of saying *something
new* in their sphere. There are endless subdivisions, of course,
but the distinctive characteristics of the two categories are
fairly well marked: the first group, that is the material, are,   50
generally speaking, by nature staid and conservative, they live
in obedience and like it. In my opinion they ought to obey
because that is their destiny, and there is nothing at all
degrading to them in it. The second group are all law-breakers
and transgressors, or are inclined that way, in the measure of
their capacities. The aims of these people are, of course,
relative and very diverse; for the most part they require, in
widely different contexts, the destruction of what exists in the
name of better things. But if it is necessary for one of them, for
the fulfilment of his ideas, to march over corpses, or wade   60
through blood, then in my opinion he may in all conscience
authorize himself to wade through blood—in proportion,
however, to his idea and the degree of its importance—mark
that. It is in that sense only that I speak in my article of their
right to commit crime. (You will remember that we really began
with the question of legality.) There is, however, not much
cause for alarm: the masses hardly ever recognize this right of
theirs, and behead or hang them (more or less), and in this way,
quite properly, fulfil their conservative function, although in
following generations these same masses put their former   70
victims on a pedestal and worship them (more or less). The first
category are always the masters of the present, but the second
are the lords of the future. The first preserve the world and
increase and multiply; the second move the world and guide it
to its goal. Both have an absolutely equal right to exist. In short,
for me all men have completely equivalent rights, and—*vive la
guerre éternelle*—until we have built the New Jerusalem, of
course!"[2]
    "You do believe in the New Jerusalem, then?"
    "Yes, I do," answered Raskolnikov firmly; he said this with   80
his eyes fixed on one spot on the carpet, as they had been all
through his long tirade.
    "A-and you believe in God? Forgive me for being so
inquisitive."
    "Yes, I do," repeated Raskolnikov, raising his eyes to Porfiry.
    "A-a-and do you believe in the raising of Lazarus?"
    "Y-yes. Why are you asking all this?"
    "You believe in it literally?"
    "Yes."
    "Ah ... I was curious to know. Forgive me. But, returning to   90
the previous subject—they are not always put to death. Some,
on the contrary ..."

[1] Raskolnikov's views are similar to those expressed by Napoleon III
in his book *Life of Julius Caesar*. The newspaper *Golos* (*Voice*) had
recently summarized the English *Saturday Review*'s analysis of
Napoleon's ideas about the right of exceptional individuals (such as
Lycurgus, Mahomet, and Napoleon I) to transgress laws and even to
shed blood. The book appeared in Paris in March 1865; the Russian
translation in April! [Lycurgus: the founder of the military regime
of ancient Sparta; Mahomet: Muhammad, the prophet of Allah and
founder of the religion Islam; Solon: statesman and reformer in
sixth-century B.C.E. Athens.]

[2] New Jerusalem, symbolic of the ideal order, after the end of time,
is a Heaven on Earth, a new paradise. See the description in
Revelation 21 (the Apocalypse). The French phrase means,
"Long live perpetual war."

"Triumph during their lifetime? Oh, yes, some achieve their ends while they still live, and then . . ."

"They begin to mete out capital punishment themselves?"

"If necessary, and, you know, it is most usually so. Your observation is very keen-witted."

"Thank you. But tell me: how do you distinguish these extraordinary people from the ordinary? Do signs and portents appear when they are born? I mean to say that we could do   100
with rather greater accuracy here, with, so to speak, rather more outward signs: please excuse the natural anxiety of a practical and well-meaning man, but couldn't there be, for example, some special clothing, couldn't they carry some kind of brand or something? . . . Because, you will agree, if there should be some sort of mix-up, and somebody from one category imagined that he belonged to the other and began 'to remove all obstacles,' as you so happily put it, then really . . ."

"Oh, that very frequently happens! This observation of yours is even more penetrating than the last."   110

"Thank you."

"Not at all. But you must please realize that the mistake is possible only among the first group, that is, the 'ordinary' people (as I have called them, perhaps not altogether happily). In spite of their inborn inclination to obey, quite a number of them, by some freak of nature such as is not impossible even among cows, like to fancy that they are progressives, 'destroyers,' and propagators of the 'new world,' and all this quite sincerely. At the same time, they really take no heed of *new people*; they even despise them, as reactionary and   120
incapable of elevated thinking. But, in my opinion, they cannot constitute a real danger, and you really have nothing to worry about, because they never go far. They might sometimes be scourged for their zealotry, to remind them of their place; there is no need even for anyone to carry out the punishment: they will do it themselves, because they are very well conducted: some of them do one another this service, and others do it for themselves with their own hands . . . And they impose on themselves various public penances besides—the result is beautifully edifying, and in short, you have nothing to worry   130
about . . . This is a law of nature."

"Well, at least you have allayed my anxieties on that score a little; but here is another worry: please tell me, are there many of these people who have the right to destroy others, of these 'extraordinary' people? I am, of course, prepared to bow down before them, but all the same you will agree that it would be terrible if there were very many of them, eh?"

"Oh, don't let that trouble you either," went on Raskolnikov in the same tone. "Generally speaking, there are extremely few people, strangely few, born, who have a new idea, or are even   140
capable of saying anything at all *new*. One thing only is clear, that the ordering of human births, all these categories and subdivisions, must be very carefully and exactly regulated by some law of nature. This law is, of course, unknown at present, but I believe that it exists, and consequently that it may be known. The great mass of men, the common stuff of humanity, exist on the earth only in order that at last, by some endeavour, some process, that remains as yet mysterious, some happy conjunction of race and breeding, there should struggle into life a being, one in a thousand, capable, in   150

however small a degree, of standing on his own feet. Perhaps one in ten thousand (I am speaking approximately, by way of illustration) is born with a slightly greater degree of independence, and one in a hundred thousand with even more. One genius may emerge among millions, and a really great genius, perhaps, as the crowning point of many thousands of millions of men. In short, I have not been able to look into the retort whence all this proceeds. But a definite law there must be, and is; it cannot be a matter of chance. . . ."

— Q **Into what two categories does Raskolnikov divide humankind?**

— Q **How does he justify the transgressions of the "lords of the future"?**

The Literary Heroines of Flaubert and Chopin

Nineteenth-century novelists shared a special interest in examining conflicts between social conventions and personal values, especially as they affected the everyday lives of women. Gustave Flaubert's *Madame Bovary* (1857), Tolstoy's *Anna Karenina* (1877), and Kate Chopin's *The Awakening* (1899) are representative of the writer's concern with the tragic consequences following from the defiance of established social and moral codes by passionate female figures. The heroines in these novels do not create the world in their own image; rather, the world—or more specifically, the social and economic environment—molds them and governs their destinies.

Flaubert (1821–1880), whom critics have called "the inventor of the modern novel," stripped his novels of sentimentality and of all preconceived notions of behavior. He aimed at a precise description of not only the stuff of the physical world but also the motivations of his characters. A meticulous observer, he sought *le mot juste* ("the exact word") to describe each concrete object and each psychological state—a practice that often prevented him from writing more than one or two pages of prose per week. One contemporary critic wittily claimed that Flaubert, the son of a surgeon, wielded his pen like a scalpel.

Flaubert's landmark novel, *Madame Bovary*, tells the story of a middle-class woman who desperately seeks to escape the boredom of her mundane existence. Educated in a convent and married to a dull, small-town physician, Emma Bovary tries to live out the fantasies that fill the pages of her favorite romance novels, but her efforts to do so prove disastrous and lead to her ultimate destruction. With a minimum of interpretation, Flaubert reconstructs the particulars of Emma's provincial surroundings and her bleak marriage. Since the novel achieves its full effect through the gradual development of plot and character, no brief excerpt can possibly do it justice. Nevertheless, the following excerpt, which describes the deterioration of the adulterous affair between Emma Bovary and the young clerk Léon, illustrates Flaubert's ability to characterize places and persons by means of the fastidious selection and accumulation of descriptive details.

In the end Léon had promised never to see Emma again; and he   1
reproached himself for not having kept his word, especially
considering all the trouble and reproaches she still probably
held in store for him—not to mention the jokes his fellow
clerks cracked every morning around the stove. Besides, he
was about to be promoted to head clerk: this was the time to
turn over a new leaf. So he gave up playing the flute and said
good-bye to exalted sentiments and romantic dreams. There
isn't a bourgeois alive who in the ferment of his youth, if only
for a day or for a minute, hasn't thought himself capable of   10
boundless passions and noble exploits. The sorriest little
woman-chaser has dreamed of Oriental queens; in a corner of
every notary's heart lie the moldy remains of a poet.

These days it only bored him when Emma suddenly burst out
sobbing on his breast: like people who can stand only a certain
amount of music, he was drowsy and apathetic amidst the
shrillness of her love; his heart had grown deaf to its subtler
overtones.

By now they knew each other too well: no longer did they
experience, in their mutual possession, that wonder that   20
multiplies the joy a hundredfold. She was as surfeited with him
as he was tired of her. Adultery, Emma was discovering, could
be as banal as marriage.

But what way out was there? She felt humiliated by the
degradation of such pleasures; but to no avail: she continued
to cling to them, out of habit or out of depravity; and every day
she pursued them more desperately, destroying all possible
happiness by her excessive demands. She blamed Léon for her
disappointed hopes, as though he had betrayed her; and she
even longed for a catastrophe that would bring about their   30
separation, since she hadn't the courage to bring it about
herself.

Still, she continued to write him loving letters, faithful to the
idea that a woman must always write to her lover.

But as her pen flew over the paper she was aware of the
presence of another man, a phantom embodying her most
ardent memories, the most beautiful things she had read and
her strongest desires. In the end he became so real and
accessible that she tingled with excitement, unable though she
was to picture him clearly, so hidden was he, godlike, under his   40
manifold attributes. He dwelt in that enchanted realm where
silken ladders swing from balconies moon-bright and flower-
scented. She felt him near her: he was coming—coming to
ravish her entirely in a kiss. And the next moment she would
drop back to earth, shattered; for these rapturous love-dreams
drained her more than the greatest orgies.

**Q What insights into Emma's personality are offered
in this brief excerpt? Into Léon's personality?**

Almost immediately after *Madame Bovary* appeared (in
the form of six installments in the *Revue de Paris*), the
novel was denounced as an offense against public and
religious morals, and Flaubert, as well as the publisher and
the printer of the *Revue*, was brought to trial before a criminal court. All three men were ultimately acquitted, but
not before an eloquent lawyer had defended all the passages (including those in Reading 30.8) that had been condemned as wanton and immoral.

A similar situation befell the American writer Kate
Chopin (1851–1904), whose novel *The Awakening* was
banned in her native city of St. Louis shortly after its
publication in 1899. The novel, a frank examination of
female sexual passion and marital infidelity, violated the
norms of the society in which Chopin had been reared.
Unlike Flaubert, whose novels convey the staleness and
inescapability of French provincial life, many of Chopin's
stories deliberately ignore the specifics of time and place.
Some are set in Louisiana, where Chopin lived for twelve
years with her husband and six children. Chopin was successful in selling her Louisiana dialect stories, many of
which explore matters of class, race, and gender within the
world of Creole society, but her novels fell into obscurity
soon after her death. *The Awakening*, whose heroine defies
convention by committing adultery, did not receive positive critical attention until the 1950s.

While Chopin absorbed the Realist strategies and social
concerns of Flaubert, she brought to her prose a sensitivity
to the nuances of human (and especially female) behavior
that challenged popular Romantic stereotypes (see chapter
28). Her work also reveals a remarkable talent for narrat-
ing a story with jewel-like precision. Her taut descriptive
style reaches unparalleled heights in the short prose piece
known as "The Story of an Hour." Here, the protagonist's
brief taste of liberation takes on an ironic fatal turn.

READING 30.9 Kate Chopin's "The Story of
an Hour" ("The Dream of
an Hour") (1894)

Knowing that Mrs. Mallard was afflicted with a heart trouble,   1
great care was taken to break to her as gently as possible the
news of her husband's death.

It was her sister Josephine who told her, in broken
sentences: veiled hints that revealed in half concealing. Her
husband's friend Richards was there, too, near her. It was he
who had been in the newspaper office when intelligence of the
railroad disaster was received, with Brently Mallard's name
leading the list of "killed." He had only taken time to assure
himself of its truth by a second telegram, and had hastened   10
to forestall any less careful, less tender friend in bearing the
sad message.

She did not hear the story as many women have heard the
same, with a paralysed inability to accept its significance. She
wept at once, with a sudden, wild abandonment, in her sister's
arms. When the storm of grief had spent itself she went away
to her room alone. She would have no one follow her.

There stood, facing the open window, a comfortable, roomy
armchair. Into this she sank, pressed down by a physical
exhaustion that haunted her body and seemed to reach into   20
her soul.

She could see in the open square before her house the tops
of trees that were all aquiver with the new spring life. The
delicious breath of rain was in the air. In the street below a

peddler was crying his wares. The notes of a distant song which some one was singing reached her faintly, and countless sparrows were twittering in the eaves.

There were patches of blue sky showing here and there through the clouds that had met and piled one above the other in the west facing her window. 30

She sat with her head thrown back upon the cushion of the chair, quite motionless, except when a sob came into her throat and shook her, as a child who has cried itself to sleep continues to sob in its dreams.

She was young, with a fair, calm face, whose lines bespoke repression and even a certain strength. But now there was a dull stare in her eyes, whose gaze was fixed away off yonder on one of those patches of blue sky. It was not a glance of reflection, but rather a suspension of intelligent thought.

There was something coming to her and she was waiting for 40 it, fearfully. What was it? She did not know; it was too subtle and elusive to name. But she felt it, creeping out of the sky, reaching toward her through the sounds, the scents, the color that filled the air.

Now her bosom rose and fell tumultuously. She was beginning to recognize this thing that was approaching to possess her, and she was striving to beat it back with her will—as powerless as her white slender hands would have been.

When she abandoned herself a little whispered word 50 escaped her slight parted lips. She said it over and over under her breath: "free, free, free!" The vacant stare and the look of terror that had followed it went from her eyes. They stayed keen and bright. Her pulses beat fast, and the coursing blood warmed and relaxed every inch of her body.

She did not stop to ask if it were not a monstrous joy that held her. A clear and exalted perception enabled her to dismiss the suggestion as trivial.

She knew that she would weep again when she saw the kind, tender hands folded in death: fixed and grey and dead. 60 But she saw beyond that bitter moment a long procession of years to come that would belong to her absolutely. And she opened and spread her arms out to them in welcome.

There would be no one to live for her during those coming years; she would live for herself. There would be no powerful will bending hers in that blind persistence with which men and women believe they have a right to impose a private will upon a fellow-creature. A kind intention or a cruel intention made the act seem no less a crime as she looked upon it in that brief moment of illumination. 70

And yet she loved him—sometimes. Often she had not. What did it matter! What could love, the unsolved mystery, count for in the face of this possession of self-assertion which she suddenly recognized as the strongest impulse of her being!

"Free! Body and soul free!" she kept whispering.

Josephine was kneeling before the keyhole, imploring for admission. "Louise, open the door! I beg: open the door—you will make yourself ill. What are you doing, Louise? For heaven's sake open the door."

"Go away. I'm not making myself ill." No: she was drinking 80 in a very elixir of life through that open window.

Her fancy was running riot along those days ahead of her.

Spring days, and summer days, and all sorts of days that would be her own. She breathed a quick prayer that life might be long. It was only yesterday she had thought with a shudder that life might be long.

She arose at length and opened the door to her sister's importunities. There was a feverish triumph in her eyes, and she carried herself unwittingly like a goddess of Victory. She clasped her sister's wrist, and together they descended the 90 stairs. Richards stood waiting for them at the bottom.

Some one was opening the front door with a latchkey. It was Brently Mallard who entered, a little travel-stained, composedly carrying his grip-sack and umbrella. He had been far from the scene of accident, and did not even know there had been one. He stood amazed at Josephine's piercing cry; at Richards' quick motion to screen him from the view of his wife.

But Richards was too late.

When the doctors came they said she had died of heart 100 disease—of joy that kills.

Q **What does this story imply about the relationship between husband and wife?**

Q **Would the story be equally effective if the roles of Louise and Brently Mallard were reversed?**

Zola and the Naturalistic Novel

Kate Chopin's contemporary Emile Zola (1840–1902) initiated a variant form of literary Realism known as *naturalism*. Naturalist fiction was based on the premise that everyday life should be represented with scientific objectivity: faithfully and with detailed accuracy. Contrary to Romantic writers, naturalists refused to embellish or idealize experience. They went beyond the Realism of Flaubert and Dickens by conceiving their characters in accordance with psychological and sociological factors, and as products of the laws of heredity. This deterministic approach showed human beings as products of environmental or hereditary factors over which they had little or no control. Just as Marx held that economic life shaped all aspects of culture, so naturalists believed that material and social elements determined human conduct and behavior.

Zola (Figure **30.7**) treated the novel as a carefully researched study of commonplace, material existence. In his passion to describe his time and place with absolute fidelity, he studied labor problems, police records, and industrial history, amassing notebooks of information on a wide variety of subjects, including coal mining, the railroads, the stock market, and the science of surgery. He presented a slice of life that showed how social and material circumstances shaped the society of late nineteenth-century France. His twenty novels (known as the Rougon-Macquart series) exploring the lives of French farmers, miners, statesmen, prostitutes, scholars, and artists constitutes a psycho-socio-biological history of his time. *The Grog Shop* (1877) offers a terrifying picture of the effects of alcoholism on industrial workers. *Nana* (1880) is a

Figure 30.7 EDOUARD MANET, *Zola*, exhibited 1868. Oil on canvas, 57 × 45 in. Manet's portrait has the quality of a snapshot. The writer is seen at his desk, which holds a copy of his short biography of the artist. Above the desk, he has posted a black-and-white reproduction of Manet's *Olympia*, a Japanese print of a sumo wrestler, and Goya's etching of a painting by Velázquez, favorite artists of both Manet and Zola.

scathing portrayal of a beautiful but unscrupulous prostitute. The most scandalous of his novels, it inspired charges of pornography and "gutter-sweeping."

A later novel in the Rougon-Macquart series, *Germinal* (1885), exposes the bitter lives of coal miners in northern France. The excerpt that follows, which relates the hellish experience of the miner Maheu, reflects Zola's talent for detailed description that transforms his writing from mere social history to powerful fiction.

READING 30.10 From Zola's *Germinal* (1885)

The four cutters [miners] had stretched themselves out, head to toe, over the whole surface of the sloping face. Separated by hooked planks that caught the loosened coal, each of them occupied about fifteen feet of the vein, which was so narrow—scarcely twenty inches at this point—that they were squashed in between the roof and the wall. They had to drag themselves along on their knees and elbows, and were unable to turn without bruising their shoulders. To get at the coal, they had to lie sideways, their necks twisted and their raised arms wielding the short-handled picks at an angle.

Zacharie was at the bottom. Levaque and Chaval above him, and Maheu at the very top. Each one was hacking away at the bed of shale with his pick, cutting two vertical grooves in the vein, then driving an iron wedge into the top of the block and freeing it. The coal was soft, and the block crumbled into pieces and rolled down

their stomachs and thighs. When these pieces, caught by the planks, had heaped up beneath them, the cutters disappeared, walled up in the narrow crevice.

Maheu was the one who suffered most. The temperature at the top climbed as high as ninety-five degrees; the air did not circulate, and the suffocating heat eventually became unbearable. In order to see clearly, he had had to hang his lamp on a nail right next to his head, and this additional heat beating down on his skull made his blood sing in his ears. But the worst was the dampness. Water was continually dripping down from the rock only a few inches above his face, and there was a never-ending stream of drops falling, with a maddening rhythm, always on the same spot. It was no use twisting his neck or turning his head: the drops kept beating against his face, splattering and spreading without stop. At the end of a quarter of an hour he was soaked through, coated with his own sweat, and steaming like a tub of laundry. That morning a drop ceaselessly trickling into his eye made him swear, but he wouldn't stop cutting, and his mighty blows jolted him so violently between the two layers of rock that he was like a plant-louse caught between two pages of a book—in constant danger of being completely crushed.

Not a word was said. They were all hammering away, and nothing could be heard except these irregular blows, muffled and seemingly far away. The sounds were harsh in the echoless, dead air, and it seemed as though the shadows had a strange blackness, thickened by the flying coal dust and made heavier by the gases that weighed down on their eyes. Behind metal screens, the wicks of their lamps gave off only reddish points of light, and it was hard to see anything. The stall opened out like a large, flat, oblique chimney in which the soot of ten winters had built up an unrelieved darkness. Phantom forms moved about, dull beams of light giving glimpses of a rounded haunch, a brawny arm, a distorted face blackened as if in preparation for a crime. Occasionally, as blocks of coal came loose, they would catch the light and shoot off crystal-like glitters from their suddenly illuminated facets. Then it would be dark again, the picks would beat out heavy dull blows, and there was nothing but the sound of panting breaths, grunts of discomfort and fatigue in the stifling air, and the dripping water from the underground streams.

Q **Which of the senses does Zola engage in this description of coal mining?**

Elements of naturalism are found in the novels of many late nineteenth-century writers in both Europe and America. Thomas Hardy (1840–1928) in England, and Stephen Crane (1871–1900), Jack London (1876–1916) and Theodore Dreiser (1871–1945) in America are the most notable of the English-language literary naturalists.

Realist Drama: Ibsen

The Norwegian dramatist Henrik Ibsen (1828–1906) brought to the late nineteenth-century stage concerns similar to those in the novels of the Realists. A moralist and a critic of human behavior, he attacked the artificial social conventions that led people to pursue self-deluding and hypocritical lives. Ibsen was deeply concerned with contemporary issues and social problems. He shocked the public with prose dramas that addressed such controversial subjects as insanity, incest, and venereal disease. At the same time, he explored universal themes of conflict between the individual and society, between love and duty, and between husband and wife.

In 1879, Ibsen wrote the classic drama of female liberation, A Doll's House. Threatened with blackmail over a debt she had incurred years earlier, Nora Helmer looks to her priggish husband Torvald for protection. But Torvald is a victim of the small-mindedness and middle-class social restraints of his time and place. When he fails to rally to his wife's defense, Nora realizes the frailty of her dependent lifestyle. Awakened to the meaninglessness of her life as "a doll-wife" in "a doll's house," she comes to recognize that her first obligation is to herself and to her dignity as a human being.

Nora's revelation brings to life, in the forceful language of everyday speech, the psychological tensions between male and female that Mill had analyzed only ten years earlier in his treatise on the subjection of women. Ibsen does not resolve the question of whether a woman's duties to husband and children come before her duty to herself; yet, as is suggested in the following exchange between Nora and Torvald (excerpted from the last scene of A Doll's House), Nora's self-discovery precipitates the end of her marriage. She shuts the door on the illusions of the past as emphatically as Ibsen shut out the world of Romantic idealism.

READING 30.11 From Ibsen's A Doll's House (1879)

Act III, Final Scene

[Late at night in the Helmers' living room. Instead of retiring, Nora suddenly appears in street clothes.]

Helmer: . . . What's all this? I thought you were going to   1
bed. You've changed your dress?

Nora: Yes, Torvald; I've changed my dress.

Helmer: But what for? At this hour?

Nora: I shan't sleep tonight.

Helmer: But, Nora dear—

Nora [looking at her watch]: It's not so very late—Sit down,
Torvald; we have a lot to talk about.

[She sits at one side of the table.]

Helmer: Nora—what does this mean? Why that stern   10
expression?

Nora: Sit down. It'll take some time. I have a lot to say to
you.

[Helmer sits at the other side of the table.]

Helmer: You frighten me, Nora. I don't understand you.

Nora: No, that's just it. You don't understand me; and I have
never understood you either—until tonight. No, don't interrupt
me. Just listen to what I have to say. This is to be a final
settlement, Torvald.

Helmer: How do you mean?   20

Nora [after a short silence]: Doesn't anything special strike
you as we sit here like this?

Helmer: I don't think so—why?

Nora: It doesn't occur to you, does it, that though we've
been married for eight years, this is the first time that we
two—man and wife—have sat down for a serious talk?

Helmer: What do you mean by serious?

Nora: During eight whole years, no—more than that—ever
since the first day we met—we have never exchanged so
much as one serious word about serious things.   30

Helmer: Why should I perpetually burden you with all my
cares and problems? How could you possibly help me to
solve them?

Nora: I'm not talking about cares and problems. I'm simply
saying we've never once sat down seriously and tried to get to
the bottom of anything.

Helmer: But, Nora, darling—why should you be concerned
with serious thoughts?

Nora: That's the whole point! You've never understood
me—A great injustice has been done me, Torvald; first by   40
Father, and then by you.

Helmer: What a thing to say! No two people on earth could
ever have loved you more than we have!

Nora [shaking her head]: You never loved me. You just
thought it was fun to be in love with me.

Helmer: This is fantastic!

Nora: Perhaps. But it's true all the same. While I was still at
home I used to hear Father airing his opinions and they became
my opinions; or if I didn't happen to agree, I kept it to myself—
he would have been displeased otherwise. He used to call me   50
his doll-baby, and played with me as I played with my dolls.
Then I came to live in your house—

Helmer: What an expression to use about our marriage!

Nora [undisturbed]: I mean—from Father's hands I passed
into yours. You arranged everything according to your tastes,
and I acquired the same tastes, or I pretended to—I'm not sure
which—a little of both, perhaps. Looking back on it all, it
seems to me I've lived here like a beggar, from hand to mouth.
I've lived by performing tricks for you, Torvald. But that's the
way you wanted it. You and Father have done me a great   60
wrong. You've prevented me from becoming a real person.

Helmer: Nora, how can you be so ungrateful and
unreasonable! Haven't you been happy here?

Nora: No, never. I thought I was; but I wasn't really.

Helmer: Not—not happy!

Nora: No, only merry. You've always been so kind to me. But our home has never been anything but a play-room. I've been your doll-wife, just as at home I was Papa's doll-child. And the children, in turn, have been my dolls. I thought it fun when you played games with me, just as they thought it fun when I played games with them. And that's been our marriage, Torvald. 70

Helmer: There may be a grain of truth in what you say, even though it is distorted and exaggerated. From now on things will be different. Play-time is over now; tomorrow lessons begin!

Nora: Whose lessons? Mine, or the children's?

Helmer: Both, if you wish it, Nora, dear.

Nora: Torvald, I'm afraid you're not the man to teach me to be a real wife to you. 80

Helmer: How can you say that?

Nora: And I'm certainly not fit to teach the children.

Helmer: Nora!

Nora: Didn't you just say, a moment ago, you didn't dare trust them to me?

Helmer: That was in the excitement of the moment! You mustn't take it so seriously!

Nora: But you were quite right, Torvald. That job is beyond me; there's another job I must do first: I must try and educate myself. You could never help me to do that; I must do it quite 90 alone. So, you see—that's why I'm going to leave you.

Helmer: *[jumping up]*: What did you say—?

Nora: I shall never get to know myself—I shall never learn to face reality—unless I stand alone. So I can't stay with you any longer.

Helmer: Nora! Nora!

Nora: I am going at once. I'm sure Kristine will let me stay with her tonight—

Helmer: But, Nora—this is madness! I shan't allow you to do this. I shall forbid it! 100

Nora: You no longer have the power to forbid me anything. I'll only take a few things with me—those that belong to me. I shall never again accept anything from you.

Helmer: Have you lost your senses?

Nora: Tomorrow I'll go home—to what was my home, I mean. It might be easier for me there, to find something to do.

Helmer: You talk like an ignorant child, Nora—!

Nora: Yes. That's just why I must educate myself.

Helmer: To leave your home—to leave your husband, and your children! What do you suppose people would say to that? 110

Nora: It makes no difference. This is something I must do.

Helmer: It's inconceivable! Don't you realize you'd be betraying your most sacred duty?

Nora: What do you consider that to be?

Helmer: Your duty towards your husband and your children—I surely don't have to tell you that!

Nora: I've another duty just as sacred.

Helmer: Nonsense! What duty do you mean?

Nora: My duty towards myself.

Helmer: Remember—before all else you are a wife and 120 mother.

Nora: I don't believe that any more. I believe that before all else I am a human being, just as you are—or at least that I

should try and become one. I know that most people would agree with you, Torvald—and that's what they say in books. But I can no longer be satisfied with what most people say—or what they write in books. I must think things out for myself—get clear about them.

Helmer: Surely your position in your home is clear enough? Have you no sense of religion? Isn't that an infallible guide to 130 you?

Nora: But don't you see, Torvald—I don't really know what religion is.

Helmer: Nora! How *can* you!

Nora: All I know about it is what Pastor Hansen told me when I was confirmed. He taught me what he thought religion was—said it was this and that. As soon as I get away by myself, I shall have to look into that matter too, try and decide whether what he taught me was right—or whether it's right for me, at least. 140

Helmer: A nice way for a young woman to talk! It's unheard of! If religion means nothing to you, I'll appeal to your conscience; you must have some sense of ethics, I suppose? Answer me! Or have you none?

Nora: It's hard for me to answer you, Torvald. I don't think I know—all these things bewilder me. But I do know that I think quite differently from you about them. I've discovered that the law, for instance, is quite different from what I had imagined; but I find it hard to believe it can be right. It seems it's criminal for a woman to try and spare her old, sick, father, or save her 150 husband's life! I can't agree with that.

Helmer: You talk like a child. You have no understanding of the society we live in.

Nora: No, I haven't. But I'm going to try and learn. I want to find out which of us is right—society or I.

Helmer: You are ill, Nora; you have a touch of fever; you're quite beside yourself.

Nora: I've never felt so sure—so clear-headed—as I do tonight.

Helmer: "Sure and clear-headed" enough to leave your 160 husband and your children?

Nora: Yes.

Helmer: Then there is only one explanation possible.

Nora: What?

Helmer: You don't love me any more.

Nora: No; that is just it.

Helmer: Nora!—What are you saying!

Nora: It makes me so unhappy, Torvald; for you've always been so kind to me. But I can't help it. I don't love you any more. 170

Helmer *[mastering himself with difficulty]*: You feel "sure and clear-headed" about this too?

Nora: Yes, utterly sure. That's why I can't stay here any longer. . . .

Q **What reasons does Nora give Helmer for leaving him?**

Q **What is Helmer's perception of Nora?**

Realism in the Visual Arts

The Birth of Photography

One of the most significant factors in the development of the materialist mentality was the birth of photography. While a painting or an engraving might bring to life the content of the artist's imagination, a photograph offered an authentic record of a moment vanished in time. Unlike the *camera obscura*, which only captured an image briefly (see chapter 23), the photograph fixed and preserved reality.

Photography—literally "writing with light"—had its beginnings in 1835, when William Henry Fox Talbot (1800–1877) fixed negative images on paper coated with light-sensitive chemicals, a process by which multiple prints might be produced from a single exposure. Slightly earlier, Talbot's French contemporary, Louis J. M. Daguerre (1787–1851), had developed a similar process that fixed the image on a polished metal plate. Unlike Talbot's prints (produced from paper negatives), however, Daguerre's images could not be reproduced—each was a one-of-a-kind object. Nevertheless, in the next decades, his more widely publicized and technically improved product, known as a *daguerreotype*, came into vogue throughout Europe and America, where it fulfilled a growing demand for portraits. Gradual improvements in camera lenses and in the chemicals used to develop the visible image hastened the rise of photography as a popular way of recording the physical world with unprecedented accuracy.

Photography presented an obvious challenge to the authority of the artist, who, throughout history, had assumed the role of nature's imitator. But artists were slow to realize the long-range impact of photography—that is, the camera's potential to liberate artists from reproducing the physical "look" of nature. Critics proclaimed that photographs, as authentic facsimiles of the physical world, should serve artists as aids to achieving greater Realism in canvas painting; and many artists did indeed use photographs as factual resources for their compositions. Nevertheless, by mid-century, both Europeans and Americans were using the camera for a wide variety of other purposes: they made topographical studies of exotic geographic sites, recorded architectural monuments, and produced thousands of portraits. Photography provided ordinary people with portrait images that had previously only been available to those who could afford painted likenesses. In the production of portraits the daguerreotype proved most popular; by 1850, some 100,000 were sold each year in Paris. Such photographs were used as calling cards and to immortalize the faces of notable individuals (see Figure 28.4), as well as those of criminals, whose "mug shots" became a useful tool for the young science of criminology.

Some photographers, such as the British pioneer Julia Margaret Cameron (1815–1879), used the camera to recreate the style of Romantic painting. Imitating the effects of the artist's paintbrush, Cameron's soft-focus portraits are Romantic in spirit and sentiment (Figure 30.8). Others

Science and Technology

1835	William H. F. Talbot (English) invents the negative–positive photographic process
1837	Louis J. M. Daguerre (French) uses a copper plate coated with silver to produce the first daguerreotype
1860	production begins on the first Winchester repeating rifle (in America)
1866	explosive dynamite is first produced in Sweden
1888	George Eastman (American) perfects the "Kodak" box camera

used the camera to document the factual realities of their time and place. The French photographer Gaspart-Félix Tournachon, known as Nadar (1820–1910), made vivid portrait studies of such celebrities as George Sand, Berlioz, and Sarah Bernhardt. Nadar was the first to experiment with aerial photography (see Figure 30.14). He also introduced the use of electric light for a series of extraordinary photographs that examined the sewers and catacombs beneath the city of Paris.

Inevitably, nineteenth-century photographs served as social documents: the black-and-white images of poverty-stricken families and ramshackle tenements (see Figure 30.5) produced by Thomas Annan (1829–1887), for

Figure 30.8 JULIA MARGARET CAMERON, *Whisper of the Muse (G. F. Watts and Children)*, ca. 1865. Photograph.

Figure 30.9 MATHEW B. BRADY or staff, *Dead Confederate Soldier with Gun, Petersburg, Virginia*, 1865. Photograph. The four-year-long American Civil War produced the largest number of casualties of any war in American history. Brady hired staff photographers to assist him in photographing the military campaigns and battles, a project that produced some 3500 photographs but left him bankrupt.

instance, record with gritty Realism the notorious slums of nineteenth-century Glasgow, Scotland. Such photographs could easily illustrate the novels of Charles Dickens. In a similar vein, the eyewitness photographs of the American Civil War (1861–1865) produced by Mathew B. Brady (1823–1896) and his staff testify to the importance of the professional photographer as a chronicler of human life. Brady's 3500 Civil War photographs include mundane scenes of barracks and munitions as well as unflinching views of human carnage (Figure **30.9**). By the end of the century, the Kodak "point and shoot" handheld camera gave vast numbers of ordinary people the freedom to take their own photographic images.

Courbet and French Realist Painting

In painting no less than in literature and photography, Realism came to challenge the Romantic style. The Realist preference for concrete, matter-of-fact depictions of everyday life provided a sober alternative to both the remote, exotic, and heroic imagery of the Romantics and the noble and elevated themes of the Neoclassicists. Obedient to the credo that artists must confront the experiences and appearances of their own time, Realist painters abandoned the nostalgic landscapes and heroic themes of Romantic art in favor of compositions depicting the consequences of industrialization (see Figure 30.3) and the lives of ordinary men and women.

The leading Realist of nineteenth-century French painting was Gustave Courbet (1819–1877). A farmer's son, he was a self-taught artist, an outspoken socialist, and a staunch defender of the Realist cause. "A painter," he protested, "should paint only what he can see." Indeed, most of Courbet's works—portraits, landscapes, and contemporary scenes—remain true to the tangible facts of his immediate vision. With the challenge "Show me an angel and I'll paint one," he taunted both the Romantics and the Neoclassicists. Not angels but ordinary individuals in their actual settings and circumstances interested Courbet.

In *The Stone-Breakers*, Courbet depicted two rural laborers performing the most menial of physical tasks (Figure **30.10**). The painting, which Courbet's friend Proudhon called "the first socialist picture," outraged the critics because its subject matter is mundane and its figures are crude, ragged, and totally unidealized. Moreover, the figures were positioned with their backs turned toward the viewer, thus violating, by nineteenth-century standards, the rules of propriety and decorum enshrined in French academic art (see chapter 21). But despite such "violations" Courbet's painting appealed to the masses. In a country whose population was still two-thirds rural and largely poor, the stolid dignity of hard labor was a popular subject.

Courbet's contemporary Jean-François Millet (1814–1875) did not share his reformist zeal; he nevertheless devoted his career to painting the everyday lives of the rural proletariat. His depictions of hard-working farm laborers earned him the title "the peasant painter." In *Gleaners* (Figure **30.11**), three ordinary peasant women pursue the menial task of gathering the bits of grain left over after the harvest. Delineated with ennobling simplicity, these stoop-laborers are as ordinary and anonymous as Courbet's stone-breakers, but, set against a broad and ennobling landscape, they appear dignified and graceful.

Figure 30.10 GUSTAVE COURBET, *The Stone-Breakers*, 1849. Oil on canvas, 5 ft. 3 in. × 8 ft. 6 in.

Figure 30.11 JEAN-FRANÇOIS MILLET, *Gleaners*, ca. 1857. Oil on canvas, approx. 2 ft. 9 in. × 3 ft. 8 in. Millet's portrayals of rural women at work—spinning, sewing, tending sheep, and feeding children—idealized the female as selfless and saintly, and offered a somewhat romanticized view of the laboring classes.

Figure 30.12 GUSTAVE COURBET, *Burial at Ornans*, 1849–1850. Oil on canvas, 10 ft. 3 in. × 21 ft. 9 in. For the introduction to the catalogue that accompanied his one-man show, Courbet wrote a *Realist Manifesto* that stated his aim "to translate the customs, the ideas, and the appearance" of his epoch according to his own estimation. A leading critic claimed that he had depicted "the modern bourgeois in all his ridiculousness, ugliness, and beauty."

While Courbet's scene has the "random" look of a snapshot, Millet's composition, in which the distant haystacks subtly echo the curved backs of the workers, appears more formal and contrived. Against Courbet's undiluted Realism, Millet's perception seems Romanticized.

A landmark even in its own time, *Gleaners* became a symbol of the dignity of hard work, a nostalgic reminder of a way of life quickly disappearing before encroaching industrialization. As such, it was copied and mass-produced in numerous engraved editions.

Courbet, however, remained brutally loyal to nature and the mundane world; he knew that the carefree peasant was an idyllic stereotype that existed not in real life, but rather in the urban imagination. He would have agreed with his contemporary, the British novelist George Eliot (Mary Ann Evans), that "no one who is well acquainted with the English peasantry can pronounce them merry."

Courbet's most daring record of ordinary life was his monumental *Burial at Ornans* (Figure **30.12**). The huge canvas (over 10 x 21 feet) consists of fifty-two life-sized

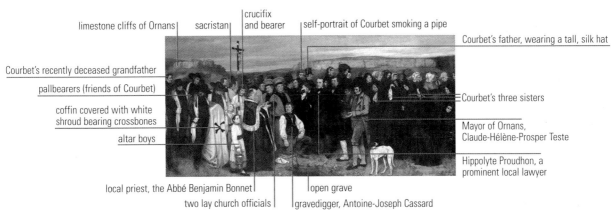

limestone cliffs of Ornans | sacristan | crucifix and bearer | self-portrait of Courbet smoking a pipe

Courbet's father, wearing a tall, silk hat

Courbet's recently deceased grandfather

pallbearers (friends of Courbet)

coffin covered with white shroud bearing crossbones

altar boys

Courbet's three sisters

Mayor of Ornans, Claude-Hélène-Prosper Teste

Hippolyte Proudhon, a prominent local lawyer

local priest, the Abbé Benjamin Bonnet

two lay church officials | open grave

gravedigger, Antoine-Joseph Cassard

figures disposed informally around the edges of a freshly dug grave. Paintings of this size normally depicted historical or religious subjects. Here, however, inspired by the funeral of his great uncle, Courbet depicts the plain-looking (and even homely) townspeople of Ornans. He minimizes the display of pomp and ceremony traditional to Western representations of Christian burial, which emphasized the ritual aspects of death and disposal. The kneeling gravedigger and the attendant dog are as important to the picture as the priest and his retinue. And the mourners, while crowded together, play a more prominent role in the composition than the deceased. With the objectivity of a camera eye, Courbet banished from his view all sentimentality and artifice. When the painting was rejected by the Universal Exhibition of 1855, Courbet rented a space near the exhibition grounds, put up a tent, and displayed the *Burial* along with thirty-eight of his paintings. He called the space "The Pavilion of Realism." For this, the first one-man show in history, Courbet charged a small admission fee.

Daumier's Social Realism

The French artist Honoré Daumier (1808–1879) left the world a detailed record of the social life of his time. He had no formal academic education, but his earliest training was in **lithography**—a printmaking process created by drawing on a stone plate (Figure 30.13). Lithography, a product of nineteenth-century print technology, was a cheap and popular means of providing illustrations for newspapers, magazines, and books.

Daumier produced over 4000 lithographs, often turning out two to three per week for various Paris newspapers and journals. For his subject matter, he turned directly to the

Figure 30.14 **HONORÉ DAUMIER**, *Nadar Raising Photography to the Heights of Art*, 1862. Lithograph. The balloonist, photographer, draftsman, and journalist Gaspard-Félix Tournachon, called Nadar, took his first photograph from a balloon. The aerial balloon, built in 1863, inspired some of the adventure novels of the science-fiction writer Jules Verne (see chapter 37). Nadar also pioneered the use of artificial lighting, by which he was able to photograph the catacombs of Paris.

world around him: the streets of Paris, the theater, the law courts. The advancing (and often jarring) technology of modern life also attracted Daumier's interest: pioneer experiments in aerial photography (Figure 30.14), the telegraph, the sewing machine, the repeating rifle, the railroad, and urban renewal projects that included widening the streets of Paris. But Daumier did not simply depict the facts of modern life; he frequently ridiculed them. Skeptical as to whether new technology and social progress could radically alter the human condition, he drew attention to characteristic human weaknesses, from the the all too familiar complacency and greed of self-serving political figures to the pretensions of the *nouveaux riches*.

One of the popular institutions mocked by Daumier was the French *Salon* (Figure 30.15). The *Salon de Paris* originated with the Royal Academy of Painting and Sculpture,

Figure 30.13 Lithography is a method of making prints from a flat surface; it is also called planography. An image is first drawn or painted with an oil-based lithographic crayon or pencil on a smooth limestone surface. The surface is wiped with water, which will not stick to the applied areas of greasy lithographic ink because oil and water do not mix. The greasy areas resist the water and are thus exposed. The surface is then rolled with printing ink, which adheres only to the parts drawn in the oil-based medium. Dampened paper is placed over the stone, and a special flatbed press rubs the back of the paper, transferring the work from the stone to the covering sheet.

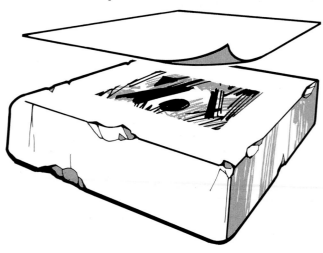

Science and Technology

1798	Aloys Senefelder (Bavarian) develops lithography
1822	William Church (American) patents an automatic typesetting machine
1844	wood-pulp production provides cheap paper for newspapers and periodicals

Figure 30.15 HONORE DAUMIER, *Free Admission Day—Twenty-Five Degrees of Heat* from the series "Le Public du Salon," published in *Le Charivari* (May 17, 1852), p.10. Lithograph. 11⅛ × 8⅝ in. The inscription reads "A day when one does not pay. Twenty-five degrees celsius."

founded in 1648 (see chapter 21). Exhibiting work at the *Salon* was a sign of royal favor and a sure path to success. Held annually during the eighteenth century at the palace of the Louvre, the juried exhibitions were public events that ran for weeks, attracting huge crowds, including newly minted art critics. Paintings were exhibited from floor to ceiling, taking up all the available space, and printed catalogues accompanied the exhibition. By the mid-nineteenth century these annual government-sponsored juried exhibitions, held in large commercial halls, had become symbols of entrenched, academic tastes. Daumier's lithographs satirized the *Salon* as a "grand occasion" attended by hoards of gaping urbanites.

The ancestors of modern-day political cartoons, Daumier's lithographs conveyed his bitter opposition to the monarchy, political corruption, and profiteering. Such criticism courted danger, especially since in mid nineteenth-century France it was illegal to caricature individuals publicly without first obtaining their permission. Following the publication of his 1831 lithograph, which depicted the French king Louis Philippe as an obese Gargantua atop a commode/throne from which he defecated bags of gold, Daumier spent six months in jail.

Primarily a graphic artist, Daumier completed fewer than three hundred paintings. In *The Third-Class Carriage*, he captured on canvas the shabby monotony of nineteenth-century lower-class railway travel (see Figure 30.1). The part of the European train in which tickets were the least expensive was also, of course, the least comfortable: it lacked glass windows (hence was subject to more than average amounts of smoke, cinders, and clatter) and was equipped with hard wooden benches rather than cushioned seats. Three generations of poor folk—an elderly woman, a younger woman, and her children—occupy the foreground of Daumier's painting. Their lumpish bodies suggest weariness and futility, yet they convey a humble dignity reminiscent of Rembrandt's figures (see chapter 22). Dark and loosely sketched oil glazes underscore the mood of cheerless resignation. Daumier produced a forthright image of common humanity in a contemporary urban setting.

The Scandalous Realism of Manet

The French painter Edouard Manet (1832–1883) presented an unsettling challenge to the world of art. A native Parisian who chose painting over a career in law, Manet was an admirer of the art of the old masters. He was equally enthralled by the life of his own time—by Parisians and their middle-class pleasures. In a large, brilliantly painted canvas entitled *Déjeuner sur l'herbe* (*Luncheon on the Grass*), he shocked public taste by taking a Classical theme and putting it in modern dress (Figure **30.16**). *Déjeuner* shows a nude woman enjoying a picnic lunch with two fully clothed male companions; a second, partially clothed woman bathes in a nearby stream. The representation of the female nude was considered the ultimate subject in academic art. Her identity in ancient sculpture, as in Western art history since the Early Renaissance, was invariably that of a mythological or allegorical figure, such as Venus or Charity. Manet's nude, however, was nothing more than an ordinary, naked woman. By picturing the female nude—and one who brazenly stares out at the viewer—in a contemporary setting occupied by clothed men, Manet offended public morality and academic tradition. He also destroyed the barrier between fantasy and everyday reality.

Figure 30.16 EDOUARD MANET, *Déjeuner sur l'herbe*, 1863. Oil on canvas, 7 ft. × 8 ft. 10 in. The still life in the lower left testifies to Manet's technical skills as a painter.

From an historical perspective, Manet's subject matter—the female nude in a landscape—was quite traditional; the artist might have had reference to such works as Titian's *Pastoral Concert* (Figure **30.17**). *Déjeuner*'s three central figures are based directly on a sixteenth-century engraving based on a Renaissance tapestry, itself derived from a lost painting by Raphael (Figure **30.18**). Nevertheless, the figures in the painting are neither woodland nymphs nor Olympian gods; rather, they are Manet's favorite model (Victorine Meurent), and his future brother-in-law (the reclining male figure).

By "updating" traditional imagery with such off-handed, in-your-face immediacy, Manet was making a statement that—as with *Madame Bovary*—targeted the degeneracy of French society. Like Flaubert, who combined authenticity of detail and an impersonal narrative style, Manet took a neutral stance that presented the subject with cool objectivity. It is no surprise that the jury of the Royal Academy rejected *Déjeuner*, refusing to hang the painting in the *Salon* exhibition of 1863. Nevertheless, that same year it was displayed in an alternate venue: the *Salon des Refusés*, a landmark exhibition of rejected paintings, was authorized by the French head of state in response to public agitation against the tyranny of the Academy. No sooner was Manet's painting hung than visitors tried to poke holes in the canvas and critics launched attacks on its coarse "improprieties." *Déjeuner* was pronounced scandalous. "The nude does

Figure 30.17 TITIAN (begun by Giorgione), *Pastoral Concert*, ca. 1505. Oil on canvas, 3 ft. 7¼ in. × 4 ft. 6¼ in.

Figure 30.18 MARCANTONIO RAIMONDI detail from *The Judgment of Paris*, ca. 1520. Engraving after Raphael tapestry.

not have a good figure," wrote one journalist, "and one cannot imagine anything uglier than the man stretched out beside her, who has not even thought of removing, out of doors, his horrible padded cap." While Manet's paintings met with repeated criticism, they were defended by his good friend Emile Zola, who penned a short biography of the artist in 1867 (see Figure 30.7). Zola praised Manet's works as "simple and direct translations of reality," observing with some acuity: "He treats figure paintings as the academic painter treats still lifes . . . He neither sings nor philosophizes. He paints, and that is all."

In a second painting of 1863, *Olympia*, Manet again "debased" a traditional subject: the reclining nude (Figure **30.19**). Lacking the subtle allure of a Titian Venus or an Ingres odalisque, the short, stocky nude (Victorine Meurent again) looks boldly at the viewer. Her satin slippers, the black ribbon at her throat, and other enticing details distinguish her as a courtesan—a high-class prostitute. Manet's urban contemporaries were not blind to this fact, but the critics were unsparingly brutal. One journalist called Olympia "a sort of female gorilla" and warned, "Truly, young girls and women about to become mothers would do well, if they are wise, to run away from this spectacle." Like Flaubert's *Madame Bovary* or Zola's *Nana*, Manet's *Olympia* desentimentalized the female image. By rendering the ideal in commonplace terms, he not only offended public taste, but challenged the traditional view of art as the bearer of noble themes.

Manet also violated academic convention by employing new painting techniques. Imitating current photographic practice, he bathed his figures in bright light and, using a minimum of shading, flattened forms in a manner inspired by Japanese prints (see Figure 31.13). His practice of eliminating halftones and laying on fresh, opaque colors

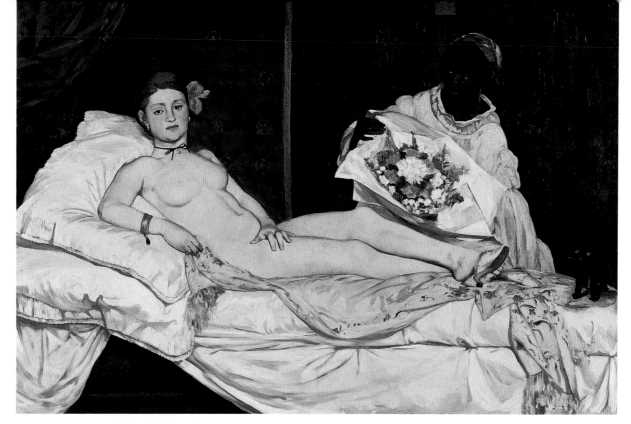

Figure 30.19 EDOUARD MANET, *Olympia*, 1863. Oil on canvas, 4 ft. 3¼ in. × 6 ft. 2¾ in. A maid presents the courtesan with a bouquet of flowers from an admirer, who, based on the startled response of the black cat, may have just entered the room. Commenting on the unmodulated flatness of the figure, Courbet compared Olympia to the Queen of Spades in a deck of playing cards.

Figure 30.20 WILLIAM MICHAEL HARNETT, *The Artist's Letter Rack*, 1879. Oil on canvas, 30 × 25 in.

(instead of building up form by means of thin, transparent glazes) anticipated impressionism, a style he embraced later in his career.

Realism in American Painting

Although most American artists received their training in European art schools, their taste for Realism seems to have sprung from a native affection for the factual and the material aspects of their immediate surroundings. In the late nineteenth century, an era of gross materialism known as the Gilded Age, America produced an extraordinary number of first-rate Realist painters. These individuals explored a wide variety of subjects, from still life and portraiture to landscape and genre painting. Like such literary giants as Mark Twain, American Realist painters fused keen observation with remarkable descriptive skills.

One of the most talented of the American Realists was William M. Harnett (1848–1892), a still-life painter and a master of *trompe l'oeil* ("fools the eye") illusionism. Working in the tradition of seventeenth-century Dutch masters, Harnett recorded mundane objects with such hair-fine precision that some of them—letters, newspaper clippings, and calling cards—seem to be pasted on the canvas (Figure **30.20**).

In the genre of portraiture, the Philadelphia artist Thomas Eakins (1844–1916) mastered the art of producing uncompromising likenesses such as that of the poet Walt Whitman (see Figure 27.12). Like most nineteenth-century American artists, Eakins received his training in European art schools, but he ultimately emerged as a painter of the American scene and as an influential art instructor. At the Pennsylvania Academy of Fine Arts, he received criticism for his insistence on working from nude models and was forced to resign for removing the loincloth of a male model in a class that included female students.

Eakins was among the first artists to choose subjects from the world of sports, such as boxing and boating. A photographer of some note, Eakins used the camera to collect visual data for his paintings. He was among the first artists to use his own photographs as the basis for true-to-life pictorial compositions.

Eakins' fascination with scientific anatomy—he dissected cadavers at Jefferson Medical College in Philadelphia—led him to produce some unorthodox representations of medical training and practice. One of his most notable canvases, *The Agnew Clinic* (see Figure 30.21), is a dispassionate view of a hospital amphitheater in which the surgeon P. Hayes Agnew lectures to students on the subject of the mastectomy that is being performed under his supervision.

Eakins' student, Henry Ossawa Tanner (1859–1937)—like many other African-American artists—found Paris more receptive than America. A talented genre painter,

MAKING CONNECTIONS

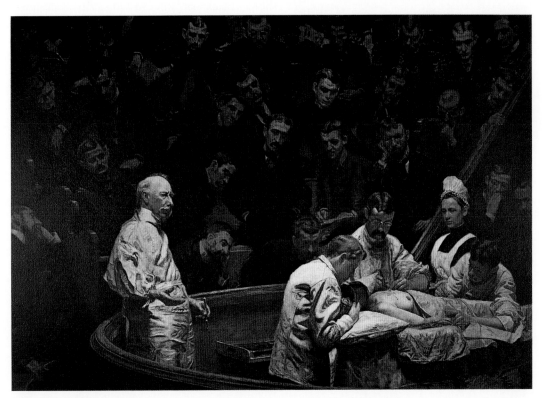

Figure 30.21 THOMAS EAKINS, *The Agnew Clinic*, 1889. Oil on canvas, 6 ft. 2½ in. × 10 ft. 10½ in. This wall-sized painting is the largest of Eakins' canvases. At the far right is the likeness of Eakins himself, painted by his wife Susan.

Figure 30.22 REMBRANDT VAN RIJN, *The Anatomy Lesson of Dr. Nicolaes Tulp*, 1632. Oil on canvas, 5 ft. 3⅜ in. × 7 ft. 1¼ in.

In 1889 Eakins accepted a commission offered by students at the University of Pennsylvania's School of Medicine to paint a portrait commemorating the retirement of a one of their favorite professors. Eakins suggested a clinic scene that would include the surgeon's collaborators and class members. In drafting the composition, he surely had in mind Rembrandt's famous group portrait, *The Anatomy Lesson of Dr. Nicolaes Tulp* (Figure **30.22**). Eakins' painting (Figure **30.21**) shares Rembrandt's dramatic staging, use of light to illuminate figures in darkened space, and dedication to realistic detail. Both paintings communicate a fresh and stubbornly precise record of the natural world.

Figure 30.23 HENRY OSSAWA TANNER, *The Banjo Lesson*, ca. 1893. Oil on canvas, 49 × 35½ in.

on-the-scene documentary paintings and drawings of the American Civil War, which *Harper's* converted to wood-engraved illustrations (Figure **30.24**). Although Homer often generalized the facts of the events he actually witnessed, he neither moralized nor allegorized his subjects (as did, for instance, Goya or Delacroix). His talent for graphic selectivity and dramatic concentration rivaled that of America's first war photographer, Mathew Brady (see Figure 30.9).

Apart from two trips to Europe, Homer spent most of his life in New England, where he painted subjects that were both ordinary and typically American. Scenes of hunting and fishing reveal his deep affection for nature, while his many genre paintings reflect a fascination with the activities of American women and children.

Homer was interested in the role of African-Americans in contemporary culture, but critical of visual representations that portrayed America's slaves as merry and content. One of his most provocative paintings, *The Gulf Stream*, shows a black man adrift in a rudderless boat surrounded by shark-filled waters that are whipped by the winds of an impending tornado (Figure **30.25**). While realistic in execution, the painting may be interpreted as a metaphor for the isolation and plight of black Americans in the decades following the Civil War. Homer shared with earlier nineteenth-century figures, including Turner, Melville, and Géricault, an almost obsessive interest in the individual's life and death struggle with the sea. However, compared (for instance) with Géricault's theatrical rendering of man against nature in *The Raft of the "Medusa"* (see Figure 29.4), which he probably saw in Paris, Homer's painting is a matter-of-fact study of human resignation in the face of deadly peril. As with many publicly displayed nineteenth-century paintings, it provoked immediate critical response.

landscape artist, and photographer, Tanner brought to his work a concern for simple, everyday events as practiced by working-class people. In *The Banjo Lesson*, he depicts an intimate domestic scene in which a young boy receives musical instruction from his grandfather (Figure **30.23**). A fine technician and a fluent colorist, Tanner showed regularly in Paris. In 1909, he was elected to the National Academy of Design, New York.

American Realists were keenly aware of the new art of photography; some, like Tanner and Eakins, were themselves fine photographers. But they were also indebted to the world of journalism, which assumed increasing importance in transmitting literate culture. Winslow Homer (1836–1910) began his career as a newspaper illustrator and a reporter for the New York magazine *Harper's Weekly*. The first professional artist to serve as a war correspondent, he produced

Figure 30.24 WINSLOW HOMER, *The War for the Union: A Bayonet Charge*, published in *Harper's Weekly*, July 12, 1862. Wood engraving, 13⅜ × 20⅝ in.

Figure 30.25 WINSLOW HOMER, *The Gulf Stream*, 1899. Oil on canvas, 28⅛ in. × 4 ft. 1⅛ in. Homer added the fully rigged sailing ship at the horizon on the left some time after the painting was exhibited.

Answering the critics, Eakins wryly replied: "The criticisms of *The Gulf Stream* by old women and others are noted. You may inform these people that the Negro did not starve to death, he was not eaten by the sharks, the water spout did not hit him, and he was rescued by a passing ship . . ."

American audiences loved their Realist painters, but, occasionally, critics voiced mixed feelings. The American novelist Henry James (1843–1916), whose novels probed the differences between European and American character, assessed what he called Homer's "perfect realism" with these words:

> He is almost barbarously simple, and, to our eye, he is horribly ugly; but there is nevertheless something one likes about him. What is it? For ourselves, it is not his subjects. We frankly confess that we detest his subjects—his barren plank fences, his glaring, bald, blue skies, his big, dreary, vacant lots of meadows, his freckled, straight-haired Yankee urchins, his flat-breasted maidens, suggestive of a dish of rural doughnuts and pie, his calico sun-bonnets, his flannel shirts, his cowhide boots. He has chosen the least pictorial features of the least pictorial range of scenery and civilization; he has resolutely treated them as if they were pictorial, as if they were every inch as good as Capri or Tangiers; and, to reward his audacity, he has incontestably succeeded. It . . . is a proof that if you will only be doggedly literal, though you may often be unpleasing, you will at least have a stamp of your own.

Late Nineteenth-Century Architecture

In the nineteenth century, the history of architecture was revolutionized by the use of an exciting new structural medium: cast iron. Providing strength without bulk, cast iron allowed architects to span broader widths and raise structures to greater heights than achieved by traditional stone masonry. Although cast iron would change the history of architecture more dramatically than any advance in technology since the Roman invention of concrete, European architects were slow to realize its potential. In England, where John Nash had used cast iron in 1815 as the structural frame for the Brighton Pavilion (see Figure 29.14), engineers did not begin construction on the first cast-iron suspension bridge until 1836; and not until mid-century was iron used as skeletal support for mills, warehouses, and railroad stations.

The innovator in the use of iron for public buildings was, in fact, not an architect but a distinguished horticulturalist and greenhouse designer, Joseph Paxton (1801–1865). Paxton's Crystal Palace (Figure **30.26**), erected for the Great Exhibition in London in 1851, was the world's first prefabricated building and the forerunner of the "functional" steel and glass architecture of the twentieth century. Consisting entirely of cast- and wrought-iron girders and 18,000 panes of glass, and erected in only nine months, the 1851-foot-long structure—its length a

Figure 30.26 JOSEPH PAXTON, interior of Crystal Palace, 1851. Cast- and wrought-iron and glass, length 1851 ft. Assembled entirely on site from prefabricated components, the Crystal Palace housed some 14,000 exhibitions. The three-story structure, illuminated mainly by natural light, anticipated today's modern shopping malls.

symbolic reference to the year of the exhibition—resembled a gigantic greenhouse. Light entered through its transparent walls and air filtered in through louvered windows. Thousands flocked to see the Crystal Palace; yet most European architects found the glass and iron structure bizarre. Although heroic in both size and conception, it had almost no immediate impact on European architecture. Dismantled after the Great Exhibition and moved to a new site, however, it was hailed as a masterpiece of prefabrication and portability decades before it burned to the ground in 1936.

Science and Technology

1773	the first cast-iron bridge is built in England
1851	the first international industrial exposition opens in London
1856	Henry Bessemer (British) perfects the process for producing inexpensive steel
1857	E. G. Otis (American) installs the first safety elevator
1863	the first "subway" (the London Underground) begins operation

Like the Crystal Palace, the Eiffel Tower (Figure **30.27**) originated as a novelty, but it soon became emblematic of early modernism. The viewing tower constructed by the engineer Gustave Eiffel (1832–1923) for the Paris World Exhibition of 1889 is, in essence, a tall (1064-foot-high) cast-iron skeleton equipped with elevators that offer visitors magnificent aerial views of Paris. Aesthetically, the tower linked the architectural traditions of the past with those of the future: its sweeping curves, delicate tracery, and dramatic verticality recall the glories of the Gothic cathedral, while its majestic ironwork anticipates the austere abstractions of International Style architecture (see chapter 32). Condemned as a visual monstrosity when it was first erected, the Eiffel Tower emerged as a positive symbol of the soaring confidence of the industrial age. This landmark of heroic materialism remained for four decades (until the advent of the American skyscraper) the tallest structure in the world.

In an age of advancing industrialization, ornamental structures such as the Crystal Palace and the Eiffel Tower gave way to functional ones. Inevitably, the skyscraper would become the prime architectural expression of modern corporate power and the urban scene. By 1850, there were seven American cities with more than 100,000 inhabitants, and before 1900 the populations of at least three of these—New York, Philadelphia, and Chicago—swelled as a result of the thousands of immigrants who came to live and work in the metropolitan community. The physical character of the premodern city, whose buildings were no more than four stories high, changed enormously with the construction of skyscrapers.

Multistoried vertical buildings were made possible by the advancing technology of steel, a medium that was perfected in 1856. Lighter, stronger, and more resilient than cast iron, steel used as a frame could carry the entire weight of a structure, thus eliminating the need for solid weight-bearing masonry walls. Steel made possible a whole new concept of building design characterized by lighter materials, flat roofs, and large windows. In 1868, the six-story Equitable Life Insurance Building in New York City was the first office structure to install an electric elevator. By the 1880s, architects and engineers united the new steel frame with the elevator to raise structures more than ten stories. William Le Baron Jenney (1832–1907) built the first all-steel-frame skyscraper, the Home Insurance Building in Chicago, which, ironically, hides its metal skeleton beneath a traditional-looking brick and masonry façade. It fell to his successor, Louis Henry Sullivan (1856–1924), to design multistory buildings, such as the Guaranty Building in Buffalo (Figure **30.28**), whose exteriors proudly reflect the structural simplicity of their steel frames. "Form should

Figure 30.27 GUSTAVE EIFFEL, Eiffel Tower, Paris, 1889.
Wrought iron on a reinforced concrete base, original height 984 ft.

Figure 30.28 LOUIS HENRY SULLIVAN and **DANKMAR ADLER**,
Guaranty Building, Buffalo, New York, 1894–1895. Steel frame.

follow function," he insisted. Within decades, the American skyscraper became an icon of modern urban culture.

Nineteenth-century steel and cast-iron technology also contributed to the construction of bridges. In 1870, work began on the first steel-wire suspension bridge in the United States: the Brooklyn Bridge (Figure **30.29**). Designed by John Augustus Roebling (1806–1926), who had earlier engineered bridges in Pennsylvania, Ohio, and Texas, the Brooklyn Bridge (upon its completion in 1883) would be the largest suspension bridge in the world. Its main span, which crosses the East River between Manhattan and Brooklyn, measures some 1600 feet. This celebrated bridge reflects the marriage of modern steel technology and Neo-Gothic design, evident in the elegant granite and limestone arches.

Realism in Music

In Italian opera of the late nineteenth century, a movement called **verismo** (literally, "truth-ism," but more generally "Realism") paralleled the Realist style in literature and art. Realist composers rejected the heroic characters of Romantic grand opera and presented the problems and conflicts of people in familiar and everyday—if somewhat melodramatic—situations. The foremost "verist" was the Italian composer Giacomo Puccini (1858–1924).

Puccini's *La Bohème*, the tragic love story of young artists (called "bohemians" for their unconventional lifestyles) in the Latin Quarter of Paris, was based on a nineteenth-century novel called *Scenes of Bohemian Life*. The colorful orchestration and powerfully melodic arias of *La Bohème* evoke the joys and sorrows of true-to-life characters. While this poignant musical drama was received coldly at its premiere in 1897, *La Bohème* has become one of the best loved of nineteenth-century operas.

Another of Puccini's operas, *Madame Butterfly*, offered European audiences a timely, if moralizing, view of the Western presence in Asia and one that personalized the clash of radically different cultures. The story, which takes place in Nagasaki in the years following the reopening of Japanese ports to the West, begins with the wedding of a young United States navy lieutenant to a fifteen-year-old *geisha* (a Japanese girl trained as a social companion to men) known as "Butterfly." The American is soon forced to leave with his fleet, while for three years Butterfly, now the mother of his son, faithfully awaits his return. When, finally, he arrives (accompanied by his new American bride) only to claim the child, the griefstricken Butterfly takes the only honorable path available to her: she commits suicide. This tragic tale, which had appeared as a novel, a play, and a magazine story, was based on a true incident. Set to some of Puccini's most lyrical music for voice and orchestra, *Madame Butterfly* reflects the composer's fascination with Japanese culture, a fascination most

evident in his poetic characterization of the delicate Butterfly. While neither the story nor the music of the opera is authentically Japanese, its *verismo* lies in its frank (though poignant) account of the bitter consequences that often accompanied the meeting of East and West.

Chronology

1830	French conquest of Algeria
1839–1850	Opium Wars in China
1848	antigovernment revolutions in France and Central Europe
1853	beginning of Meiji rule in Japan
1860	unification of Italy
1861–1865	United States Civil War
1869	completion of the U.S. transcontinental railroad
1871	unification of Germany

Figure 30.29 JOHN AUGUSTUS and **WASHINGTON AUGUSTUS ROEBLING**, Brooklyn Bridge, New York, 1869–1883. Currier and Ives print, 1877.

LOOKING BACK

The Global Dominion of the West

- During the second half of the nineteenth century, as Western industrialization accelerated, Realism came to rival Romanticism both as a style and as an attitude of mind.
- Western industrialization and the materialistic values with which it was allied precipitated imperialism and colonialism, both of which had a shaping influence on the non-Western world. The heavy hand of Western imperialism in some parts of Africa, Asia, and in the Middle East had a crippling effect on independent growth and productivity.

Nineteenth-Century Social Theory

- The ideologies of liberalism, conservatism, utilitarianism, and socialism offered varying solutions to nineteenth-century social and economic inequities. Marxist communism called for violent proletarian revolution that would end private ownership of the means of economic production.
- The leading proponent of liberalism, John Stuart Mill, defended the exercise of individual liberty as protected by the state.
- Mill's opposition to the subordination of women gave strong support to nineteenth-century movements for women's rights.

Realism in Literature

- In literature, Realism emerged as a style concerned with recording contemporary subject matter in true-to-life terms.
- Such novelists as Dickens in England, Dostoevsky and Tolstoy in Russia, Flaubert and Zola in France, and Twain and Chopin in America described contemporary social conditions sympathetically and with fidelity to detail.
- Flaubert and Chopin provided alternatives to Romantic idealism in their realistic characterizations of female figures.
- Zola's naturalistic novels pictured human beings as determined by hereditary and sociological factors, while Ibsen's fearless portrayal of class and gender opened a new chapter in modern drama.

Realism in the Visual Arts

- By the mid nineteenth century the camera was used to document all aspects of contemporary life as well as to provide artists with detailed visual data.
- In painting, Courbet led the Realist movement with canvases depicting the activities of humble and commonplace men and women. Daumier employed the new technique of lithography to show his deep concern for political and social conditions in rapidly modernizing France.
- With the landmark paintings *Déjeuner sur l'herbe* and *Olympia*, Edouard Manet shocked public taste by modernizing Classical subjects and violating conventional painting techniques.
- American Realism is best represented by the *trompe l'oeil* paintings of William Harnett and the down-to-earth subjects of Thomas Eakins and Winslow Homer.

Late Nineteenth-Century Architecture

- Paxton's Crystal Palace, the world's first prefabricated cast-iron structure, offered a prophetic glimpse into the decades that would produce steel-framed skyscrapers.
- In an age of advancing industrialization, ornamental structures such as the Crystal Palace and the Eiffel Tower gave way to functional ones. Inevitably, the skyscraper would become the prime architectural expression of modern corporate power and the urban scene.

Realism in Music

- *Verismo* opera departed from Romantic tradition by seeking to capture the lives of men and women with a truth to nature comparable to that of Realist novels and paintings.
- In the opera *Madame Butterfly*, the Italian "verist" Giacomo Puccini presented a timely view of America's imperialistic presence in Asia.

Glossary

capitalist one who provides investment capital in economic ventures

entrepreneur one who organizes, manages, and assumes the risks of a business

lithography a printmaking process created by drawing on a stone plate; see Figure 30.13

proletariat a collective term describing industrial workers who lack their own means of production and hence sell their labor to live

verismo (Italian, "realism") a type of late nineteenth-century opera that presents a realistic picture of life, instead of a story based in myth, legend, or ancient history

Chapter

31

The Move Toward Modernism

ca. 1875–1900

"Is not the nineteenth century ... a century of decadence?"
Nietzsche

Figure 31.1 CAMILLE PISSARRO, *Le Boulevard Montmartre: Rainy Weather, Afternoon*, 1897. Oil on canvas, 20⅝ × 26 in. In his long career, Pissarro painted hundreds of rural and urban landscapes. His techniques in capturing the effects of light influenced the work of his fellow Impressionists. Nevertheless, he sold very few paintings in his lifetime.

LOOKING AHEAD

During the last quarter of the nineteenth century, France emerged as the center of Western artistic production. Paris became the melting pot for artists and intellectuals, composers and journalists. London and Paris hosted World's Fairs that brought the arts and cultures of Japan, Africa, and Oceania to the attention of astonished Westerners. In an era of relative world peace and urban prosperity, Western artists were preoccupied with the pleasures of life and the fleeting world of the senses. They initiated styles—Symbolism, Impressionism, and Postimpressionism —that neither idealized the world nor described it literally. Much of their art was driven by aesthetic principles that—similar to music—communicated no specific meaning, but rather, evoked feeling by way of pure form and color. Their goals were described by Walter Pater in 1868 with the slogan *l'art pour l'art*, or "art for art's sake."

Late nineteenth-century science and technology helped to drive this new approach in the arts. The last decades of the century saw the invention of synthetic oil paints available in portable tubes. In 1873, the British physicist James Clerk Maxwell (1831–1879) published his *Treatise on Electricity and Magnetism*, which explained that light waves consisting of electromagnetic particles produced radiant energy. In 1879, after numerous failures, the American inventor Thomas Edison (1847–1931) moved beyond scientific theory to create the first efficient incandescent light bulb. Edison's light bulb provided a sharper perception of reality that—along with the camera—helped to shatter the world of romantic illusion. By the year 1880, the telephone transported the human voice over thousands of miles. In the late 1880s, Edison developed the technique of moving pictures. The invention of the internal combustion engine led to the production of automobiles in the 1890s, a decade that also witnessed the invention of the X-ray and the genesis of radiotelegraphy. Such technologies accelerated the tempo of life and drew attention to the role of the senses in defining experience.

Late Nineteenth-Century Thought

Nietzsche's New Morality

The most provocative thinker of the late nineteenth century was the German philosopher and poet Friedrich Wilhelm Nietzsche (1844–1900). Nietzsche was a Classical philologist, a professor of Greek at the university of Basle, and the author of such notable works as *The Birth of Tragedy* (1872), *Thus Spoke Zarathustra* (1883–1892), and *On the Genealogy of Morals* (1887). In these, as in his shorter pieces, Nietzsche voiced the sentiments of the radical moralist. Deeply critical of his own time, he called for a revision of traditional values. He rejected organized religion, attacking Christianity and other institutionalized religions as contributors to the formation of a "slave morality." He was equally critical of democratic institutions, which he saw as rule by mass mediocrity. His goal for humanity was the emergence of a "superman" (*Übermensch*), whose singular vision and courage would, in his view, produce a "master" morality.

Nietzsche did not launch his ideas in the form of a well-reasoned philosophic system, but rather as aphorisms, maxims, and expostulations whose visceral force bear out his claim that he wrote "with his blood." Reflecting the spiritual cynicism of the late nineteenth century, he asked, "Is man merely a mistake of God's? Or God merely a mistake of man's?"

Nietzsche shared with Dostoevsky the view that European materialism had led inevitably to decadence and decline. In *The Antichrist*, published in 1888, shortly before Nietzsche became insane (possibly a result of syphilis), he wrote:

> Mankind does not represent a development toward something better or stronger or higher in the sense accepted today. "Progress" is merely a modern idea, that is, a false ideal. The European of today is vastly inferior in value to the European of the Renaissance: further development is altogether not according to any necessity in the direction of elevation, enhancement, or strength.

The following readings demonstrate Nietzsche's incisive imagination and caustic wit. The first, taken from *The Gay Science* (1882) and entitled "The Madman," is a parable that harnesses Nietzsche's iconoclasm to his gift for prophecy. The others, excerpted from *Twilight of the Idols* (or *How One Philosophizes with a Hammer*, 1888), address the fragile relationship between art and morality and the art for art's sake spirit of the late nineteenth century.

READING 31.1 From the Works of Nietzsche

The Gay Science (1882)

The Madman. Have you not heard of that madman who lit a   1
lantern in the bright morning hours, ran to the market place,
and cried incessantly, "I seek God! I seek God!" As many of
those who do not believe in God were standing around just
then, he provoked much laughter. Why, did he get lost? said
one. Did he lose his way like a child? said another. Or is he
hiding? Is he afraid of us? Has he gone on a voyage? or
emigrated? Thus they yelled and laughed. The madman jumped
into their midst and pierced them with his glances.

"Whither is God" he cried. "I shall tell you. *We have killed*   10
him—you and I. All of us are his murderers. But how have we
done this? How were we able to drink up the sea? Who gave
us the sponge to wipe away the entire horizon? What did we

do when we unchained this earth from its sun? Whither is it moving now? Whither are we moving now? Away from all suns? Are we not plunging continually? Backward, sideward, forward, in all directions? Is there any up or down left? Are we not straying as through an infinite nothing? Do we not feel the breath of empty space? Has it not become colder? Is not night and more night coming on all the while? Must not lanterns be lit in the morning? Do we not hear anything yet of the noise of the gravediggers who are burying God? Do we not smell anything yet of God's decomposition? Gods too decompose. God is dead. God remains dead. And we have killed him. How shall we, the murderers of all murderers, comfort ourselves? What was holiest and most powerful of all that the world has yet owned has bled to death under our knives. Who will wipe this blood off us? What water is there for us to clean ourselves? What festivals of atonement, what sacred games shall we have to invent? Is not the greatness of this deed too great for us? Must not we ourselves become gods simply to seem worthy of it? There has never been a greater deed; and whoever will be born after us—for the sake of this deed he will be part of a higher history than all history hitherto."

Here the madman fell silent and looked again at his listeners; and they too were silent and stared at him in astonishment. At last he threw his lantern on the ground, and it broke and went out. "I come too early," he said then; "my time has not come yet. This tremendous event is still on its way, still wandering—it has not yet reached the ears of man. Lightning and thunder require time, the light of the stars requires time, deeds require time even after they are done, before they can be seen and heard. This deed is still more distant from them than the most distant stars—*and yet they have done it themselves.*"

It has been related further that on that same day the madman entered divers churches and there sang his *requiem aeternam deo.* Led out and called to account, he is said to have replied each time, "What are these churches now if they are not the tombs and sepulchers of God?"

Twilight of the Idols (1888)

L'art pour l'art. The fight against purpose in art is always a fight against the moralizing tendency in art, against its subordination to morality. *L'art pour l'art* means, "The devil take morality!" But even this hostility still betrays the overpowering force of the prejudice. When the purpose of moral preaching and of improving man has been excluded from art, it still does not follow by any means that art is altogether purposeless, aimless, senseless—in short, *l'art pour l'art,* a worm chewing its own tail. "Rather no purpose at all than a moral purpose!"—that is the talk of mere passion. A psychologist, on the other hand, asks: what does all art do? does it not praise? glorify? choose? prefer? With all this it strengthens or weakens certain valuations. Is this merely a "moreover"? an accident? something in which the artist's instinct had no share? Or is it not the very presupposition of the artist's ability? Does his basic instinct aim at art, or rather at the sense of art, at life? at a desirability of life? Art is the great stimulus to life: how could one understand it as purposeless, as aimless, as *l'art pour l'art*?

One question remains: art also makes apparent much that is ugly, hard, and questionable in life; does it not thereby spoil life for us? And indeed there have been philosophers who attributed this sense to it: "liberation from the will" was what Schopenhauer taught as the over-all end of art; and with admiration he found the great utility of tragedy in its "evoking resignation." But this, as I have already suggested, is the pessimist's perspective and "evil eye." We must appeal to the artists themselves. What does the tragic artist communicate of himself? Is it not precisely the state *without* fear in the face of the fearful and questionable that he is showing? This state itself is a great desideratum;[1] whoever knows it, honors it with the greatest honors. He communicates it—*must* communicate it, provided he is an artist, a genius of communication. Courage and freedom of feeling before a powerful enemy, before a sublime calamity, before a problem that arouses dread—this triumphant state is what the tragic artist chooses, what he glorifies. Before tragedy, what is warlike in our soul celebrates its Saturnalia;[2] whoever is used to suffering, whoever seeks out suffering, the heroic man praises his own being through tragedy—to him alone the tragedian presents this drink of sweetest cruelty.

. . . .

One might say that in a certain sense the nineteenth century *also* strove for all that which Goethe as a person had striven for: universality in understanding and in welcoming, letting everything come close to oneself, an audacious realism, a reverence for everything factual. How is it that the over-all result is no Goethe, but chaos, a nihilistic sigh, an utter bewilderment, an instinct of weariness which in practice continually drives toward a recourse to the eighteenth century? (For example, as a romanticism of feeling, as altruism and hypersentimentality, as feminism in taste, as socialism in politics.) Is not the nineteenth century, especially at its close, merely an intensified, *brutalized* eighteenth century, that is, a century of *decadence*? So that Goethe would have been—not merely for Germany, but for all of Europe—a mere interlude, a beautiful "in vain"? But one misunderstands great human beings if one views them from the miserable perspective of some public use. That one cannot put them to any use, that in itself may belong to greatness. . . .

Q. If art excludes moral purpose, what, according to Nietzsche, might be the purpose of art?

Bergson: Intellect and Intuition

While Nietzsche anticipated the darker side of modernism, Henri Bergson (1859–1941) presented a more positive point of view. Bergson, the most important French philosopher of his time, offered a picture of the world that paralleled key developments in the arts and sciences and anticipated modern notions of time and space. Bergson viewed life as a vital impulse that evolved creatively, much like a work of art.

---

[1] Something desired as essential.
[2] An orgy, or unrestrained celebration.

According to Bergson, two primary powers, intellect and intuition, governed the lives of human beings. While intellect perceives experience in individual and discrete terms, or as a series of separate and solid entities, intuition grasps experience as it really is: a perpetual stream of sensations. Intellect isolates and categorizes experience according to logic and geometry; intuition, on the other hand, fuses past and present into one organic whole. For Bergson, instinct (or intuition) is humankind's noblest faculty, and *duration*, or "perpetual becoming," is the very stuff of reality—the essence of life.

In 1889, Bergson published his treatise *Time and Freewill*, in which he described true experience as durational, a constant unfolding in time, and reality, which can only be apprehended intuitively, as a series of qualitative changes that merge into one another without precise definition.

Poetry in the Late Nineteenth Century: The Symbolists

Bergson's poetical view of nature had much in common with the aesthetics of the movement known as *symbolism*, which flourished from roughly 1885 to 1910. The Symbolists held that the visible world does not constitute a true or universal reality. Realistic, objective representation, according to the Symbolists, failed to convey the pleasures of sensory experience and the intuitive world of dreams and myth. The artist's mission was to find a language that embraced the mystical, the erotic, and the ineffable world of the senses. For the Symbolists, reality was a swarm of sensations that could never be described but only *suggested* by poetic symbols—images that elicited moods and feelings beyond literal meanings.

In literature, the leading Symbolists were the French poets Charles Baudelaire (1821–1867), Paul Verlaine (1844–1896), Arthur Rimbaud (1854–1891), and Stéphane Mallarmé (1842–1898), and the Belgian playwright Maurice Maeterlinck (1862–1949). Arthur Rimbaud, who wrote most of his poetry while in his teens, envisioned the poet as seer. Freeing language from its descriptive function, his prose poems shattered the rational sequence of words and phrases, detaching them from their traditional associations and recombining them so as to create powerful sense impressions. In one of the prose poems from his *Illuminations*, for example, Rimbaud describes flowers as "Bits of yellow gold seeded in agate, pillars of mahogany supporting a dome of emeralds, bouquets of white satin and fine rods of ruby surround the water rose." The Symbolists tried to represent nature without effusive commentary, to "take eloquence and wring its neck," as Verlaine put it. In order to imitate the indefiniteness of experience itself, they might string words together without logical connections. Hence, in Symbolist poetry, images seem to flow into one another, and "meaning" often lies between the lines.

Mallarmé

For Stéphane Mallarmé, the "new art" of poetry was a religion, and the poet–artist was its oracle. Inclined to melancholy, he cultivated an intimate literary style based on the "music" of words. He held that art was "accessible only to the few" who nurtured "the inner life." Mallarmé's poems are tapestries of sensuous, dreamlike motifs that resist definition and analysis. To name a thing, Mallarmé insisted, was to destroy it, while to suggest experience was to create it.

Mallarmé's pastoral poem, "L'après-midi d'un faune" ("The Afternoon of a Faun") is a reverie of an erotic encounter between two mythological woodland creatures, a faun (part man, part beast) and a nymph (a beautiful forest maiden). As the faun awakens, he tries to recapture the experiences of the previous afternoon. Whether his elusive memories belong to the world of dreams or to reality is uncertain; but, true to Bergson's theory of duration, experience becomes a stream of sensations in which past and present merge. As the following excerpt illustrates, Mallarmé's verbal rhythms are free and hypnotic, and his images, which follow one another with few logical transitions, are intimately linked to the world of the senses.

READING 31.2 From Mallarmé's "The Afternoon of a Faun" (1876)

I would immortalize these nymphs: so bright	1
Their sunlit coloring, so airy light,	
It floats like drowsing down. Loved I a dream?	
My doubts, born of oblivious darkness, seem	
A subtle tracery of branches grown	5
The tree's true self—proving that I have known,	
Thinking it love, the blushing of a rose.	
But think. These nymphs, their loveliness . . . suppose	
They bodied forth your senses' fabulous thirst?	
Illusion! which the blue eyes of the first,	10
As cold and chaste as is the weeping spring,	
Beget: the other, sighing, passioning,	
Is she the wind, warm in your fleece at noon?	
No; through this quiet, when a weary swoon	
Crushes and chokes the latest faint essay	15
Of morning, cool against the encroaching day,	
There is no murmuring water, save the gush	
Of my clear fluted notes; and in the hush	
Blows never a wind, save that which through my reed[1]	
Puffs out before the rain of notes can speed	20
Upon the air, with that calm breath of art	

---

[1] A pipe or flute.

That mounts the unwrinkled zenith visibly,
Where inspiration seeks its native sky.
You fringes of a calm Sicilian lake,
The sun's own mirror which I love to take,   **25**
Silent beneath your starry flowers, tell
How here I cut the hollow rushes, well
Tamed by my skill, when on the glaucous gold
Of distant lawns about their fountain cold
A living whiteness stirs like a lazy wave;   **30**
And at the first slow notes my panpipes gave
These flocking swans, these naiads, rather, fly
Or dive.

                . . . .

See how the ripe pomegranates bursting red
To quench the thirst of the mumbling bees have bled;   **35**
So too our blood, kindled by some chance fire,
Flows for the swarming legions of desire.
At evening, when the woodland green turns gold
And ashen grey, 'mid the quenched leaves, behold!
Red Etna[2] glows, by Venus visited,   **40**
Walking the lava with her snowy tread
Whene'er the flames in thunderous slumber die.
I hold the goddess!
                Ah, sure penalty!
But the unthinking soul and body swoon
At last beneath the heavy hush of noon.   **45**
Forgetful let me lie where summer's drouth
Sifts fine the sand and then with gaping mouth
Dream planet-struck by the grape's round wine-red star.
Nymphs, I shall see the shade that now you are.

Q **How does this poem compare with those of Wordsworth and Shelley (Readings 27.1 and 27.2)?**

Q **What aspects of Mallarmé's poem do you detect in the music of Debussy and the paintings of Monet?**

Music in the Late Nineteenth Century: Debussy

It is no surprise that Symbolist poetry, itself a kind of music, found its counterpart in music. Like the poetry of Mallarmé, the music of Claude Debussy (1862–1918) engages the listener through nuance and atmosphere. Debussy's compositions consist of broken fragments of melody, the outlines of which are blurred and indistinct. "I would like to see the creation . . . of a kind of music without themes and motives," wrote Debussy, "formed on a single continuous theme, which is uninterrupted and which never returns on itself."

Debussy owed much to Richard Wagner and the romantic composers who had abandoned the formal clarity of classical composition (see chapter 29). He was also indebted

Figure 31.2 Vaslav Nijinsky, "Afternoon of a Faun," 1912. Photo: L. Roosen. Dancing the part of the faun, Nijinsky moved across the stage in profile in imitation of the frieze on an ancient Greek vase. While he performed professionally for only ten years, his provocative choreography ushered in modern dance.

to the exotic music of Bali in Indonesia, which he had heard performed at the World's Fair of 1889. Debussy experimented with nontraditional kinds of harmony, such as the five-tone scale found in East Asian music. He deviated from the traditional Western practice of returning harmonies to the tonic, or "home tone," introducing shifting harmonies with no clearly defined tonal center. His rich harmonic palette, characterized by unusually constructed chords, reflects a fascination with tone color that may have been inspired by the writings of the German physiologist Hermann von Helmholtz (1821–1894)—especially his treatise *On the Sensations of Tone as a Physiological Basis for the Theory of Music* (1863). But Debussy found his greatest inspiration in contemporary poetry and painting. A close friend of the Symbolist poets, he set a number of their texts to music. His first orchestral composition, *Prelude to "The Afternoon of a Faun"* (1894), was (in his words) a "very free illustration of Mallarmé's beautiful poem," which had been published eighteen years earlier. Debussy originally intended to write a dramatic piece based on the poem, but instead produced a ten-minute orchestral prelude that shares its dreamlike quality.

In 1912, his score became the basis for a twelve-minute ballet choreographed by Vaslav Nijinsky (1888–1950; Figure **31.2**). This brilliant Russian choreographer violated the formalities of classical dance by introducing sexually

---

[2] A volcanic mountain in Sicily.

🎼 See Music Listening Selections at end of chapter.

Figure 31.3 FERDINAND HODLER, *The Chosen One*, 1893–1894. Tempera and oil on canvas, 7 ft. 3½ in. × 9 ft. 10½ in. Six angelic figures float above the ground on which a nude boy sits before a barren tree. While the images suggest renewal and rejuvenation, no clear narrative attaches to the scene.

charged gestures and by dancing portions of the ballet bare-foot. He outraged critics who attacked the ballet for its "vile movements of erotic bestiality and gestures of extreme shamelessness."

Debussy had little use for the ponderous orchestras of the French and German romantics. He scored the *Prelude* for a small orchestra whose predominantly wind and brass instruments might recreate Mallarmé's delicate mood of reverie. A sensuous melody for unaccompanied flute pro-vides the composition's opening theme, which is then developed by flutes, oboes, and clarinets. Harp, triangle, muted horns, and lightly brushed cymbals contribute luminous tonal textures that—like the images of the poem itself—seem based in pure sensation. Transitions are subtle, and melodies seem to drift without resolution. Shifting harmonies with no clearly defined tonal center

engulf the listener in a nebulous flood of sound that calls to mind the shimmering effects of light on water and the ebb and flow of ocean waves. Indeed, water—a favorite subject of Impressionist painters—is the subject of many of Debussy's orchestral sketches, such as *Gardens in the Rain* (1903), *Image: Reflections in the Water* (1905), and *The Sea* (1905).

Painting in the Late Nineteenth Century

Symbolism

In the visual arts, Symbolists gave emphasis to the simpli-fication of line, arbitrary color, and expressive, flattened form. *The Chosen One* (Figure **31.3**) by the Swiss artist Ferdinand Hodler (1853–1918) employs these features in depicting a young male child surrounded by a circle of angelic figures. The painting does not represent a specific event; rather, it suggests a mysterious and unnamed rite of passage. Symbolist emphasis on suggestion rather than depiction constituted a move in the direction of Modernist Abstraction and Expressionism (see chapters 32 and 33 respectively).

Impressionism

The nineteenth-century art style that captured most fully the intuitive realm of experience, and thus, closely paralleled the aesthetic ideals of Bergson, Mallarmé, and

Science and Technology	
1841	John G. Rand invents the collapsible metal paint tube
1879	Edison produces the incandescent light bulb
1889	Edison invents equipment to take and show moving pictures
1898	Wilhelm C. Röntgen (German) discovers X-rays

Debussy, was *Impressionism*. Luminosity, the interaction of light and form, subtlety of tone, and a preoccupation with sensation itself were the major features of Impressionist art.

Impressionist subject matter preserved the romantic fascination with nature and the Realist preoccupation with daily life. But Impressionism departed from both the romantic effort to idealize nature and the Realist will to record the natural world with unbiased objectivity. Often called an art of pure sensation, Impressionism was, in part, a response to nineteenth-century research into the physics of light, the chemistry of paint, and the laws of optics. *The Principles of Harmony and the Contrast of Colors* by the nineteenth-century French chemist Michel Chevreul (1786–1889), along with treatises on the physical properties of color and musical tone by Hermann von Helmholtz mentioned above, offered new insights into the psychology of perception. These complemented the earliest appearance of synthetic pigments, which replaced traditional earth pigments. Of particular importance were chrome yellow, synthetic ultramarine, viridian, and emerald green, all of which gave the impressionists a brighter range of color. Until the mid nineteenth century, paint was stored in a pig's bladder, which was tapped and resealed as paint was needed. But the invention of the collapsible metal tube made it possible for artists to freely transport paint to outdoor sites and store paint longer.

Monet: Pioneer Impressionist

In 1874 the French artist Claude Monet (1840–1926) exhibited a canvas that some critics consider the first modern painting. *Impression: Sunrise* (Figure **31.4**) is patently a seascape; but the painting says more about *how* one sees than about *what* one sees. It transcribes the fleeting effects of light and the changing atmosphere of water and air into a tissue of small dabs and streaks of color—the elements of pure perception. To increase luminosity, Monet coated the raw canvas with gesso, a chalklike medium. Then, working in the open air and using the new synthetic paints, he applied brushstrokes of pure, occasionally unmixed, color. Monet ignored the brown underglazes artists traditionally used to build up form. Maintaining that there were no "lines" in nature, he avoided fixed contours. Instead of blending his colors to create a finished effect, he placed them side by side, building up a radiant impasto. In order to intensify visual effect, he juxtaposed complementary colors, putting touches of orange (red and yellow) next to blue and adding bright tints of rose, pink, and vermilion. He rejected the use of browns and blacks to create shadows; instead, he applied colors complementary to the hue of the object casting the shadow, thus approximating the prismatic effects of light on the human eye. Monet's canvases capture the external envelope: the instantaneous visual sensation of light itself.

Figure 31.4 CLAUDE MONET, *Impression: Sunrise*, 1873. Oil on canvas, 19⅝ × 25¼ in.

Figure 31.5 CLAUDE MONET, *Water-Lily Pond, Symphony in Green* (*Japanese Bridge*), 1899. Oil on canvas, 35 in. × 3 ft. ⅜ in. The reflections of dense foliage in the surface of the waterlily pond eliminate distinctions between foreground and background and suggest a shifting play of light. Such paintings inspired the Symbolist Charles Morice to call Monet "master and king of the ephemeral."

Monet was by no means the first painter to deviate from academic techniques. Constable had applied color in rough dots and dabs, Delacroix had occasionally juxtaposed complementary colors to increase brilliance, and Manet had often omitted halftones. But Monet went further by interpreting form as color itself—color so rapidly applied as to convey the immediacy of a sketch. Consequently, *Impression: Sunrise* struck the art world as a radically new approach. One critic dismissed the painting as "only an impression," no better than "wallpaper in its embryonic state," thus unwittingly giving the name "impressionism" to the movement that would dominate French art of the 1870s and 1880s.

Monet's early subjects include street scenes, picnics, café life, and boating parties at the fashionable tourist resorts that dotted the banks of the River Seine near Paris. However, as Monet found the intangible and shifting play of light more compelling than the pastimes of Parisian society, his paintings became more impersonal and abstract. Wishing to fix sensation, or as he put it, to "seize the intangible," he painted the changing effects of light on such mundane objects as poplar trees and haystacks. Often working on a number of canvases at once, he might generate a series that showed his subject in morning light, under the noon sun, and at sunset. After visiting London in the 1890s, during which time he studied the works of Constable and Turner, his canvases became even more formless and radiant. At his private estate in Giverny, he lovingly painted dozens of views of the lily ponds, and the lavish gardens that he himself designed and cultivated (Figure 31.5). These ravishing paintings brought him pleasure and fame at the end of his long career.

Monet may be considered an ultrarealist in his effort to reproduce with absolute fidelity the ever-changing effects of light. His freedom from preconceived ideas of nature prompted his contemporary Paul Cézanne to exclaim that he was "only an eye," but, he added admiringly, "what an eye!" Ironically, Monet's devotion to the physical truth of nature paved the way for modern abstraction—the concern with the intrinsic qualities of the subject, rather than with its literal appearance.

Renoir

Impressionism was never a single, uniform style. Nevertheless, it characterized the art of the group of Parisian artists who met regularly at the Café Guerbois and who showed their works together at no less than eight public exhibitions held between 1874 and 1886. To a greater or lesser extent, their paintings reflected Monet's manner of rendering nature in short strokes of brilliant color. Above all, they brought painterly spontaneity to a celebration of the leisure activities and diversions of urban life: dining, dancing, theater going, boating, and socializing.

In this sense, the most typical Impressionist painter might be Pierre-Auguste Renoir (1841–1919). Le Moulin de la Galette, a popular outdoor café and dance hall located in Montmartre (the bohemian section of nineteenth-century Paris), provided the setting for one of Renoir's most seductive tributes to youth and informal pleasure (Figure 31.6). In the painting, elegantly dressed young men and women—artists, students, and working-class members of Parisian society—dance, drink, and flirt with one another in the flickering golden light of the late afternoon sun.

Pissarro

Renoir's colleague, Camille Pissarro (1830–1903), was born in the West Indies but settled in Paris in 1855. The oldest and one of the most prolific of the Impressionists, he exhibited in all eight of the Impressionist group shows. Like Monet and Renoir, Pissarro loved outdoor subjects: peasants working in the fields, the magical effects of freshly fallen snow, and sunlit rural landscapes. Late in his career, however, as his eyesight began to fail, he gave up painting out-of-doors. Renting hotel rooms that looked out upon the streets of Paris, he produced engaging cityscapes (see Figure 31.1)—sixteen of Paris boulevards in 1897 alone.

Strikingly similar to popular panoramic photographs of turn-of-the-century Paris, Pissarro's luminous scenes capture the rhythms of urban life; throngs of horse-drawn carriages and pedestrians are bathed in the misty atmosphere that envelops Paris after the rain. Asked by a young artist for advice on "how to paint," Pissarro responded that one should record visual perceptions with immediacy, avoid

Figure 31.6 PIERRE-AUGUSTE RENOIR, *Le Moulin de la Galette*, 1876. Oil on canvas, 4 ft. 3½ in. × 5 ft. 9 in. Montmartre, the semirural working-class district of Paris, was not incorporated into the city limits until 1860. The Moulin ("mill") marked the spot of one of Montmartre's famous old windmills. *Galettes*, that is, buckwheat pancakes, were a specialty of the house.

Figure 31.7 EDGAR DEGAS, *Two Dancers on a Stage*, ca. 1874. Oil on canvas, 24⅛ × 18 in. A comparison of this composition with that of the far left woodcut in Figure 31.10 reveals a similar treatment of negative space, a raked perspective, and the off-center arrangement of figures.

defining the outlines of things, observe reflections of color and light, and honor only one teacher: nature.

Degas

Edgar Degas (1834–1917) regularly exhibited with the Impressionists; but his style remained unique. Classically trained—he began copying Poussin at the Louvre when he was eighteen—he never sacrificed line and form to the beguiling qualities of color and light. He produced thousands of drawings and pastels, ranging from quick sketches to fully developed compositions. Whether depicting the urban world of cafés, racetracks, theaters, and shops, or the demimonde of laundresses and prostitutes, he concentrated his attention on the fleeting moment. He rejected the traditional "posed" model, seeking instead to capture momentary and even awkward gestures, such as stretching and yawning. Degas was a consummate draftsman and a master designer. His innovative compositional techniques balance spontaneity and improvisation with artifice and calculation. In *Two Dancers on a Stage* (Figure **31.7**), for example, he presents two ballerinas as if seen from above and at an angle that leaves "empty" the lower left portion of the painting. In this feat of breathtaking

asymmetry, part of the figure at the right seems to disappear off the edge of the canvas, while the body of a third figure at the left is cut off by the frame. The deliberately "random" view suggests the influence of photography, with its accidental "slice of life" potential, as well as the impact of Japanese woodcuts, which Degas enthusiastically collected after they entered Europe in the 1860s.

During the 1860s, Degas became interested in the subject of horse racing, which, like the theater, had become a fashionable leisure activity and social event (Figure **31.8**). His drawings and paintings of the races focused primarily on the anatomy and movement of the horses. In his studies of physical movement, he learned much from the British artist, photographer, and inventor Eadweard Muybridge (1830–1904), whose stop-action photographs of the 1870s and 1880s were revolutionary in their time (Figure **31.9**).

Japanese Woodblock Prints and Western Art

Japanese woodblock prints entered Europe along with Asian trade goods (often as the wrappings for those goods) in the late nineteenth century. Though they were new to Europeans, they represented the end of a long tradition in

Figure 31.8 EDGAR DEGAS, *The False Start*, ca. 1870. Oil on canvas, 12⅝ × 15¾ in. The English sport of horse racing took hold in France in the 1830s when a track was built at Chantilly. In 1857, a fashionable racetrack was established at Longchamp in the Bois de Boulogne on the outskirts of Paris.

Figure 31.9 EADWEARD MUYBRIDGE, *Photo Sequence of Racehorse*, 1884–1885. Photograph.

Japanese art, one that began declining after Japan was forced to open its doors to the West in the 1860s. Produced in great numbers between 1660 and 1860, and sold as popular souvenirs, they recorded the pleasures of *ukiyo*, "the floating—or fleeting—world" of courtesans, actors, and dancers (see Figure 31.13) that enlivened the streets of bustling, urban Edo (now Tokyo). Like the magnificent folding screens commissioned by wealthy patrons (see chapter 21), the prints feature flat, unmodulated colors, undulating lines, and compositions that are cropped or include large areas of empty space. Their daring use of **negative space** and startling perspective were often the consequence of unusual vantage points, such as the bird's-eye view seen in the prints of Kunisada (Figure **31.10**). Such prints were mass-produced, most often by men, despite Kunisada's rendering.

During the mid nineteenth century, Japanese woodblock artists added landscapes to their repertory. The landscape prints, often produced as a series of views of local Japanese sites, resemble the topographical studies of European artists. But they operated out of entirely different stylistic imperatives: unlike the

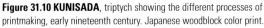

Figure 31.10 KUNISADA, triptych showing the different processes of printmaking, early nineteenth century. Japanese woodblock color print.

Left: the printer has just finished taking an impression by rubbing the *baren* (a round pad made of a coil of cord covered by a bamboo sheath) over the paper on the colored block; numerous brushes and bowls of color are visible. Kunisada has made the design more interesting by using women, though the craftsmen were almost always men (information from Julia Hutt, *Understanding Far Eastern Art.* New York: Dutton, 1987, 53).

Center: a woman (in the foreground) sizing paper sheets that are then hung up to dry; another is removing areas with no design from the block with a chisel.

Right: a woman with an original drawing pasted onto a block conversing with another who is sharpening blades on a whetstone.

Romantics, the Japanese had little interest in the picturesque; rather, they gave attention to bold contrasts and decorative arrangements of abstract shapes and colors. The absence of chiaroscuro and aerial perspective reduced the illusion of spatial depth and atmospheric continuity between near and far objects. All of these features are evident in one of the most famous mid nineteenth-century Japanese landscape prints: *Mount Fuji Seen Below a Wave at Kanagawa* (Figure **31.11**), from the series "Thirty-six Views of Mount Fuji" by Katsushika Hokusai (1760–1849).

When Japanese prints arrived in the West (see Figure 31.13), they exercised an immediate impact on fine and commercial art, including the art of the lithographic poster (see Figure 31.12). Monet and Degas bought them (along with Chinese porcelains) in great numbers, and van Gogh, a great admirer of Hokusai, insisted that his own work was "founded on Japanese art."

Théodore Duret, a French art critic of the time and an enthusiast of impressionist painting, was one of the first writers to observe the impact of Japanese prints on nineteenth-century artists. In a pamphlet called "The Impressionist Painters" (1878), Duret explained:

> We had to wait until the arrival of Japanese albums before anyone dared to sit down on the bank of a river to juxtapose on canvas a boldly red roof, a white wall, a green poplar, a yellow road, and blue water. Before Japan it was impossible; the painter always lied. Nature with its frank colors was in plain sight, yet no one ever saw anything on canvas but attenuated colors, drowning in a general halftone.
>
> As soon as people looked at Japanese pictures, where the most glaring, piercing colors were placed side by side, they finally understood that there were new methods for reproducing certain effects of nature.

Japonisme, the influence of Japan on European art of the late nineteenth century, proved to be multifaceted: the prints coincided with the Impressionist interest in casual urban subjects (especially those involving women) and

inspired a new way of reconciling the illusion of the three-dimensional world with the flatness of the two-dimensional canvas. At the same time, the elegant naturalism and refined workmanship of Asian *cloisonné* enamels, ceramics, lacquerwares, ivories, silks, and other collectibles were widely imitated in the Arts and Crafts movements that flourished at the end of the century (see Figure 31.18).

Cassatt

One of the most notable artists to come under the influence of Japanese prints was the American painter Mary Cassatt (1844–1926). Cassatt spent most of her life in Paris, where she became a friend and colleague of Degas, Renoir, and other Impressionists, with whom she exhibited regularly. Like Degas, she painted mainly indoors, cultivating a style that combined forceful calligraphy, large areas of unmodulated color, and unusual perspectives—the major features of the Japanese woodcuts—with a taste for female subjects.

Cassatt brought a unique sensitivity to domestic themes that featured mothers and children enjoying everyday tasks and diversions (Figure **31.14**). These gentle and optimistic images appealed to American collectors and did much to increase the popularity of Impressionist art in the United States. Yet the so-called "Madonna of American art" preferred life in Paris to that in prefeminist America. "Women do not have to fight for recognition here if they do serious work," wrote Cassatt.

Figure 31.11 KATSUSHIKA HOKUSAI, *Mount Fuji Seen Below a Wave at Kanagawa*, from "Thirty-six Views of Mount Fuji," Tokugawa Period. Full-color woodblock print, width 14¾ in.

Figure 31.12 HENRI DE TOULOUSE-LAUTREC,
Jane Avril, 1899. Lithograph, printed in color, 22 × 14 in.

MAKING CONNECTIONS

The lithographic technique made possible the late nineteenth-century art of the publicity poster. While he was not the first to produce these commercial artworks, Toulouse-Lautrec was among the pioneers of modern poster design. In the last ten years of his life he would create some thirty lithographic posters. Commissioned to design posters advertising the popular cabaret known as the Moulin Rouge ("Red Mill"), he produced some magnificent images of its famous can-can dancer Louise Weber, known as La Goulue (the "greedy one"), whose risqué high-kicking displays attracted enthusiastic audiences. A poster of the Parisian entertainer who replaced La Goulue, Jane Avril (Figure **31.12**), shows the artist's brilliant combination of bright, flat colors, sinuous lines, and the sensitive integration of positive and negative space—stylistic features that reflect the direct influence of Japanese *kabuki* prints (Figure **31.13**).

**Figure 31.13
TORII KIYONOBU,**
*Actor as a Monkey
Showman*, ca. 1720.
Woodblock print,
13¼ × 6¼ in.

Toulouse-Lautrec

Cassatt's gentle visions of domestic life stand in strong contrast to the paintings of Henri de Toulouse-Lautrec (1864–1901). Toulouse-Lautrec, the descendant of an aristocratic French family, practiced many of the stylistic principles of Impressionism, but his choice of subject matter was often so intimate that members of his own family condemned his work as unacceptable to "well-bred people."

The art of Toulouse-Lautrec captured the seamy side of Parisian life—the life of cabaret dancers and prostitutes who, like Zola's Nana, lived on the margins of middle-class society. Toulouse-Lautrec self-consciously mocked traditional ideas of beauty and propriety. He stylized figures—almost to the point of caricature—in bold and forceful silhouettes. Flesh tones might be distorted by artificial light or altered by the stark white make-up (borrowed from Japanese theater) that was current in European fashion. At *The Moulin Rouge* shows the patrons and entertainers of the famous Montmartre cabaret that opened in late 1889 (Figure **31.15**). The unconventional perspective forces the eye into the space above the diagonal axis of a balustrade, where one encounters the jaded-looking assembly of stylishly hatted men and women.

Toulouse-Lautrec's cousin, | Toulouse- | La Goulue fixing her
Dr. Tapié de Céleyran | Lautrec | hair before a mirror

Jane Avril | bentwood café chairs designed | the performer
by Michael Thonet in 1830 | May Milton

Figure 31.15 HENRI DE TOULOUSE-LAUTREC, *At The Moulin-Rouge,* 1893–1895. Oil on canvas, 4 ft. ⅜ in. × 4 ft. 7¼ in.

Figure 31.14 MARY CASSATT, *The Bath,* 1891–1892. Oil on canvas, 3 ft. 3½ in. × 26 in. Cassatt offers a bird's-eye view of all elements in the painting with the exception of the pitcher in the lower right foreground and the chest of drawers in the background.

Art Nouveau

The posters of Toulouse-Lautrec bear the seductive stamp of *Art Nouveau* (French for "new art"), an ornamental style that became enormously popular in the late nineteenth century. *Art Nouveau* artists shared with members of the English Arts and Crafts movement a high regard for the fine artisanship of the preindustrial Middle Ages, an era that achieved an ideal synthesis of the functional and the decorative in daily life. The proponents of the new style also prized the decorative arts of Asia and Islam, which tended to favor bold, flat, organic patterns and semi-abstract linear designs. Acknowledging the impact of the Japanese woodcut style, one French critic insisted that Japanese blood had mixed with the blood of *Art Nouveau* artists.

Art Nouveau originated in Belgium among architects working in the medium of cast iron, but it quickly took on an international reach that affected painting, as well as the design of furniture, textiles, glass, ceramics, and jewelry. The Belgian founder of the style, Victor Horta (1861–1947), brought to his work the Arts and Crafts

Figure 31.16 VICTOR HORTA, Tassel House, Brussels, 1892–1893.

veneration for fine craftsmanship and the Symbolist glorification of the sensuous and fleeting forms in nature. A distinguished architect and a great admirer of Eiffel's 1064-foot-high tower (see Figure 30.27), Horta translated the serpentine lines and organic rhythms of flowers and plants into magnificent glass and cast-iron designs for public buildings and private residences (Figure **31.16**).

"Art in nature, nature in art" was the motto of *Art Nouveau*. The sinuous curves of blossoms, leaves, and tendrils, executed in iron, were immortalized in such notable monuments as the rapid transport system known as the Paris Métro. They also appear in wallpaper, poster design, book illustration, tableware, and jewelry. In *Art Nouveau*, as in late nineteenth-century literature and painting, women were a favorite subject: the female, often shown with long, luxuriant hair, might be pictured as

Figure 31.18 TIFFANY GLASS AND DECORATING CO., Peacock vase, 1892–1902. Iridescent "favrile" glass, blues and greens with feather and eye decorations, height 14⅛ in. A student of ancient and medieval glass practices, Tiffany patented in 1874 a way of mixing different colors of heated glass to produce the iridescent art glass he called "favrile" (a name derived from a Saxon word meaning "handmade").

seductress or enchantress. She might appear as a fairy or water nymph (Figure **31.17**), a poetic, sylphlike creature. In *Art Nouveau* pins, bracelets, and combs, she is the human counterpart of vines and flowers fashioned in delicately crafted metal armatures and semiprecious stones.

Such images suggest that *Art Nouveau*, although modern in its effort to communicate meaning by way of shapes, patterns, and decoration, was actually a waning expression of a century-long romantic infatuation with nature.

In America, *Art Nouveau* briefly attracted the attention of such architects as Louis Sullivan (see chapter 30), who embellished some of his otherwise austere office buildings and department stores with floral cast-iron ornamentation. It also inspired the magnificent glass designs of Louis Comfort Tiffany (1848–1933). The son of Charles L. Tiffany, founder of the famed New York jewelry house, Louis was a great admirer of Chinese *cloisonnés* and ancient glass techniques. His innovative studio methods included assembly-line production, the use of templates, and the employment of female artisans who received the same wages as males—a policy that caused great controversy in Tiffany's time. Tiffany's inventive art glass, which featured floral arabesques and graceful geometric patterns, made him one of the masters of the international *Art Nouveau* style (Figure **31.18**).

Figure 31.17 EUGÈNE GRASSET, Comb, ca. 1900. ¼ × 2¾ in.

Sculpture in the Late Nineteenth Century

Degas and Rodin

The two leading European sculptors of the late nineteenth century, Edgar Degas and Auguste Rodin (1840–1917), were masters at capturing the physical vitality of the human figure. Like the Impressionists, they were interested in lifelike movement and the sensory effects of light. To catch these fleeting qualities, they modeled their figures rapidly in wet clay or wax. The bronze casts made from these originals preserve the spontaneity of the additive process. Indeed, many of Degas' bronze sculptures, cast posthumously, retain the imprints of his fingers and fingernails.

Figure 31.19 EDGAR DEGAS, *Little Dancer Aged Fourteen*, ca. 1880–1881 (cast ca. 1919–32). Bronze with net tutu and hair ribbon, 3 ft. 2½ × 14½ in. × 14¼ in. In Degas' time, young female dancers, called "little rats," usually came from working-class families for whom they provided income.

Figure 31.20 AUGUSTE RODIN, *Dancing Figure*, 1905. Graphite with orange wash, 12⅛ × 9⅜ in.

Degas often executed sculptures as exercises preliminary to his paintings. Throughout his life, but especially as his vision began to decline, the artist turned to making three-dimensional "sketches" of racehorses, bathers, and ballerinas—his favorite subjects. At his death, he left some 150 sculptures in his studio, some fully worked and others in various stages of completion. Only one of these sculptures, the *Little Dancer Aged Fourteen*, was exhibited as a finished artwork during Degas' lifetime. The reddish-brown wax original, made eerily lifelike by the artist's addition of a tutu, stockings, bodice, ballet shoes, a green satin ribbon, and hair from a horsehair wig (embedded strand by strand into the figure's head), was the subject of some controversy in the Parisian art world of 1881 (a world that would not see such mixed-media innovations for another half-century). The bronze cast of Degas' *Dancer* (Figure **31.19**), whose dark surfaces contrast sensuously with the fabric additions, retains the supple grace of the artist's finest drawings and paintings.

Like Degas, Rodin was keenly interested in movement and gesture. In hundreds of drawings, he recorded the dancelike rhythms of studio models whom he bid to move about freely rather than assume traditional, fixed poses (Figure **31.20**). But it was in the three-dimensional media that Rodin made his greatest contribution. One of his earliest sculptures, *The Age of Bronze* (Figure **31.21**), was so lifelike that critics accused him of forging the figure from plaster casts of a live model. In actuality,

Figure 31.21 AUGUSTE RODIN, *The Age of Bronze*, 1876. Bronze, 25½ × 9⅜ × 7½ in. The influence of Rodin's teacher, Jean-Baptiste Carpeaux, can be detected in a comparison of this sculpture with Carpeaux's *The Dance*, executed some eight years earlier (see Figure 29.20).

Rodin had captured a sense of organic movement by recreating the fleeting effects of light on form. He heightened the contrasts between polished and roughly textured surfaces, deliberately leaving parts of the piece unfinished. "Sculpture," declared Rodin, "is quite simply the art of depression and protuberance."

But Rodin moved beyond naturalistic representation. Moving toward modernism, he used expressive distortion to convey a mood or mental disposition. He renounced formal idealization and gave his figures a nervous energy and an emotional intensity that he found lacking in both Classical and Renaissance sculpture. "The sculpture of antiquity," he explained, "sought the logic of the human body; I seek its psychology." In this quest, Rodin was joined by his close friend, the American dancer Isadora Duncan (1878–1927). Duncan introduced a language of physical expression characterized by personalized gestures and improvised movements that were often fierce, earthy, and passionate (Figure **31.22**). Insisting that the rules of classical ballet produced

Figure 31.22 Isadora Duncan in *La Marseillaise*. Notorious for flouting the rules of academic dance as well as those of middle-class morality, the California-born Duncan achieved greater success in Europe than in the United States. She adopted the signature affectation of wearing scarves, one of which accidentally strangled her in a freak car mishap.

Figure 31.23 AUGUSTE RODIN, *The Gates of Hell*, 1880–1917. Bronze, 20 ft. 8 in. × 13 ft. 1 in. Below the Three Shades, in the center of the lintel (where Jesus is usually found in a traditional Christian Judgment scene) sits the Thinker, the human Creator, contemplating humankind doomed by its passions.

ugly choreography, Duncan danced barefoot, often wearing Greek-style tunics in reference to ancient dance. "I have discovered the art that has been lost for two thousand years," claimed Duncan.

Rodin's most ambitious project was a set of doors he was commissioned to design for the projected Museum of Decorative Arts in Paris. Loosely modeled after Ghiberti's *Gates of Paradise* (see Figure 17.20), *The Gates of Hell* (Figure **31.23**) consists of a swarm of figures inspired by the tortured souls of Dante's "Inferno" (see chapter 12). Rodin worked on the project for eight years, making hundreds of drawings and sculptures based on Dante's poem; but he never completed the doors, which were cast in bronze only years after his death. The figures that occupy *The Gates*, not all of which are identifiable, writhe and twist in postures of despair and yearning. Arrived at intuitively—like the images in a Mallarmé poem or a Monet landscape—they melt into each other without logical connection. Rodin admitted that he projected no fixed subject, "no scheme of illustrations or intended moral purpose." "I followed my own imagination," he explained, "my own sense of movement and composition." Collectively, his figures evoke a world of flux and chaos; their postures capture the restless discontent voiced by Nietzsche and Gauguin, and their random arrangement gives substance to Bergson's view of reality as a perpetual stream of sensations.

Throughout his career, Rodin remained compelled by the contents of *The Gates*. He cast in bronze many of its individual figures, and recreated others in marble. The two most famous of these are *The Kiss* (Figure **31.24**), based on the figures of the lovers Paola and Francesca (on the lower left door), and *The Thinker*. The latter—one of the best known of Rodin's works—originally represented Dante contemplating his imagined underworld from atop its portals.

Figure 31.24 AUGUSTE RODIN,
The Kiss, 1886–1898. Marble, over life-size.

The Arts of Africa and Oceania

During the late nineteenth century, expanding Western commercialism and colonialism brought Europeans in closer contact with Africa and Oceania (the islands of the South and Central Pacific, Map 31.1). Nineteenth-century Africa and Oceania were essentially preindustrial and preliterate. Their social organization was usually highly stratified with clear distinctions between and among various classes: royalty, priests, and commoners held different ranks. Their economies were agricultural, and their gods and spirits were closely associated with nature and natural forces that were the object of communal and individual worship (see chapter 18). In some parts of Africa, kingdoms with long-standing traditions of royal authority were destroyed by colonial intrusion. But in other parts of Africa, ancient ways of life persisted. The royal traditions of Benin, Dahomey, Kongo, Yoruba, and other West African kingdoms (Map 31.2) continued to flourish well into the modern era. During the nineteenth century, the oral traditions of African literature came to be recorded in written languages based on the Arabic and Western alphabets.

Africa and Oceania consisted of thousands of tightly knit communities in which reverence for the gods and the spirits of deceased ancestors was expressed by means of elaborate systems of worship. Reliquaries, masks, and other power objects were created by local artists to channel the spirits, celebrate rites of passage, and ensure the continuity and well-being of the community. As vessels for powerful spirits, they functioned to transmit supernatural energy. While sharing with some Western styles (such as Symbolism) a disregard for objective representation, the arts of these indigenous peoples stood far apart from nineteenth-century Western academic tradition. On the other hand, they had their roots in long-established cultural traditions—some extending back over thousands of years. Much of the art created in these regions during the nineteenth (and twentieth) century had its origins in conventional forms handed down from generation to generation. So, for example, masks produced in the nineteenth century by the Bambara people of Mali preserve the techniques and styles practiced almost without interruption since the founding of Mali's first empire in the thirteenth century (see chapter 18, Figure 18.8).

Although productivity from region to region in Africa and from island to island in Oceania varies dramatically, parts of Africa and Oceania generated some of their finest artwork during the nineteenth century. The classic period in Kenya-Kayan art, from the island of Borneo, for instance, dates from the mid nineteenth to the early twentieth century. And among the Maori peoples of New Zealand, the art of woodcarving, usually employed in the construction of elaborate wooden meeting houses, flourished during the

Map 31.1 The Islands of the South and Central Pacific.

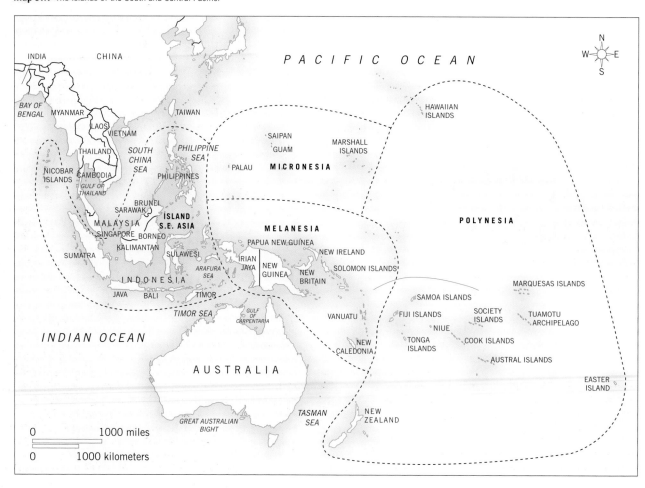

1800s. Teams of woodcarvers using European tools produced expressive totemic images embellished with elaborate patterns of tattoos that—similar to African scarification—were popular throughout the South Pacific (see Figure 31.29).

In Africa, even as the incursions of the French disrupted the Yoruba kingdoms of Nigeria (Map 31.2), royal authority asserted itself in the increased production of magnificent beaded objects, some of which served to identify and embellish the power and authority of the king. The beaded conical crown that belonged to King Glele (1858–1889) of Dahomey (the modern Republic of Benin) is surmounted by a bird that symbolizes potent supernatural powers and the all-surpassing majesty of the ruler (Figure **31.25**). Beadwork had been practiced in West Africa since the sixteenth century, when the Portuguese introduced the first Venetian glass beads to that continent. However, the golden age of beadwork occurred in the late nineteenth century, when uniformly sized European "seed beads" in a wide variety of colors first became available. It is noteworthy that in West Africa beading was an activity reserved exclusively for men.

A second example of high artistic productivity in nineteenth-century Africa comes from the genre of freestanding sculpture: the image of the war god Gu, commissioned by King Glele as a symbol of his own military might, was carved from wood and covered with hammered brass (said to have come from spent bullet shells). Brandishing two scimitars, the figure served to guard the gate that led into the city of Abhomey. Its fierce, scarified face with its jutting jaw, the wide flat feet, and taut, stylized physique reflect a powerful synthesis of naturalism and abstraction that typifies nineteenth-century African art, but, at the same time, adheres to a long tradition of West African sculpture (Figure **31.26**). The figure failed, however, in its protective mission: shortly after the death of King Glele in 1889, his kingdom fell to French colonial forces.

Primitivism

Europe had been involved in Africa and Oceania since the sixteenth century. By the nineteenth century, trade in goods, guns, and slaves had transformed African culture. In some areas, the availability of guns had led to violence and mayhem. Apart from imperialistic ambition, the Western penetration of the so-called "Dark Continent" was the product of intellectual curiosity, which had been stirred by Napoleon's Egyptian campaign (see chapter 29). Following the French invasion of Nigeria in 1830, and especially after medical science had recognized that quinine was effective against the dreaded malaria, Africa began to attract Western travelers and adventurers. Delacroix visited Morocco in 1831, bringing back to Europe seven sketchbooks of drawings and numerous watercolors. The British explorers David Livingstone (1813–1873) and Henry M. Stanley (1841–1904) spent years investigating Africa's vast terrain. Journalistic records of such expeditions drew attention

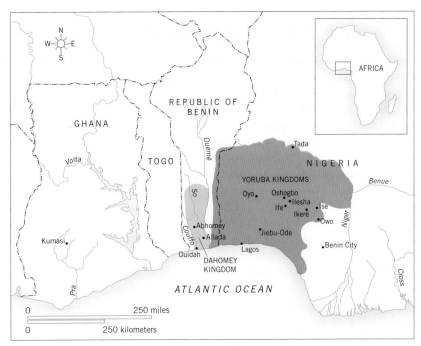

Map 31.2 The Kingdoms of Yoruba and Dahomey.

Figure 31.25 Yoruba headdress, nineteenth century. Beads and mixed media. This crown of a Yoruba tribal prince is ornamented with figures of birds, chameleons, lizards, and human faces.

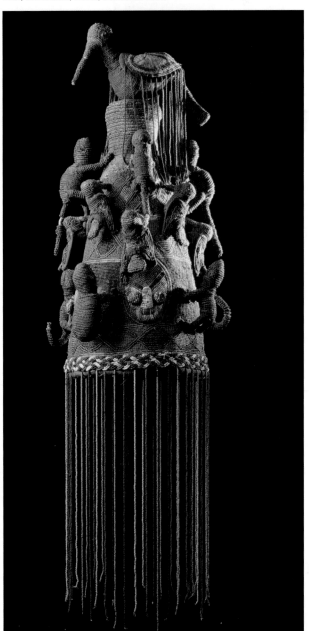

Figure 31.26 GANHU HUNTONDJI (attributed), *The war god Gu*, nineteenth century. Brass and wood, height 41½ in.

"primitive," implying simplicity and lack of sophistication. The French word "*primitif*" carried as well a positive charge, implying a closeness to nature exalted by those who decried the damaging effects of proto-modern industrialized society.

Contributing to the European infatuation with non-Western culture was the *Exposition Universelle* (World's Fair) held in Paris in 1889, which brought to public view the arts of Asia, Africa, and Oceania. Reconstructions of villages from the Congo and Senegal, Japan and China, Polynesia and other South Sea islands introduced the non-Western world to astonished Europeans. Non-Western societies and their artistic achievements quickly became objects of research for the new disciplines of anthropology (the science of humankind and its culture) and ethnography (the branch of anthropology that studies preliterate peoples or groups). In 1890, the Scottish anthropologist Sir James Frazer (1854–1941) published *The Golden Bough*, a pioneer study of magic and religion as reflected in ancient and traditional folk customs. Collections of non-Western art filled the galleries of ethnographic museums, such as the American Museum of Natural History, which opened in New York in 1869, and the Musée d'Ethnographie du Trocadero in Paris, founded in 1878. Tragically, however, it was often the case that even as these cultures were coming to be valued and their art collected and installed in Western museums, their brilliance and originality began to wane. The French painter Paul Gauguin, who recorded his impressions of Tahiti in his romanticized journal *Noa Noa* (*Fragrance*), lamented:

> The European invasion and monotheism have destroyed the vestiges of a civilization which had its own grandeur. . . . [The Tahitians] had been richly endowed with an instinctive feeling for the harmony necessary between human creations and the animal and plant life that formed the setting and decoration of their existence, but this has now been lost. In contact with us, with our school, they have truly become "savages" . . .

Gauguin objected to colonial efforts to impose French legal and economic policies on the Tahitians; he condemned the eradication of local religious beliefs by Catholic and Protestant missionaries. The appeal of "the primitive" among late nineteenth-century figures such as Gauguin reflected a more than casual interest in the world beyond the West. It provoked protests against what Gauguin called the "reign of terror" imposed by the West upon native non-Western populations. It also constituted a rebellion against Western values and societal taboos—a rebellion that would become full-blown in the primitivism of early modern art.

Postimpressionism

The art that followed the last of the Impressionist group shows in 1886 is generally designated as "Postimpressionist." Seeking a style that transcended the fleeting, momentary

to cultural traditions that differed sharply from those of the West. What often emerged was an oversimplified (and often distorted) understanding of the differences between and among a multitude of cultures, some of which were perceived as exotic, violent, and fundamentally inferior. Many Westerners characterized indigenous peoples as

impression, the Postimpressionists gave increased emphasis to color and compositional form. They embraced an art-for-art's sake aestheticism that prized pictorial invention over pictorial illusion. Strongly individualistic, they were uninterested in satisfying the demands of public and private patrons; most of them made only sporadic efforts to sell what they produced. Like the Impressionists, the Postimpressionists looked to the natural world for inspiration. But unlike their predecessors, they brought a new sense of order to their compositions, following the incisive observation of the French Symbolist Maurice Denis (1870–1943) that a painting, before being a pictorial representation of reality, is "a flat surface covered with shapes, lines, and colors assembled in a particular order." This credo, as realized in Postimpressionist art, would drive most of the major modern art movements of the early twentieth century (see chapter 32).

Van Gogh

The Dutch artist Vincent van Gogh (1853–1890) was a passionate idealist whose life was marred by loneliness,

poverty, depression, and a hereditary mental illness that ultimately drove him to suicide. During his career he produced over 700 paintings and thousands of drawings, of which he sold less than a half-dozen in his lifetime.

Van Gogh painted landscapes, still lifes, and portraits in a style that featured flat, bright colors, a throbbing, sinuous line, short, choppy brushstrokes, and bold compositions that betray his admiration for Japanese woodblock prints. His heavily pigmented surfaces were often manipulated with a palette knife or built up by applying paint directly from the tube. Deeply moved by music (especially the work of Wagner), he shared with the romantics an attitude toward nature that was both inspired and ecstatic. His emotional response to an object, rather than its physical appearance, influenced his choice of colors, which he likened to orchestrated sound. As he explained to his brother Theo, "I use color more arbitrarily so as to express myself more forcefully."

Van Gogh's painting *The Starry Night* (Figure **31.27**), a view of the small French town of Saint-Rémy, is electrified by thickly painted strokes of white, yellow, orange, and

Figure 31.27 VINCENT VAN GOGH, *The Starry Night*, 1889. Oil on canvas, 29 in. × 3 ft. ¼ in. In 1889 Van Gogh began a year's stay at the mental hospital in Saint-Rémy near Arles, an area of southern France renowned for its intermittent fierce winds, known as "the mistral." Mistral winds and clear night skies filled with shooting stars may have provided inspiration for this painting.

that evoke the coiling heavens in *The Starry Night*, charge the surface with undulating rhythms that sharply contrast with the immobile figure. This visual strategy underscores the artist's monkish alienation. Indeed, van Gogh confessed to his colleague Gauguin that he saw himself in this portrait as a simple Buddhist monk.

Gauguin

Van Gogh's friend and colleague, Paul Gauguin (1848–1903) shared his sense of alienation from middle-class European society. Part-Peruvian, his earliest childhood was spent in South America; in his teens he joined the merchant marines before settling down in Paris. After ten years of marriage, he abandoned his wife, his five children, and his job as a Paris stockbroker to devote himself to painting. He traveled to Brittany in northwest France,

Figure 31.29 Fragment of a Maori doorpost (*poupou*) in the style of Te Arawa, from New Zealand. Wood.

Figure 31.28 VINCENT VAN GOGH, *Self-Portrait*, 1889. Oil on canvas, 25½ × 21¼ in.

blue. Cypresses writhe like flames, stars explode, the moon seems to burn like the sun, and the heavens heave and roll like ocean waves. Here, van Gogh's expressive use of color invests nature with visionary frenzy.

In his letters to Theo (an art dealer by profession), van Gogh pledged his undying faith in the power of artistic creativity. In 1888, just two years before he committed suicide, he wrote: "I can do without God both in my life and in my painting, but I cannot, ill as I am, do without something which is greater than I, which is my life—the power to create. And if, defrauded of the power to create physically, a man tries to create thoughts in place of children, he is still part of humanity." Assessing his own creativity, van Gogh claimed that making portraits allowed him to cultivate what was "best and deepest." "Altogether," he explained, "it is the only thing in painting which moves me to the depths, and which more than anything else makes me feel the infinite." For van Gogh, the challenge of portraiture lay in capturing the heart and soul of the model. His many portraits of friends and neighbors, and the twenty-four self-portraits painted between 1886 and 1889, elevate romantic subjectivity to new levels of confessional intensity. In the *Self-Portrait* of 1889 (Figure **31.28**), for instance, where the pale flesh tones of the head are set against an almost monochromatic blue field, the skull takes on a forbidding, even spectral presence—an effect enhanced by the lurid green facial shadows and the blue-green eyes, slanted (as he related to Theo) so as to make himself look Japanese. His brushstrokes, similar to those

Figure 31.30 PAUL GAUGUIN, *The Day of the God (Mahana no Atua)*, 1894. Oil on canvas, 27⅜ × 35⅝ in. The blues in the background are of the same intensity as those in the foreground, thereby flattening space to create a tapestrylike surface. Gauguin denied that his paintings carried specific meanings. "My dream is intangible," he wrote a friend, "it comprises no allegory."

to Martinique in the West Indies, to Tahiti in the South Seas, and to southern France, returning for good to the islands of the South Pacific in 1895.

Gauguin took artistic inspiration from the folk culture of Brittany, the native arts of the South Sea islands, and from dozens of other nontraditional sources. What impressed him was the self-taught immediacy and authenticity of indigenous artforms, especially those that made use of powerful, totemic abstraction (Figure **31.29**). His own style, nurtured in the Symbolist precepts (discussed earlier in this chapter) and influenced by Japanese woodcuts and photographs of Japanese temple reliefs on view at the *Exposition Universelle* in 1889, featured flat, often distorted and brightly colored shapes that seem to float on the surface of the canvas.

In *The Day of the God* (Figure **31.30**), bright blues, yellows, and pinks form tapestrylike patterns reminiscent of Japanese prints and *Art Nouveau* posters. Gauguin's figures cast no shadows; his bold, unmodeled colors, like those of van Gogh, are more decorative than illusionistic. Like the verbal images of the Symbolist poets, Gauguin's colored shapes carry an intuitive charge that lies beyond literal description. For example, the languid, organic shapes in the

foreground pool of water and the fetal positions of the figures lying on the shore are suggestive of birth and regeneration. These and other figures in the painting seem spiritually related to the totemic guardian figure (pictured at top center of the canvas), who resembles the creator god and supreme deity of Maori culture (compare Figure 31.29).

Gauguin joined van Gogh at Arles in southeastern France in the fall of 1888, and for a brief time the two artists lived and worked side by side. Volatile and temperamental, they often engaged in violent quarrels, during one of which part of van Gogh's ear was cut off, either by van Gogh himself, or (as some historians claim) by Gauguin. But despite their intense personal differences, the two artists were fraternal pioneers in the search for a provocative language of form and color. Gauguin's self-conscious effort to assume the role of "the civilized savage" was rooted in the notion of the *primitif*, the condition of unspoiled nature celebrated by Rousseau, Thoreau, and others. His flight to the South Seas represents the search for a lost Eden, and reflects the fascination with exotic non-Western cultures that swept through late nineteenth-century Europe. As such, Gauguin's bohemian nonconformity may have been the "last gasp" of Romanticism.

Figure 31.31 GEORGES SEURAT, *Sunday Afternoon on the Island of La Grande Jatte*, 1884–1886. Oil on canvas, 6 ft. 9½ in. × 10 ft. ⅜ in. Nothing is left to chance in this highly formalized vision of the good life. Seurat died of diphtheria at the age of thirty-one, having completed barely a decade of mature work.

Seurat

Rejecting the formlessness of Impressionism, George Seurat (1859–1891) introduced formal pictorial construction. Trained academically, Seurat brought a degree of balance and order to his compositions that rivaled the works of Poussin and David. The figures in a Seurat painting seem plotted along an invisible grid of vertical and horizontal lines that run parallel to the picture plane. Every form assumes a preordained place. A similar fervor for order may have inspired Seurat's novel use of tiny dots of paint (in French, *points*). These he applied side by side (and sometimes one inside another) to build up dense clusters that intensified color and gave the impression of solid form—a style known as *pointillism*. He arrived at the technique of dividing color into component parts after studying the writings of Chevreul and other pioneers in color theory, such as the American physicist Ogden N. Rood (1831–1902), whose *Modern Chromatics, with Applications to Art and Industry* (translated into French in 1880) showed that optical mixtures of color were more intense than premixed colors. Leaving nothing to chance (Gauguin called him "the little green chemist"), Seurat applied each colored dot so that its juxtaposition with the next would produce the desired degree of vibration to the eye of the beholder.

Although Seurat shared the impressionists' fascination with light and color, he shunned spontaneity, for while he made his sketches out-of-doors, he executed his paintings inside his studio, usually at night and under artificial light.

Seurat's monumental *Sunday Afternoon on the Island of La Grande Jatte* shows a holiday crowd of Parisians relaxing on a sunlit island in the River Seine (Figure **31.31**). Although typically impressionistic in its subject matter—urban society at leisure—the painting (based on no less than twenty drawings and 200 oil studies) harbors little of the impressionist's love for intimacy and fleeting sensation. Every figure is isolated from the next as if it were frozen in space and unaware of another's existence. Seurat claimed that he wished to invest his subjects with the gravity of the figures in a Greek frieze. Nevertheless, one critic railed, "Strip his figures of the colored fleas that cover them; underneath you will find nothing, no thought, no soul." Seurat's universe, with its atomized particles of color and its self-contained figures, may seem devoid of human feeling, but its exquisite regularity provides a comforting alternative to the chaos of experience. Indeed, the lasting appeal of *La Grande Jatte* lies in its effectiveness as a symbolic retreat from the tumult of everyday life and the accidents of nature.

Cézanne

More so than Seurat, Paul Cézanne (1839–1906) served as a bridge between the art of the nineteenth century and that of the twentieth. Cézanne began his career as an Impressionist in Paris, but his traditional subjects—landscapes, portraits, and still lifes—show a greater concern for the formal aspects of a painting than for its subject matter. His effort to "redo nature after Poussin," that is, to find the enduring forms of nature that were basic to all great art, made Cézanne the first modernist painter.

Cézanne's determination to invest his pictures with a strong sense of three-dimensionality (a feature often neglected by the Impressionists) led to a method of building up form by means of small, flat planes of color, larger than (but not entirely unlike) Seurat's colored dots. Abandoning the intuitive and loosely organized compositions of the impressionists, Cézanne also sought to restore to painting the sturdy formality of academic composition. His desire to achieve pictorial unity inspired bold liberties of form and perspective: he might tilt and flatten surfaces; reduce (or abstract) familiar objects to basic geometric shapes—cylinders, cones, and spheres; or depict various objects in a single composition from different points of view. Cézanne's still lifes are not so much tempting likenesses of apples, peaches, or pears as they are architectural arrangements of colored forms (Figure **31.32**). In short, where narrative content often seems incidental, form itself takes on meaning.

Cézanne's mature style developed when he left Paris and returned to live in his native area of southern France. Here he tirelessly studied the local landscape: dozens of times he painted the rugged, stony peak of Mont Sainte-Victoire near his hometown of Aix-en-Provence. Among his last versions of the subject is a landscape in which trees and houses have become an abstract network of

Figure 31.32 PAUL CÉZANNE, *The Basket of Apples*, ca. 1895. Oil on canvas, 25¾ × 32 in. The rear edge of the tabletop marks the horizon line at two different places; the top two lady-fingers are seen from above, while those below and the plate itself are seen straight on. Such deliberate deviations from optical Realism characterize many of Cézanne's still lifes.

colored facets of paint (Figure **31.33**). By applying colors of the same intensity to different parts of the canvas—note the bright green and rich violet brushstrokes in both sky and landscape—Cézanne challenged traditional distinctions between foreground and background. In Cézanne's canvases, all parts of the composition, like the flat shapes of a Japanese print, have become equal in value. Cézanne's methods, which transformed an ordinary mountain into an icon of stability, led the way to modern abstraction.

Figure 31.33 PAUL CÉZANNE, *Mont Sainte-Victoire*, 1902–1904. Oil on canvas, 27½ × 35¼ in. Between 1880 and his death in 1906, the so-called Master of Aix produced no less than twenty-five oil paintings and watercolors of his favorite mountain as seen from the countryside around his native city. In this rendering, dense patches of color come close to pure abstraction.

LOOKING BACK

Late Nineteenth-Century Thought

- The provocative German thinker Friedrich Wilhelm Nietzsche, who detected in European materialism a deepening decadence, called for a revision of traditional values.
- While Nietzsche anticipated the darker side of modernism, Henri Bergson presented a positive view of life as a vital impulse that evolved creatively and intuitively.

Poetry in the Late Nineteenth Century: The Symbolists

- Symbolist poets, such as Paul Verlaine and Arthur Rimbaud, devised a language of sensation that evoked rather than described feeling.
- In Stéphane Mallarmé's *L'après-midi d'un faune*, sensuous images unfold as discontinuous literary fragments.

Music in the Late Nineteenth Century: Debussy

- Symbolist poetry found its counterpart in music. The compositions of Claude Debussy engage the listener through nuance and atmosphere.
- Inspired by Indonesian music, Wagnerian opera, and Symbolist poetry, Debussy created a mood of reverie in the shifting harmonies of his *Prelude to "The Afternoon of a Faun."*

Painting in the Late Nineteenth Century

- The Impressionists, led by Monet, were equally representative of the late nineteenth-century interest in sensation and sensory experience. These artists tried to record an instantaneous vision of their world, sacrificing the details of perceived objects in order to capture the effects of light and atmosphere.
- Renoir, Degas, and Pissarro produced informal, painterly canvases that offer a glimpse into the pleasures of nineteenth-century urban life.
- Two major influences on late nineteenth-century artists were stop-action photography and Japanese woodblock prints. The latter, originally popularized as souvenirs, entered Europe along with Asian trade goods.
- In the domestic interiors of Cassatt and the cabarets of Toulouse-Lautrec, scenes of everyday life show the influence of Japanese prints.

Art Nouveau

- Originating in Belgium, *Art Nouveau* ("new art") was an ornamental style that became enormously popular in the late nineteenth century.

- The proponents of the style prized the arts of Asia and Islam, which featured bold, flat, organic patterns and semiabstract linear designs. In America, the style was advanced in the art glass of Louis Comfort Tiffany.

Sculpture in the Late Nineteenth Century

- The works of Degas and Rodin reflect a common concern for figural gesture and expressive movement.
- Rodin's efforts to translate inner states of feeling into physical form were mirrored by Isadora Duncan's innovations in modern dance.

The Arts of Africa and Oceania

- The late nineteenth century was a time of high artistic productivity in Africa and Oceania. Reliquaries, masks, and freestanding sculptures were among the power objects created to channel the spirits of ancestors, celebrate rites of passage, and ensure the well-being of the community.
- While sharing with some Western styles (such as Symbolism) a general disregard for objective representation, the visual arts of Africa and Oceania stood apart from nineteenth-century Western academic tradition.

Primitivism

- Colonialism and travel to Africa and Oceania worked to introduce the West to cultures that were perceived by some as exotic and violent, and by others as "primitive" and blissfully close to nature.
- The Paris *Exposition Universelle* of 1880 brought non-Western culture to public attention, encouraging the establishment of ethnographic collections and a broader interest in the world beyond the West.

Postimpressionism

- Renouncing their predecessors' infatuation with the fleeting effects of light, the Postimpressionists explored new pictorial strategies.
- Van Gogh and Gauguin used color not as an atmospheric envelope but as a tool for personal, symbolic, and visionary expression.
- Seurat and Cézanne reacted against the formlessness of Impressionism by inventing styles that featured architectural stability.

Music Listening Selections

CD Two Selection 16 Debussy, *Prélude à "L'après-midi d'un faune,"* 1894.

Glossary

negative space the background or ground area seen in relation to the shape of the (positive) figure

literature 114
Bell, Alexander Graham 73
Bentham, Jeremy 76
Bergson, Henri 113–14, 116, 131
Time and Freewill 114
Berlioz, Hector 62–3, 69, 93, **29.16**
Damnation of Faust 63
Harold in Italy 62
Symphonie fantastique 46, 62–3
Bernhardt, Sarah 93
Bessemer, Henry 106
Bhagavad-Gita 18
Bierstadt, Albert 21
The Rocky Mountains, Lander's Peak 21–2, **27.14**
Birth of Tragedy, The (Nietzsche) 112
Bizet, Georges: *Carmen* 46, 60
Blake, William 10–11
Songs of Innocence 11
Songs of Experience 11
"The Tiger" 11 (quoted), **27.5**
blues, the 39
Bodrigue, William *see* Renwick, James
Bohème, La (Puccini) 108–9
Bolívar, Simón 29
Boris Godunov (Pushkin) 35
Borneo: Kenya-Kayan art 132
Boulevard Montmartre: Rainy Weather (Pissarro) 119, **31.1**
Brady, Matthew B. 94, 104
Dead Confederate Soldier with Gun 94, **30.9**
"Brahma" (Emerson) 18 (quoted)
Brahms, Johannes 62
brass instruments 59, 60
Brave Deeds Against the Dead (Goya) 51, **29.3**
bridges
cast iron 105, 106
suspension 108
Brighton, England: Royal Pavilion (Nash) 59, 105, **29.14**
Britain 2, 71, 73, 75
architecture 57–8, 59, 105–6
industrialism 2, 73, 75
literature 5–11, 32–5, 46–7, 58, 81–2, 89, 91
painting 11, 14–16
photography 93–4, 120
social theorists 76–7, 81
Brontë, Charlotte: *Jane Eyre* 46
Brontë, Emily: *Wuthering Heights* 46
Brooklyn Bridge, New York (Roebling) 108, **30.29**
Brothers Karamazov, The (Dostoevsky) 85
Brueghel, Pieter the Elder 13
Brussels: Tassel House (Horta) 127, **31.16**
Buddhism 18
Buffalo, New York, Guaranty Building (Sullivan and Adler) 107, **30.28**
Burial at Ornans (Courbet) 96–8, **30.12**
Byron, George Gordon, Lord 2, 34–5, 53, **28.1**
Childe Harold's Pilgrimage 34, 62
Don Juan 34, 35
"Prometheus" 34, 35 (quoted)

C

cameras 71, 93, 94, 112
Cameron, Julia Margaret 93
Whisper of the Muse (G. F. Watts and Children) **30.8**
capitalism 75, 76, 77, 81, 110
Carlyle, Thomas 81
On Heroes and Hero-Worship 29
Carmen (Bizet) 46, 60
Carmen (Mérimée) 46
Carpeaux, Jean-Baptiste: *The Dance* 65, **29.20**
Cassatt, Mary 123

The Bath 123, **31.14**
cast iron 105–8, 127
Castle of Otranto, The (Walpole) 32
Catlin, George 22, 23, 24, 57
The White Cloud, Head Chief of the Iowas 22, **27.16**
Cézanne, Paul 119, 139–40
The Basket of Apples 139, **31.32**
Mont Sainte-Victoire 139–40, **31.33**
Charles IV, King of Spain 50
Charles X, King of France 53–5
Chevreul, Michel: *The Principles of Harmony and the Contrast of Colors* 117, 138
Chicago: Home Insurance Building (Jenney) 107
Childe Harold's Pilgrimage (Byron) 34, 62
China 73–5, 78, 134
literature 11–12
opium trade 73–4, 109
painting 12–13
Chopin, Frédéric 2, 47, 63–4, **29.17**
Etude in G-flat Major, Opus 10, No. 5 64
Chopin, Kate 88
The Awakening 87, 88
"The Story of an Hour" 88–9 (quoted)
Chosen One, The (Hodler) 116, **31.3**
Church, Frederic Edwin 22
Niagara 22, **27.15**
Church, William 98
Close No. 37 High Street (Annan) 94, **30.5**
coal 2, 71
Cole, Thomas 21, 22
The Oxbow (View from Mount Holyoke . . .) 21, **27.13**
Coleridge, Samuel Taylor 18
Lyrical Ballads 5
Rime of the Ancient Mariner 15
colonialism 4, 59, 71, 72–3, 75, 132, 133, 134, **Map 30.1**
Colt, Samuel 55
communism 77, 78
Communist Manifesto (Marx and Engels) 77, 78–80 (quoted)
concerto 60
Congo 73, 134
conservatism 76, 77
Constable, John 14, 16, 118
The Haywain 14, **27.1**
Wivenhoe Park, Essex 14, **27.8**
Cooper, James Fenimore 17
Cordier, Charles-Henri-Joseph 57
African in Algerian Costume 57, **29.11**
Corot, Jean-Baptiste-Camille 16–17
Ville d'Avray 16, **27.11**
Courbet, Gustave 94, 96
Burial at Ornans 96–8, **30.12**
The Stone-Breakers 94, **30.10**
Crane, Stephen 91
creationism 3, 5
Crime and Punishment (Dostoevsky) 85, 86–7 (quoted)
Crystal Palace, London (Paxton) 105–6, 107, **30.26**
Cuba 73

D

Daguerre, Louis J. M. 93
daguerreotypes 93, **28.4**
Damnation of Faust (Berlioz) 63
dance 64, 129–31 *see also* ballet
Dance, The (Carpeaux) 65, **29.20**
Dancing Figure (Rodin) 128, **31.20**
Darwin, Charles 3–5, **27.2**
The Descent of Man 3

The Origin of Species 3, 4–5 (quoted)
Darwinism, social 4, 71
Daumier, Honoré 98–100
Free Admission Day – Twenty-Five Degrees of Heat **30.15**
Nadar Raising Photography to the Heights of Art 93, 98, **30.14**
The Third-Class Carriage 99–100, **30.1**
David Copperfield (Dickens) 82
David, Jacques-Louis 50
Napoleon Crossing the Great Saint Bernard Pass 30, **28.2**
The Oath of the Horatii 54, **29.7**
Day of the God, The (Gauguin) 137, **31.30**
Dead Confederate Soldier with Gun (Brady) 94, **30.9**
Debussy, Claude 115–16, 117
Gardens in the Rain 116
Image: Reflections in the Water 116
Prelude to "The Afternoon of a Faun" 115–16, **31.2**
The Sea 116
Declaration of Rights (P. B. Shelley) 8
Defence of Poetry (P. B. Shelley) 8
Degas, Edgar 120, 122, 123, 128
The False Start 120, **31.8**
Little Dancer Aged Fourteen 128, **31.19**
Two Dancers on a Stage 120, **31.7**
Déjeuner sur l'herbe (Manet) 100–1, **30.16**
Delacroix, Eugène 53–5, 60, 63, 64, 104, 118, 133
Arabs Skirmishing in the Mountains 53, **29.5**
Fréderic Chopin 63, **29.17**
Liberty Leading the People 53–5, **29.6**
Mephistopheles Appearing to Faust in his Study 53, **28.5**
Portrait of George Sand 47, **28.6**
Denis, Maurice 135
Descartes, René 3
Descent of Man, The (Darwin) 3
dialectic, Hegelian 3, 26
Dickens, Charles 81–2, 89
David Copperfield 82
Nicholas Nickleby 82
The Old Curiosity Shop 82–3 (quoted)
Oliver Twist 82
Diesel, Rudolf 114
"Disasters of War" (Goya) 51, **29.3**
Disraeli, Benjamin 75
Doll's House, A (Ibsen) 91–2 (quoted)
Don Juan (Byron) 34, 35
Donizetti, Gaetano: *Lucia di Lammermoor* 66
Dostoevsky, Fyodor 85–6, 112
The Brothers Karamazov 85
Crime and Punishment 85, 86–7 (quoted)
The Possessed 85
Douglass, Frederick 29, 37, **28.4**
My Bondage and My Freedom 37–8 (quoted)
drama, realist 91–2
Dreiser, Theodore 91
Dumas, Alexandre 29
Duncan, Isadora 129–31, **31.22**
Dürer, Albrecht 13
Duret, Théodore: "The Impressionist Painters" 122 (quoted)
Dutch painting *see* Gogh, Vincent van; Rembrandt van Rijn
dynamics (musical) 60–1, 69
dynamite 93
dynamo, first 78

E

Eakins, Thomas 102–3, 104, 105
The Agnew Clinic 103, **30.21**
Walt Whitman 103, **27.12**

Eastman, George 93
Eckhart, Johannes 2
Edison, Thomas 112, 114, 116
Egypt 29, 57, 75
Eiffel, Gustave
    Eiffel Tower 107, 127, **30.27**
    Statue of Liberty (framework) **29.8**
1812 Overture (Tchaikovsky) 62
electricity 71, 78, 112
elevators 106, 107
Elgin marbles 9
Eliot, George (Mary Anne Evans) 46, 96
Emerson, Ralph Waldo 4, 17–18
    "Brahma" 18 (quoted)
    "Nature" 17–18 (quoted)
Engels, Friedrich 77, 78
    Communist Manifesto 77, 78–80 (quoted)
engines/power 2, 71 *see also* internal combustion
    engines
England *see* Britain
entrepreneurs 75, 110
Equitable Life Insurance building, New York 107
"Erlkönig" (Schubert) 62
Etude in G-flat Major, Opus 10, No. 5 (Chopin)
    64
études 64, 69
Eugene Onegin (Pushkin) 35, 60
Eugene Onegin (Tchaikovsky) 60
eugenics 4, 26
Evolution, Theory of (Darwin) 3–5, **27.2**
exploration 133–4

F
fairy tales (Grimm brothers) 29
False Start, The (Degas) 120, **31.8**
Faust (Goethe) 39–40, 40–6 (quoted), 46, 48, 62,
    53, 63, **28.5**
Faust Symphony (Liszt) 62
Fichte, Gottlieb 2
Flaubert, Gustave 87, 89
    Madame Bovary 87, 88 (quoted), 101
folk art, American 24–5, **27.19, 27.20**
Ford, Henry 114
Forever Free (Lewis) 55, **29.10**
Four Seasons, The (Vivaldi) 61–2
France 29, 55, 71, 75, 81, 112, 134, **Map 28.1**
    architecture 107
    literature 46, 47–8, 87–8, 89–90, 114–15
    music 62–4, 115–16
    painting and lithography 16–17, 51–5, 94–102,
        117–20, 124, 138–40
    philosophy 113–14
    photography 93, 98
    sculpture 55, 57, 65, 128–31
Frankenstein . . . (M. Shelley) 32–4 (quoted), **28.3**
Frazer, Sir James: *The Golden Bough* 134
Free Admission Day – Twenty-Five Degrees of Heat
    (Daumier) **30.15**
free verse 19, 26
Friedrich, Caspar David 13
    Two Men Looking at the Moon 13, **27.7**
Fustel de Coulanges, Numa Denis 81

G
Gandhi, Mohandas Karamchand 18
Gardens in the Rain (Debussy) 116
Garnier, J. L. Charles: Opéra, Paris 64–5, **29.18,
    29.19**
Gates of Hell, The (Rodin) 128, **31.23**
Gauguin, Paul 131, 134, 136–7, 138
    The Day of the God (Mahana no Atua) 137,
    31.30
Gay Science, The (Nietzsche) 112–13 (quoted)

Geiger, Andrew: *A Concert of Hector Berlioz in
    1846* 63, **29.16**
genetics, molecular 4, 5
Géricault, Théodore 2, 51–2, 104
    The Raft of the "Medusa" 15, 51–2, 104, **29.4**
Germany 2, 57, 71, 75, 109
    architecture 57
    historicism 81
    literature 39–47, 46
    music 46, 60–2
    opera 46, 67
    painting 13
    philosophy 2–3, 112–13
    social theorists 77–80
Germinal (Zola) 90 (quoted)
Gilbert, Olive 38
Gilded Age 102
Giorgione: *Pastoral Concert* **30.17**
Giselle (ballet) 66
glass, Tiffany 127, **31.18**
Gleaners, The (Millet) 94–6, **30.11**
Glele, King of Dahomey 133
Godwin, William 32
Goethe, Johann Wolfgang von 3, 39, 67
    Faust 39–40, 40–6 (quoted), 46, 48, 60, 62, 63,
    28.5
    Sorrows of Young Werther 46
Gogh, Vincent van 122, 135–6, 137
    Self-Portrait 136, **31.28**
    The Starry Night 135–6, **31.27**
Golden Bough, The (Frazer) 134
Goodyear, Charles 78
gospel music 39
Gothic novels 32
Gothic Revival architecture 57, 58
Goya, Francisco 50, 104
    Brave Deeds Against the Dead 51, **29.3**
    *The Third of May, 1808: The Execution of the
        Defenders of Madrid* 50–1, **29.1**
Grasset, Eugène: comb 127, **31.17**
"Gretchen am Spinnrade" (Schubert) 62
Grimm, Jacob and Wilhelm: fairy tales 29
Grog Shop, The (Zola) 89
Gros, Antoine-Jean 2, 50
    Napoleon Visiting the Plague Victims at Jaffa
        50, **29.2**
Guaranty Building, Buffalo, New York (Sullivan
    and Adler) 107, **30.28**
Gulf Stream, The (W. Homer) 104–5, **30.25**
Gypsies, The (Pushkin) 60

H
Hardy, Thomas 91
Harnett, William Michael 102
    The Artist's Letter Rack 102, **30.20**
Harold in Italy (Berlioz) 62
Harper's Weekly 104, **30.24**
Harvard University 58
Hawthorne, Nathaniel 17, 29
Haydn, Franz Joseph 59, 60, 61
Haywain, The (Constable) 14, **27.1**
Hegel, Georg Wilhelm Friedrich 3, 77, 78
    The Philosophy of History 3
Heine, Heinrich 46, 62
    "You are Just Like a Flower" 46 (quoted)
Helmholtz, Hermann von: *On the Sensations of
    Tone . . .* 115, 117
heroes
    Promethean 32–5, 60, 62
    romantic 29–30, 34, 39, 46, 50, 55
Hicks, Edward 24
    The Peaceable Kingdom 24, **27.20**
Hinduism 2, 17, 18

historicism 81
Hodler, Ferdinand: *The Chosen One* 116, **31.3**
Hoffmann, E. T. A. 59
Hokusai, Katsushika: *Mount Fuji Seen Below a
    Wave at Kanagawa* 122, **31.11**
Home Insurance Building, Chicago (Jenney) 107
Homer, Winslow 104
    The Gulf Stream 104–5, **30.25**
    The War for the Union: A Bayonet Charge
        104, **30.24**
Horta, Victor 126–7
    Tassel House, Brussels 127, **31.16**
Houses of Parliament, London (Barry and Pugin)
    58, **29.12**
Howe, Elias 78
Hudson River school 21
Hugo, Victor 29
    Les Misérables 29
Hungary 60, 62
Huntondji, Ganhu: The war god Gu 133, **31.26**

I
Ibsen, Henrik 91
    A Doll's House 91–2 (quoted)
idealism, German 2
idée fixe 62–3, 67, 69
Idylls of the King (Tennyson) 57–8
Illuminations (Rimbaud) 114
Image: Reflections in the Water (Debussy) 116
imperialism 4, 29, 71–3, 132 *see also* colonialism
Impression: Sunrise (Monet) 117, **31.4**
impressionism 102, 112, 116–17, 118, 122, 124,
    128, 134, 135, 139
impromptus 64, 69
India 72, 73, 75
Industrial Revolution/industrialism 2, 5, 17, 71,
    73, 75, 94, **30.3**
Interior of Tintern Abbey (Turner) 6, 15, **27.3**
internal combustion engines 71, 78, 112, 114
Iran 75
Iron Mill (Menzel) **30.3**
Islam 75
Italy 29, 71, 109
    music 60
    opera 19, 66, 108–9

J
James, Henry 105
Jane Avril (Toulouse-Lautrec) 124, **31.12**
Jane Eyre (C. Brontë) 46
Japan 13, 73, 109, 134
    woodblock prints 101, 120–3, 124, 126, 135,
        137, 140, **31.10, 31.11, 31.13**
Japonisme 122
jazz 39
Jefferson, Thomas 57
Jenney, William Le Baron: Home Insurance
    Building, Chicago 107
journalism 104
Judgement of Paris (Raimondi after Raphael)
    101, **30.18**

K
Kant, Immanuel 2
Kapital, Das (Marx) 77
Keats, John 2, 9, 11
    "Ode on a Grecian Urn" 9, 10 (quoted)
Kenya-Kayan art (Borneo) 132
King, Martin Luther 18
Kipling, Rudyard: "The White Man's Burden"
    71, 72 (quoted)
Kiss, The (Rodin) 131, **31.24**
Kiyonobu, Torii: *Actor as a Monkey Showman* 124,